DATE DUE			

Down on Parchman Farm

The Great Prison in the Mississippi Delta

William Banks Taylor

Foreword by Peggy Whitman Prenshaw

Ohio State University Press
Columbus

Cover photo of the superintendent's home at Parchman, ca. 1916, courtesy Mississippi
Department of Archives & History, Archives and Library Division, Special Collections Section.

Library of Congress Cataloging-in-Publication Data

Taylor, William Banks.
    Down on Parchman Farm : the great prison in the Mississippi Delta / William Banks
Taylor ; foreword by Peggy Whitman Prenshaw
        p.   cm.
    Includes bibliographical references.
    ISBN 0-8142-5023-8 (pa : alk. paper)
    1. Mississippi State Penitentiary—History.   2. Prisons—Mississippi—History.
3. Prisoners—Crimes against—Mississippi.   4. Criminal justice, Administration of—
Mississippi—History.   5. Mississippi—Politics and government.   I. Title.
HV9475.M7T394   1999
365'.9762—dc21   99-17998
                                                                                                        CIP

Cover design: Dan O'Dair.
Type set in Adobe Galliard by Nighthawk Design.
Printed by McNaughton & Gunn, Inc.

The paper used in this publication meets the minimum requirements of the American
National Standard for Information Sciences—Permanence of Paper for Printed Library
Materials. ANSI Z39.48–1992.

9   8   7   6   5   4   3   2   1

Contents

Foreword

Throughout the twentieth century the name *Parchman* has been a powerful signifier in American penal history, conferring vivid life upon the institution of prisons as well as calling to mind one particular state facility, the notorious Mississippi penal farm. It would be difficult to exaggerate the dimensions of Parchman's presence in the history of Mississippi, for in its way the penitentiary has played a central role in the politics and culture of the state and region.

Year after year, for the first seven decades of the twentieth century, Parchman-related controversies occupied the legislature and filled the state's—and often the nation's—newspapers with stories of mismanagement, followed by reform efforts; stories of abusive treatment of inmates, followed by reform policies; reports of blatant exploitation of political patronage, followed by reform laws; and further reports of outright graft, followed always by promises of reform. None of it came to much, but in 1972 real reform did begin at last, the consequence of litigation in federal court brought by inmates claiming unconstitutional conditions. There followed a two-decade judicial inquisition involving well over 150 orders for relief, but by 1976 the old convict farm had been dismantled.

A decade later, United States District Judge William C. Keady, recalling the old Parchman and pondering the fatal blows he had dealt it, told a reporter: "We are seeing an institution come from being a very backward, shabby, trusty-run plantation, to a modern operation" (Jackson *Clarion-Ledger,* June 15, 1986).

The shabby plantation to which Judge Keady referred was described in a 1938 Works Progress Administration (WPA) publication, *Mississippi: A Guide to the Magnolia State,* as simply a "typical" one:

At PARCHMAN . . . is the MISSISSIPPI PENAL FARM, a prison operated on an agricultural system. The farm is a typical Delta plantation, consisting of 15,497 acres planted in cotton, corn, and truck, with cotton the
leading crop. The prisoners, separated into small groups, live in camps.
The present (1937) number of prisoners is 1,989. A brick yard, a machine shop, a gin, and a storage plant are operated by convict labor. The
prison is self-supporting and operates at a profit when the price of cotton
is good.

This description was accurate enough, but it failed to mention the antebellum features of the penal farm. With its vast cotton acreage, black
field hands, and white overseers, the plantation would have been quite
at home in the Mississippi of 1860. Nor did the WPA description relate
the countless stories—both media accounts and gossipy tales—told of
the punishments inflicted to keep the "long line" chopping and picking
in the cotton fields. Unmentioned were the notorious strap, "Black
Annie," the use of which Hodding Carter opposed so vehemently in the
pages of his Greenville *Delta Democrat-Times;* the bloodhounds and
German shepherds, carefully bred and trained by the convicts themselves; and the fabled "trusty-shooters," aptly named "headhunters,"
who guarded and sometimes felled convicts in the fields.

All of this remained intact, out of step with the nation's evolving
standard of decency, until Parchman came under the constitutional
scrutiny of the federal courts, and the institution fell along with the
South's other convict farms—Angola in Louisiana, Cummins in Arkansas. Yet Parchman Farm had its defenders then and, retrospectively,
has them today, for in many ways it was a remarkably successful penal
institution. The old penal farm was distinguished, moreover, by the
prominent place it did—and does—occupy in the literary and musical
imaginations of Mississippians, who tell not only of a brutal, oppressive
prison but also of a place capable of harboring some sustaining warmth
and camaraderie.

The extraordinary attention devoted to Parchman by musicians and
writers owes perhaps to the power of the old convict farm to give such
a rich image of human beings contending with bad times. The farm
offered a visual manifestation of the blues. Set in the Yazoo Delta of
isolated Sunflower County, it lay in the heart of blues country, and the
inmates, always predominantly black, sang of back-breaking labor and
love miseries, themes that characterize the blues everywhere.

In the 1930s John A. Lomax and his son Alan went to Parchman

Farm in their search for American folk songs, and there they recorded work chants and blues. Seventeen years later, Alan Lomax returned to record more songs, and these were released by Tradition Records as *Negro Prison Songs from the Mississippi State Penitentiary.* On the record jacket, Lomax wrote that "the singers were all Negro prisoners, who, according to the practice of Mississippi, were serving out their time by working on a huge state cotton plantation in the fertile Yazoo Delta." Lomax went on to write that "the songs, quite literally, kept the men alive and normal. As the gangs 'rolled under the hot broilin' sun,' the roaring choruses of the songs revived flagging spirits, restored energy to failing bodies, brought laughter to silent misery."

The translation of misery into song does not negate the misery, of course, but the outpouring of music does point up some of the anomalies of the old penal farm, at least when compared to today's prison practices. In fact, a reconsideration of the seemingly retrograde features of the prison suggests that some of these produced humane, ameliorative effects upon the condition of the prisoners.

Old Parchman Farm was a prison without walls, the front gate being attached to nothing, and convicts came and went with astonishing frequency. So too did "lewd women" from the "free world," who plied their trade squarely in the middle of Dixie's Bible Belt, constrained hardly at all by the prison administrators. Except for the maximum security unit, "Little Alcatraz," there were no cells, only dormitories known as "cages" that closely resembled military barracks. By and large, convicts ran the penitentiary. "Cagebosses" were virtually sovereign in the cages, trusty-shooters oversaw the fields, and scattered about the place were all manner of support services managed by felons. Parchman had a brickyard, a canning plant, a dairy, a laundry—in fact, all the establishments that one would typically find in any Delta town, including, of course, a railroad depot with a gin and adjacent warehouses.

In Shelby Foote's 1950 novel, *Follow Me Down* (New York: Dial Press, 1950), the county jailer, Roscoe Jeffcoat, describes Parchman to one of his prisoners:

> It ain't so bad, considering. . . . They don't have no cells like this, for one thing. No walls, no bob wire. Nothing like that. . . . Its a farm . . . a plantation like back in slavery days—eighteen thousand acres, mostly cotton. They give you your own mule and everything. You go out in the morning, eat in the field, and come back in at sundown. Thats during

the season. Off-season, Sundays, rainy days, you sit around the bunk
house, reading, talking. It aint bad. Stay in line, youll be all right. Otherwise the sergeant's got a strap—Black Annie. . . . Its better than solitary.
(They dont have solitary like most prisons. Solitary's inhuman, the warden says.) And the first Sunday in every month is visiting day. Thats when
the women come. (268)

The special celebrity of Parchman Farm beyond the state's borders owes
arguably to the celebrity of Mississippi's writers and blues artists. To
these Mississippians, Parchman is a special place, and through their
artistry they have made it so to all who have read their stories or heard
their songs. William Faulkner's convict in *Old Man* (New York: New
American Library, 1948) goes from Parchman on an unforgettable
journey to fight the flood of 1927 and finds life in the "free world" un-
predictable and worrisome. As he struggles to avoid entanglements
with the woman he has rescued, he thinks of "the barracks at night,
with screen against the bugs in summer and good stoves in winter and
someone to supply the fuel and the food too; the Sunday ball games
and the picture shows—things which, with the exception of the ball
games, he had never known before." The woman and her baby em-
body all the complications of civilization, which he flees in order to return to the monastic life offered by his prison in the Delta.

In Eudora Welty's 1970 Pulitzer Prize–winning novel, *Losing Battles*
(New York: Random House, 1970), Jack Renfro makes exactly the op-
posite choice, escaping the day before he completes his sentence to return home to his family's reunion. Describing the penitentiary to the
assembled group ("Aunt Birdie," he says, "Parchman is too big to
fence"), Jack explains to everyone, including the judge who sentenced
him, how he managed to escape: "I come out on Dexter. . . . He knows
me. There's a overseer that rides him every day but Sunday. The kind
of horse Dexter is, he's almost an overseer himself. He took me over-
seeing all over those acres, and finally he conducted me out onto a
little road that meant business." The judge's wife hoots, "He just rode
a plough horse out of Parchman" (196).

In Welty's work, as in Faulkner's, Parchman is a powerful symbol of
separateness. Welty even makes fictive use of the name *Parchman,* for
Jack's absence coincides with a parching drought that intensifies the
impoverishment of his already poor hill-country family.

As symbol and setting, Parchman is a looming presence. In the
1950s Mose Allison sang his version of "Parchman Farm Blues," telling

of sweating, downtrodden men dragging cotton sacks along the sweltering floor of the Yazoo Delta. His rendition of the old work-song lament, however, was but one in a long line of songs about Parchman. Many of my generation of teenagers in the 1950s danced to the rock-and-roll version of "The Midnight Special," blissfully ignorant of the song's origins and subject—a hard-core Delta blues song reflecting the feelings of black convicts awaiting the train that brought them "mama" on visiting day. The strains of these and many other old songs about the state penitentiary, their convict-composers long forgotten, are heard today at the annual Delta Blues Festival in Greenville.

For those who know the blues of the Mississippi Delta, the huge penal farm is as real and present a place as it is to those who know the works of Faulkner. When Mink Snopes kills Jack Houston in Faulkner's *The Mansion* (New York: Random House, 1959), he is sentenced to Parchman, his "destination, doom." There, Mink finds "the tall wire stockade with its single gate guarded day and night by men with shotguns, and inside it the low grim brick buildings with their barred windows . . . " (48–49).

In another, less well known novel, Robert Rylee's *Deep Dark River* (New York: Farrar and Rinehart, 1935), the convict Mose Southwick wonders how the "land about him could sometimes be so beautiful and sympathetic." The last lines of the novel capture something of the paradox of Parchman, the ambiguities signified by the prison, as Mose looks out "across those fields of toil, across the wide ridge of the levee and the black mud flats, to where lay the river, silent, majestic, silver in the moonlight. On the other side . . . the sweep of other fields and over all the limitless night, holy, touched by the hands of peace" (308).

In Taylor's history of Parchman Farm, the ambiguities of this extraordinary prison unfold, mirroring much of the broader history of Mississippi and the South in the twentieth century. It is a remarkable story of personalities and politics, of debates about the functions of prisons in society, of controversies about the responsibility of government to protect and to punish.

Nathaniel Hawthorne's novel *The Scarlet Letter* counterpoised the prison to the wilderness, presenting a classic American image of wild freedom balanced by the constraints of civilization. In this history of Parchman, the author offers an even more provocative image: a prison in the wilderness that fundamentally challenges a governing society and its jailers and prisoners to envision and establish an outpost of civilization. Though no *Heart of Darkness,* Parchman's story does call upon its readers to acknowledge the many contradictions that shape Americans' understandings of retribution and redemption, criminal justice and racial justice, and, inevitably, our clashing impulses toward darkness and light.

Peggy Whitman Prenshaw

Acknowledgments

This book is both an abridged and expanded version of my *Brokered Justice: Race, Politics, and Mississippi Prisons, 1798–1992*, published by the Ohio State University Press in 1993. It is an abridgement because it focuses more narrowly on the history of Mississippi's fabled Parchman Farm, an expansion because it has a lot more to say about Parchman than did the earlier volume. The story begins with the political jockeying of the late nineteenth century that in 1900 resulted in the first of several land deals delivering acreage in Sunflower County to the state penal system. It ends in 1972, on the eve of United States District Judge William C. Keady's holding in *Gates v. Collier*—the death warrant for the old penal farm.

While this volume contains a substantial amount of new information about Parchman Farm, it is essentially the product of the long research project that resulted in *Brokered Justice*. I must therefore acknowledge those who inspired, facilitated, and contributed to the earlier volume.

Research on the history of the Mississippi penal system was undertaken at the request of John Watkins, Mississippi commissioner of corrections during the last years of the administration of Governor Cliff Finch (1976–80). Initially the Mississippi Department of Corrections (MDOC) supported the project, providing me with a research assistant and covering the expense of research, but that support ended abruptly when Finch and Watkins left office. Afterward the University of Southern Mississippi (USM) extended a small research grant and continued to cover essential expenses until the project was completed.

Several former state legislators were also quite helpful. Con Maloney, chairman of the senate corrections committee, boldly supported the project at its inception despite well-founded reservations about the legal and political ramifications of "skeletons in the closet." Convinced that the exposure of a few skeletons might well prove useful to the public interest, the late senator Bill Harpole, formerly Governor J. P. Coleman's superintendent at Parchman (1956–60), also lent a hand, reviewing the manuscript and advancing helpful suggestions. Other state politicians, agreeing with Senator Harpole but frankly admitting that they were among the skeletons, assisted on condition of anonymity.

A number of former and current employees of Mississippi's penal system devoted time and effort to the project as well. Leonard Vincent, now senior legal counsel for the MDOC, wrote an insightful legal treatise that proved quite useful in the early stages of research. Dr. Joe Cooke, formerly assistant commissioner of corrections, furnished official statistics and insightful analyses. Dr. Donald Cabana, formerly warden at Parchman and interim commissioner of corrections, and Professor Tyler Fletcher of USM, the last chairman of the state penitentiary's board of commissioners, advanced valuable comment on the old penal farm and its place within state politics. Mr. Lonnie Herring, training officer at Parchman, and Mr. Ken Jones, MDOC director of public relations, provided reproductions of photographs. Others, too numerous to name, contributed rare documents and useful leads, among them whispered instructions that sent me stamping through the wilds of the Yazoo Delta in search of old-timers with tales to tell.

The old-timers interviewed included former employees of the penal system, former convicts, and a number of others who, in one way or another, had some association with the pre-*Gates* Parchman. In the end, over 350 hours of such testimony was taken, and the best of it was obtained on condition of anonymity.

I have been extremely careful with the anonymous ones, always taking care to draw a clear line between fact and opinion. Yet even the opinions have been valuable—indeed essential—in the attempt to understand and relate the complex story of Parchman Farm, and I must express a debt of gratitude to those who were willing to share their memories of the old days.

I must also acknowledge those who coauthored chapters in *Brokered Justice,* thereby contributing indirectly to this volume. One of them, Ruby E. Cooley Reid, served as my research assistant during 1979 and early 1980, afterward producing a master's thesis that examined Parchman's early history. Not only her research but also her perspective as an African American have proved valuable. Dr. Warrick R. Edwards, instructor of history at Tallahassee Community College, and Dr. Ronald G. Marquardt, professor of political science at USM, also coauthored chapters in *Brokered Justice*. The work of the former, Dr. Edwards, dealt with Mississippi's notorious convict lease system, which preceded the commencement of penal farming. That of the latter, Professor Marquardt, focused on the initial holding in *Gates v. Collier*, the federal case that brought Parchman down.

Others read the manuscript, clarified matters of fact, and prevented errors of judgment. Useful indeed were the suggestions of Dr. Charles A. Marx, formerly chief assistant to the Mississippi attorney general, executive assistant to Governor Bill Allain, and Mississippi commissioner of revenue. I am similarly indebted to Dr. William K. Scarborough, professor of history at USM, whose expertise in antebellum plantation management shed light on many curious facets of life at Parchman Farm, and to Dr. E. Duane Davis, professor of criminal justice at Western Carolina University, whose valuable advice inadvertently went unacknowledged in *Brokered Justice*.

Special thanks also go to the staff of the Mississippi Department of Archives and History and that of the William David McCain Library and Archives at USM. Especially valuable was the assistance of Henry Simmons of the McCain Library and Archives, who spent much time leading me through the nooks and crannies of his beloved Mississippi Collection.

Finally, I am indebted to Barbara Hanrahan, the director of the Ohio State University Press, who solicited and brought this volume to fruition.

Introduction

Beginning in the mid-1970s, and continuing for the remainder of the decade, the residents of Alligator, Sledge, and the other little towns dotting Mississippi's Yazoo Delta sometimes saw a blood-red glow in the evening sky. Many of them, especially the older folk, looked on with troubled faces. For the glow, they knew, emanated from burning buildings on Parchman Farm, an institution whose presence framed so much of their history, and of their parents' and grandparents' before them.

The burning buildings were "cages"—barracks that had housed Mississippi's felons for the better part of the twentieth century—and they burned as a result of orders handed down by the United States Court for the Northern District of Mississippi, signaling yet another in a series of blows inflicted since late 1972, when Judge William C. Keady issued his initial holding in the landmark case of *Gates v. Collier*. Already the judge's construction of constitutional law had struck down most of the institution's long-standing principles of organization and management. Now, as the cages were consumed by flames, rumor held that soon thousands of the penitentiary's alluvial acres would be leased to private planters. It was clear to every observer that the old penal farm was in the throes of death.

To the north, in the river town of Greenville, the remnants of Hodding Carter's old circle shed no tears, instead basking in the sunshine of long-delayed vindication. For Carter, the Pulitzer Prize–winning editor of the Greenville *Delta Democrat-Times,* had waged war on the state's political establishment for decades, and since the early fifties he and his allies had increasingly regarded Parchman Farm as a mirror image of all that was wrong in Mississippi.

Their rationale was quite simple. Far from being a correctional institution, a place promoting the ideals of American criminal justice, the state penitentiary was a rundown, corrupt pork barrel that had been exploited by the state's ruling Delta oligarchy for as long as anyone could remember. But all the stories about sweetheart contracts, "walking" cotton bales, and vanishing livestock merely underscored the real complaint: the lingering presence of a penal institution organized and administered on principles that were remarkably similar to those which had governed antebellum slave management. And indeed, even in 1972, when Parchman first came under the constitutional scrutiny of the federal court, the place remained a plantation of some twenty thousand acres where convicts, the bulk of them black men, toiled in cotton fields under the sway of mounted white overseers.

Worse still, they had toiled under conditions that were, to say the very least, shocking to people of reasonable sensibility. The cages were unfit for human habitation, especially the showers, where convicts often stood ankle-deep in raw sewage. Within the rat-infested barracks, a convict hierarchy reigned supreme, reportedly inflicting atrocities at will. In the cotton rows, "trusty-shooters" guarded shuffling convict field hands with .30–.30 Winchester rifles, and stories of slaughter had filtered out of the penitentiary for years. At "Little Alcatraz," the prison's ugly, low-slung maximum security unit, naked men were confined in darkness, knocked to and fro by water propelled through high-pressure hoses, and deprived of adequate food for days on end. And more than one convict claimed that "Black Annie," the blunt strap of antebellum vintage, continued to reign on the penal farm, the white overseers' principal instrument of terror despite an official policy banning it.

All this had been exploited very effectively by the convict-plaintiffs' attorney in the federal court, with state actors backpedaling every step of the way; and as the judicial inquisition proceeded, many of Parchman's convicts, especially the younger ones, celebrated the burning cages, the termination of field work, and the promise of improved living conditions. Among them, Nazareth Gates and his fellow inmate-plaintiffs were regarded as heroes, Judge Keady as a Lincoln:

> Ole Jege Keady come to da farm,
> Supah say, we mean no harm,
> But Naz'reth tole dat jege a thang or two,
> 'Bout Annie an' da hole where men turn blue,
> Now da Cap'n he ride da rows alone,

No niggahs dare t' call 'is own,
An' supah say it gwine t' pass,
While dat jege keep on whuppin' Miss'sippi's ass.[1]

Some of the older convicts, amused by all the ass-whuppin', joined the celebration, and a number of them talked of the bad old days to the lawyers, politicians, journalists, and scholars who descended on the suddenly accessible penitentiary. Their stories were shocking, those who heard them duly shocked, and the word went forth, feeding—not unlike *Uncle Tom's Cabin* had fed well over a century earlier—the moral indignation so essential for a sustained assault on one of the South's peculiar institutions.

There was, to be sure, much to criticize about old Parchman Farm, especially if one viewed the institution from the pervasive civil rights perspective of the early 1970s. Some people, though, thought that the issues involved were not that simple. Among them were a number of Parchman's veteran employees.

Several of these men and women stood motionless near the fire trucks as the flames engulfed an old cage. Their eyes, reflecting the red glow before them, betrayed consternation, even disgust, at what they beheld. At last they had seen enough; and as they turned and walked away, toward the vehicles that would convey them back to Front Camp, they mumbled among themselves, their heads shaking in disapproval.

Not many of these employees were educated people. Most of them, in fact, qualified as "rednecks," or whatever other derogatory term one might choose to describe the deprived class of rural white folk who inhabit the Mississippi Delta. But uneducated people of humble origins are not necessarily stupid, and an outsider who prodded, displaying interest in their thoughts and feelings, heard an interesting assessment of what was transpiring at Parchman Farm. One such conversation occurred at Front Camp, near Parchman's administration building, where several employees, having just watched the destruction of the old cage, were both surprised and pleased to learn that at least one outsider thought their opinions mattered.

All of them agreed, more or less, that the hand of the federal judge had been forced—forced by the greed and boneheadedness of state politicians. Such behavior, they were quick to add, was nothing new:

Mississippi's politicians had always exploited the patronage, produce, and labor pool of Parchman Farm, and nobody had ever accused them of having much sense when it came to the penitentiary. Still, things had gone on pretty well until the late fifties, when the bottom fell out of the cotton market and all the ruckus about civil rights started. Afterward, a lower breed of state politician had appeared, and these guys had gone too far. They had forgotten that Parchman was a penitentiary. They had entrusted it to political hacks. And they had bled the place dry, allowing the physical plant to deteriorate terribly, ignoring the welfare of staff members and convicts alike, and displaying astonishing disregard for the legal facts of life. Inevitably, the state had been bludgeoned in the federal court.

This resigned point of view was offered somewhat timidly; but the more the employees talked, the more animated they became, and soon their numbers grew as others stopped by to investigate all the hubbub. One of the newcomers was a grizzled old man, and for some time he listened quietly, his hard, gray eyes betraying utter disdain for the prattle of his colleagues.

This, one sensed immediately, was a prison man of the old school, and one who seldom shared his opinions with others. He was, though, a thoughtful fellow, and he had given much thought to the subject at hand. Now, at last, he had decided to have his breath out, and the others conceded the stage to him, obviously surprised that he would speak at all.

The old man began slowly, and with carefully measured words. Yes, he conceded, the Mississippi legislature had its share of shysters and boneheads; and yes, their hanky-panky and stupidity had left Parchman a sitting duck, a plaintiff attorney's dream come true. But Mississippi had no monopoly on either sorry politicians or prison problems. The fact was, politics and prisons did not mix real well anywhere in the country, never had, and other states had prison woes much worse than those of Mississippi. So the question was, Why Parchman? Why not one of those awful Big-House joints up North? Why was Judge Keady so hot to destroy Mississippi's penitentiary? Where was he coming from? Where did he think he was heading?

At first, the man admitted, he had enjoyed watching Keady slap state politicians around a little. They certainly deserved a slap or two, and early on there was reason to believe that the judge, a native Mississippian after all, might force the politicians to do what was right for

Parchman. But somewhere along the way Keady had lost perspective, he thought, and all the court-ordered remedies were now sacrificing substance to form. The substance was effective prison administration, the form, a shaky notion of civil rights focusing on black felons. The judge was ignorant of the former, consumed by the latter, and unwittingly compromising the interests of both.

If Keady had bothered to educate himself on the subject of prisons, the veteran told his listeners, he would have found that Parchman Farm, even with its warts, stacked up pretty well with other American penal institutions. For the first fifty-odd years of the prison's existence, he stressed, its agricultural yield had provided the state with its greatest source of income other than tax revenues, and afterward the institution had operated with relatively little public support. No American prison of the twentieth century, in fact, had been as cost-effective, and surely no reasonable person could object to a penal institution whose felons contributed to their own maintenance.

All the while, the veteran added, Parchman's convict population had remained remarkably small and stable, usually at well below two thousand, except for the years of the Great Depression. That, he reckoned, said something for the value of the prison as a deterrent of crime among the state's general population, and the fact that a relatively small number of inmates found their way back to the farm suggested that not many of them had been eager to return.

Or maybe, just maybe, the failure of convicts to return constituted a rare triumph for convict rehabilitation, the man suggested with a hint of a grin. For old Parchman Farm, after all, was much more than a cotton plantation: it was a largely self-sufficient community, a place where convicts worked in a wide variety of very practical jobs, many of them managerial positions, and a number of the jobs taught skills that were as marketable outside the prison as within it. That, surely, was better than the idleness that characterized the lives of convicts in so-called progressive prisons. At any rate, more than a few of Mississippi's convicts had profited from a labor system that closely resembled the free world.

Many other good things could be said about old Parchman Farm, the veteran insisted. Certainly it was a secure prison: attempted escapes were rare, successful ones even more so. Nor had the institution fallen prey to the horrible riots that plagued so many other American penal institutions. And there was also better food, better health, and a much smaller number of deaths among Parchman's convicts than among those elsewhere. Indeed, by virtually every objective standard of evaluation, the old penal farm had been remarkably effective.

Effective prison administration, though, was not the focus of this judge, the veteran emphasized. Quite the contrary, Keady was married to abstraction, unwilling to consider the facts of prison life, and sacrificing a good, if politically troubled, penitentiary on the altar of the newfangled racial politics.

Yes, the bulk of Parchman's inmates had been black, members of Mississippi's unfortunate underclass, when the penitentiary came under the scrutiny of the federal court; and that, more than anything else, the veteran thought, had influenced the judge. The presence of a predominantly black inmate population, though, was nothing extraordinary: a majority of convicts in every state prison were members of an underclass. That was an unhappy state of affairs, and perhaps it reflected poorly on the country, but it was hardly reason to criticize a penal institution. Prisons did not manufacture criminals; they merely received and dealt with the offspring of criminal process. Mississippi's convicts had been predominantly black yesterday; they were predominantly black today; they would remain predominantly black until somebody figured out a way to reverse the tide of history, to change the economic and social facts of life. Judge Keady had not done that: not one order of his court promised to alter the racial profile of the state's convict population.

The man's tone was more hostile now. Yes, he conceded, Parchman's camps had been racially segregated, and that had also riled the judge. Yet racial integration was another high-blown social abstraction, a thing that got little more than lip-service even in Judge Keady's affluent social circle, and prisons could not afford such hypocrisy. Racism, however unpleasant, was a fact of life; it was most prevalent among the lowest classes, not only in Mississippi, but everywhere else as well; and not many of Parchman's convicts were aristocrats. There was, then, good reason for racial segregation: it stopped black and white gangs from forming, thereby preventing attacks on what was surely the most precious of all constitutional rights, that protecting life and limb. Former judges, federal and state alike, had understood this, the old man emphasized, but not this Keady fellow.

Here the speaker paused, glancing downward and collecting his thoughts for what was obviously going to be a closing argument. Given the large number of black inmates and the social climate of the day, he began, Parchman's labor system had conjured up "thoughts of slav'ry" in Judge Keady's courtroom, and the attorney for the convict-plaintiffs had "stopped at nothin' in drivin' that point home." Such a point of view was "superficial bull shit," however, and scored points only because the state's attorneys were "as ignorant as th' judge." The parallel ignored the fact that "ever' big farm in th' South works the same way more or less." But above all, it ignored the fact that "lockin' folks up is ah lot lak slav'ry ever'where." Was not imprisonment a means of punishment that took away a man's freedom and put masters over him? Was not that the whole idea, "th' nature of th' beast?"

Of course it was; and with that fact established, questions about old Parchman Farm could be asked and answered in reasonable context. Was forced labor in a cotton patch any more slavish than the "shit that goes on in them Yankee cellblocks?" Had not Parchman's white gunmen been subjected to the same regimen as its black ones, "workin' th' fields on th' same terms?" Had not all of them, black and white, been allowed "t' move up oudda th' rows after they behaved themselves fer ah while?" Had not this system of promotion made Parchman the nation's only "Nigra-run prison," a place where almost all middle-management positions were filled by black people? And amid all the indignant talk about Black Annie and Little Alcatraz, had anyone considered the fact that prisons housed convicted felons, some of them as "mean as rattlesnakes," and that such folk, "no matter what th' color of their skin," had to be dealt with "jis lak ah man deals with ah rattler."

None of that mattered to this judge; with him, form mattered more than substance, and it was "damned if ya do an' damned if ya don't." All of a sudden, field work at Parchman reminded Keady of the days of slavery, "even though 'e's seen white folk, jis like colored folk, workin' free-werl farms all 'is life." But the judge did not like the alternative either. Convicts who "sat on their asses" at Parchman made trouble, "jis lak they do up Nawth." And when they made trouble, Keady "didn't like spankin's," even though he had "had 'is own ass wo' out along wid ever'body else at school when 'e acted up." Instead, he thought that "lockin' a man down" was more humane. But Keady "rilly din't lak that neither." He refused to believe that "th' filthy sum-bitches that wuz locked down trashed their cells," and thought "th' po' thangs wuz bein' mistreated," regardless of whether staff members "let 'em waller in their own shit or hosed 'em down." The central problem, concluded the veteran, was that the judge "didn't know a goddamn thang 'bout prisons, thought they wuz church camps or somethin'," and he therefore did not understand that he was "playin' wid fire." Instead of "doin' what 'e ought," Keady was dismantling a workable scheme of prison administration. He was destroying a functional inmate social structure. He was assuring more convict-on-convict violence through racial integration. And, adding insult to injury, he was emasculating the staff, thereby giving reign to the "law of th' jungle."

Meanwhile, criminal convictions were soaring, and among those being committed to the penitentiary were an unprecedented number of alumni. Not surprisingly, tensions were mounting, costs were skyrocketing, and nobody seemed to understand that increased appropriations for the penal system would come out of the hide of social services, especially public education. That was a "helluva note," the veteran thought, since "ah po' edgycation brings most people up heah in th' fust place."

This judge had "his nose in law books too long." Or maybe he had been "runnin' with th' wrong people." Or maybe "old political scars," inflicted during Keady's days in the state senate, were behind it all. Or maybe he was bucking for promotion, "ah move up to th' Fifth Circuit." Whatever the case, the man was "meddlin' in somethin' 'e didn't know ah fuckin' thang about an' puttin' square pegs in round holes."

With that, the old man rested his case and ambled, head down, toward Parchman's administration building amid the congratulatory remarks of his colleagues.

The opinions of the veteran and his nodding colleagues were perhaps understandable: Judge Keady's finding of fact and orders for relief hardly complimented Parchman's employees, and many of them regarded themselves as victims, even martyrs, caught squarely between a doctrinaire federal judge and a dysfunctional state political apparatus. Strangely, though, their views on the effects of the court-ordered changes were shared by a number of the penitentiary's supposed victims.

During the years immediately following the initial holding in *Gates,* Parchman's convicts were about evenly divided in opinion on the court's notion of relief, and a degree of tension, which sometimes produced physical confrontation, existed between the opposing groups. The division of opinion was essentially generational in nature. By and large, the older convicts were staunch defenders of their sergeants and the old regime, and some of the most adamant of them were the graybeards among Parchman's black population. One group of such men, four strong, loitered near the hospital, acting for all the world like employees; and they too were willing enough to express their opinions, even to a white city boy.

These aging wards of the state were mortified by the destruction of Parchman Farm. They were "lifers." They had adapted to the regimen of prison life. Now, with their world collapsing around them, they looked to the future with trepidation and recalled the past fondly, finding comfort in what had existed before all the trouble.

The old rules were simple enough, their hunched, graying leader related in the rhythmic African American dialect of the Yazoo Delta. "Mine y' own bus'ness, eyes down an' lips zipped," when the camp sergeant, "da Main Mos' Man," came around. Heed the orders of the cageboss, "da Man's baw in da cage." Keep on the right side of the canteen-man, "da Man's hip-baw an' Main Mos' Snitch." Follow the orders of the Cap'n, "da Man's drivah in da rows." Chop and pick real steady, "elbow t' elbow wid da udder gunmen on da long line." Shuffle forward to the cadence "odda callah," always "keepin' ah reel close eye on da gun line." Freeze, knee to the ground, "when dare be ah rabbit in da row." Never, never, piss off a shooter.

Sure, the work on the line was tough, the old convict recalled, and more than a few gunmen fell prey to the scorching Delta sun. But a sensible fellow, one who knew how to pace himself, made out "jis fine," and boys like these got their reward on the weekends.

There were the perfumed women, "legs spread wide," ready for a good romp on the stained, yellowing mattresses in the cages. There was more of the same, though not quite so rough, when "mama come to da tonk on visitin' day." There were the ball games, "wid pleny ah bucks up fer grabs," and "da bone-rollin'," where good money changed hands, too. There was the "cawn likka," made "rat cheer on da farm." There was "da pickin' in da cages," often accompanied by a jig and a 'bone. And if the prostate acted up, or if the legs or back "be givin' out," a man could "jis sleep, gittin' ready fer da werk bell an' da shouts odda shoodahs" at dawn on Monday.

The food "be purty good, too, jis lak grammaw's table": butter beans, field peas, okra, corn, squash, tomatoes, poke salad, and corn bread—as much as a man could eat. Along with it came a decent ration of milk and enough pork, chicken, and turkey "t' keep da skin colah rat." And if the canteen-man had connections with the boys who handled the beef herd, a steak dinner, gobbled down with a little hooch, "make ah buthday reel nice."

In many ways, the old man recalled, life on the farm had been just like the free world, or at least what he remembered of the free world. Field work was field work, whether at Parchman or at any other farm; and if a man played by the rules, several years of it led him out of the rows. The route for the "dummies" was clearly marked:

> Do ya time in da rows. Neber complain. Say yassir an' nosir to da Cap'n. Fine Jesus—da whyt fok lak dat. Grab da chance t' werk some big shot's farm, maybe eben da sen'tor's place. Ack reel happy when da pol'ticians come up da farm. Keep up da yassirs an' da nosirs. Trabel up da trusty laddah, leavin' da gunmen in da rows. Start out as ah shoodah. Or try to land ah job at da cannin' plant, da dairy, da laundry, da horspital, or da gues' house. Or go da servant route, sweepin' up da Cap'n's shack or da Man's cottage, maybe eben movin' up da Big House some day.

Either way, even a dummy could get out of the rows, improve his lot, and maybe earn a ticket home.

The route for the "smart baws" was shorter. For money "mean bus'ness, reel bus'ness, on da farm, jis lak da free werl," and there were plenty of ways to get it. "Suck up to da canteen-man," trying to land a job on his staff. "Sell smokes, reefer, candy, an' all da udder shit to da gunmen," taking care not to shortchange the canteen-man. Move up to procurement, wheeling and dealing with the stash that fell off the backs of the trucks. Continue on up the ladder, exploiting connections to get the gunmen what they wanted, maybe even becoming the sergeant's hip-boy yourself some day.

Or maybe go to work for the cageboss, "whuppin' ah li'l ass, makin' book, pimpin', brewin' 'shine." Play by the boss's rules. Get promoted, "climbin' up da laddah in da cage." Be at the right place when the boss cashed in his chips: his syndicate was worth inheriting. And always give the sergeant and the driver their due: "a baw hadda have da Man an' da Cap'n on 'is side when 'e made 'is move," paying up and going for that pardon, suspended sentence, or parole. Then walk "da sweet wauk, out da front gate, 'cross dem tracks, an' home t' mama."

Sure, a fellow who refused to play by the rules paid—paid dearly sometimes, the old-timer continued. The sergeant was in charge and only a fool messed with him, but "da Man purty much let thangs shift fer demselves," never doing anything that might undermine the cage-boss and staying on top of things through the Cap'n, the canteen-man, the shooters, and his "udder snitches in da cage." So long as things in the cage went well, and so long as the field work got done, "nobody see da Man vere much."

The guys who kept the lid on were cons, the cageboss and the shooters. Play by the boss's rules, get along fine; cross the boss, "go hawngry," stand on "da coke crate fer ah spell," get a "nuccah sammich," or become free game for "da gal-baws." Play by the shooters' rules, get along fine; "turn rabbit in da row, be dead."

Back in the old days, the lifer remembered, the sergeant came down to the cage whenever "da boss an' da Cap'n couldn't git ah noo baw t' nuccah unner." But he "dint come reel offen": calling him down made the cageboss and the Cap'n look bad, "lak dey couldn't take care ah bus'ness." When the sergeant came, though, "fur flew." He rode that horse up in the yard, "da strop" hanging from his belt, and dismounted, "mad as ah hornet." Then the trusties, and "sometime da Man hisself," got rough, "givin' ah spankin' rat dare on da flo' da cage."

"Da strop git ah noo baw's 'tention, dat's fer shore," but "ah trip ov' ta Li'l Alcatraz"—some time in the hole—"be ah lot worse," the old convict remembered. "Dare be no werk in da hole, jis sittin'," and that sounded real good to new boys who had never hoed or picked before. But a little time in the hole went a long way, especially on summer days when the heat and humidity made skin feel like rubber. Then, too, the sergeant and the shooters at Li'l Alcatraz were "bad dudes"; the food was awful, usually nothing more than a few hard field peas and some of yesterday's pasty grits; and most of the inmates were "shit-slingin' muddah-fuckahs" who never shut up. But the worst thing about the hole was "d' feel d' place." The gas chamber "be rat nex doe," and everybody "hear tell 'bout dat cy'nide hittin' da acid." After a day or two, "mos' baws be ready 'nough t' git back da line."

Folks in the free world "fussed 'bout Annie an' da hole, sayin' dey be crool an' all," the old convict remembered. Truth was, though, that Annie had been "mainly show fer ah long time," a thing that "scart da noo baws," and a trip over to the hole was pretty rare, too: "supah say it be ah vacation from da rows." So nobody was sent to the hole "'less dey turn't rabbit an' live t' tell it."

Instead, the boss did his thing in the cage, keeping everybody right "one way d' udder," while the Cap'n simply made "da baws what buck da line" stand in the rows all alone with the sun beating down. That usually made them rethink matters, especially if the mercy-man failed to bring his water barrel around, and then they had to deal "widda boss an' 'is baws back da cage." Next day, "if dey still be uppidy," they stood in the rows all alone again and so on "'til dey come rat." And of course they lost their privileges, their chance to move up out of the rows, and "dare ticket home." A man just had "t' hunkah down."

Yes, "da whyt fok down Jacksun" had ignored the farm for a long time, the lifer mused with a pained expression, his head shaking slowly. But things "werk purty good back da ole days, 'speshly when Mr. Marvin be heah." Everybody "knowed da rules." Everybody "had dare place." Everybody "be real tight." A man could get "mos' anythang 'e want." Life "be perdic'able," and a man felt safe and secure. Now, though, "da lid be offen da farm 'cause dat jege."

Piddling around the cages had pleased everyone at first, but now all the piddling "be brewin' big trouble," and "dis int'gration shit jis ain't gon' go down." Black and white people "be diff'rent, 'speshly dem wild town-niggahs an' crazy 'necks." They had been tough enough to manage in the old segregated cages, even with their own kind in charge, but now this judge was creating a war zone. Already, knots of young black guys and white guys were facing off, shanks were everywhere, and people "be gittin' cut."

Back in the old days, "afo all da trouble," the cageboss "woulda stopped dat shit," the old man stressed: "da boss an' 'is baws be da onliest gang." But now the authority of the cagebosses, even the toughest of them, had been undermined, and with nobody controlling the cages, everything was coming unraveled. The hands of the sergeants and drivers were tied. In fact, they were toothless, what with "dat jege an' dem shystahs lookin' ovah dare shouldahs," and they seemed willing enough to let the boys with the shanks sort things out for themselves.

The judge had also taken away most of the perks held out in the old days. The flow of women had been reduced to a trickle, and now only the married guys were entertaining female visitors. So a man had to watch his back, and "'speshly 'is ass," in the shower these days, and everybody was competing for the females "ovah da woman's camp," the "dawg-ugly gals what werk up da Front Camp," and "da free-werl gals what come up heah lookin' fer sparrahs wid broke wings."

It was also a lot tougher for a man to pick up money nowadays. The work on neighboring plantations had stopped. Income from whoring and gambling had fallen off. Nobody was making 'shine. The sergeants and drivers had gone straight. Not much was falling off the backs of the trucks anymore, and the word from Front Camp was that trusties would no longer keep the farm's books. Everyone was watching his p's and q's, life was getting dangerous, and every day it was getting tougher for the smart boys to buy a ticket home.

"Dese young gunmen be fools," the old-timer pronounced with a tone of disgust. They whooped and hollered about the burning cages, but none of them were giving much thought to what would replace them. Construction was already under way—one could hear the bull-dozers at work—and rumors were about that the new Parchman would be a real prison, a place with cramped cells and razor wire and hacks. That, the four old men agreed, their heads shaking almost violently, might sound "reel good t' jeges an' uddah fok out dare da free werl," but not to anybody who knew anything about prisons.

They are all gone now—Judge Keady, the indignant veteran employees, and the troubled lifers alike—and Parchman Farm has gone with them, replaced, sure enough, by a real prison with towering cellblocks, razor wire, and hacks. Yet the new Parchman surpasses the old in precious few categories of penological evaluation, and even today there are many old-timers who agree with those who criticized Judge Keady over two decades ago.

Perhaps the most notable of them is Donald Cabana, whose book *Death at Midnight*[2] relates his experiences as Parchman's warden during the 1980s, especially his role in the execution of a convict. But Cabana, a native of Massachusetts, also tells of his earlier days at Parchman—of the days before the *Gates* case when, as the Cap'n, he supervised the fabled long line.

Cabana minces no words: old Parchman Farm, he contends, was a remarkably effective penal institution, notwithstanding its abuses and rundown condition on the eve of *Gates*. Indeed, drawing on his experiences as a prison administrator in the states of Florida, Massachusetts, and Missouri, Cabana argues that Mississippi's old penal farm was a "prison administrator's dream come true" and a place where uncommonly close relationships existed between staff members, convicts, and the families of convicts. Cabana, however, goes much further, actually comparing the pre-*Gates* Parchman favorably with the prison of today and asserting that Judge Keady "threw out the baby with the bath water" in a misguided attempt to bring improvement.

Cabana's point of view certainly runs afoul of contemporary interpretation, which holds that Mississippi's former penal farm was little more than a twentieth-century extension of slavery. The opinions of the former warden, however, are hardly uninformed, and at all events they merit a backward glance, one that transcends the rather simplistic image of Parchman Farm that has emerged in the years since the advent of the civil rights movement.

This book makes that attempt, drawing on a wide range of sources and inducing from them a historical account most notable for paradox and not a little irony.

Part I

Mr. Vardaman's Farm
1900–1934

Think of 16,000 acres of land stretching out before us as level as a floor and as fertile as the Valley of the Nile, in the very finest state of cultivation.

—Report of the Joint Penitentiary Committee
to the Mississippi Legislature, 1912

1

Born of Politics

By 1900 most of the damage inflicted on Jackson by General Sherman's army had been repaired, and residents no longer referred to Mississippi's capital city as "Chimneyville." Commerce thrived in the central business district on and around Capital Street. More and more fashionable homes, all of them adorned with spindles and gables, were springing up along State Street. The development reached north, out toward the high ground where Joe Johnston's little army had dug in some thirty-seven years earlier, grimly awaiting the Federal onslaught.

Similar progress was noticeable elsewhere around the state. The river towns were certainly recovering. Natchez, largely unscathed by the war, was prosperous as always, helped along by the money of social-climbing carpetbaggers and now boasting an aggressive mulatto commercial class. Greenville, too, had come a long way. Even ravished Vicksburg had been brought nearly right.

Inland from the old Confederate fortress, up the churning Yazoo, where the flat bottomland stretched as far as the eye could see, old-timers spoke of a miracle. The fields flowered with the white bolls, bringing unprecedented prosperity. The little towns were lively, a far cry from the stagnation of yesteryear. And the city of Greenwood, where the muddy waters of the Yazoo and Tallahatchie converged near the crumbling Confederate rifle-pits below old Fort Pemberton, was booming, well on the way toward becoming the world's greatest inland cotton market.

Much of the progress was owing to the state's improved infrastructure. The levees along the Mississippi River and its tributaries were repaired for the most part, enabling planters once again to produce their bales. The roads were also much better. But the real change had been wrought by the railroad men.

To the east of Jackson, the rail junction of Meridian, which Sherman had left a tangle of twisted iron, was back in business, rebuilt and improved, if not yet thriving. Much the same was true of Corinth, up north, from which Sidney Johnston had launched his furious assault on the Federal lines around Shiloh Church. To the south, Brookhaven, Hattiesburg, and McComb were developing along with the railroads, bringing the formerly stagnant Piney Woods into the pale of the state's economy, and there was much reason to expect great commercial growth along the coastal strip bordering the Gulf of Mexico.

Things, it seemed, were looking up; and in early 1900, when the state legislature convened in Jackson, the politicians noted increasing tax revenue and pondered ways to spend it.

The Bill

One of the bills on the table called for the construction of a new state capitol. Mississippi's old statehouse had its virtues, but the years had not been kind to the structure, and for about a decade its chambers had been hopelessly overcrowded. Symbolism, too, bore on the matter, for the past thirty-odd years had not been a happy era for Mississippians, and in the minds of many, the old capitol stood as a monument to the indignities of black Republican rule.

Ten years earlier, back in 1890, what the legislators regarded as the worst of those indignities had been rooted out by the ratification of a state constitution with provisions that virtually disfranchised the state's large African American underclass.[1] Now, the political legacy of the Civil War was all but destroyed, the state was prospering, and the old democracy of General Jackson was reemerging with the new century. All in all, the time was right for the construction of a grand statehouse, one symbolizing Mississippi's economic and political recovery.

The proposed site was the acreage on which the state penitentiary stood. Built in the 1830s, the institution had been a source of civic pride during the late antebellum era, rising with feudal majesty over central Jackson. Sherman, though, had razed the penitentiary along with everything else, leaving only a burnt-out shell; and after the war, despite a number of renovations, the state had progressively abandoned the old prison, leasing its convicts to private planters and railroad syndicates.[2]

During the 1880s, the competition of leased convict labor had inspired vigorous protest among the small farmers of the state, and the delegates representing the farmers at the constitutional convention of 1890 had secured a ban on leasing and a provision mandating the placement of all convicts on lands owned or operated by the state. Some four years later the state had purchased three large tracts of land outside Jackson for its penal system. Afterward, convicts had been employed to develop these properties, with others being distributed to levee commissioners in the Delta and, temporarily it was said, to a small number of planters who shared the profits of convict labor with the state.[3]

The future of the penal system, then, had pointed away from Jackson for some time, and public officials had allowed the old penitentiary to degenerate terribly. So there the thing stood, an eyesore and a health hazard occupying six choice lots squarely in the center of the otherwise resurrected capital city. Its walls were collapsing, its buildings rotting. Cattle, horses, and swine made up most of the institution's inmates, and their waste leaked onto adjoining streets, blending with kitchen slops to generate an overpowering odor. Only the previous year, in 1899, the Hinds County grand jury had described the prison as a "public disgrace" and an "insult to the City of Jackson."[4]

Jacksonians lobbied vigorously for the removal of the old penitentiary. Of course, those wanting a new state capitol joined the chorus, all the while casting covetous eyes toward the land the penitentiary occupied. The lower chamber of the legislature was willing enough to go along, but the senate balked. After much wrangling, a deal was struck.

The Deal

The 1900 legislature mandated the razing of the old penitentiary and the construction of a new state capitol on its grounds. Along with that statute came another, one that sanctioned the purchase of "an additional penitentiary farm or farms" consisting of up to 15,000 acres. And, showing that they meant business, the legislators adopted two joint resolutions pertaining to the penal system, one calling for a detailed statement of receipts and expenditures, the other for an investigation of management and control.[5]

The statute mandating the purchase of additional acreage for the penal system was shocking to some. After all, the state already possessed penal farms in Hinds, Holmes, and Rankin Counties. Together these properties constituted some 8,000 acres, and little had been done to develop them. So why authorize the purchase of 15,000 additional acres? What would the penal system do with 23,000 acres? And why should Mississippi employ its convicts at large-scale agriculture, thereby competing with farmers? What had happened to the old idea of placing felons behind bars, where they belonged, and engaging them in textile manufacturing, as the state had done before the war?

Speculation was rife in the capital, and more than a few political observers saw the hand of avarice, a new state capitol purchased with a sweetheart land deal. The defenders of the legislative package, however, pointed out that it signaled the realization of a long-standing political plank of Mississippi's Agrarian Democrats: the establishment of a large state penal farm where the proceeds of convict labor might benefit the public instead of private individuals.[6]

The practice of placing convicts on the plantations of well-heeled planters and at the construction sites of land-grabbing railroad syndicates was indefensible, these parties argued. The exploitation of convict labor had enabled contractors to amass colossal fortunes since the war, and along the way criminal process had become a brokerage most notable for graft and human abuse.[7] From all points of view, the state had to reassume control of its penal system.

That done, the only remaining question was whether Mississippi should place its convicts in a traditional cellblock prison or on penal farms. The answer was obvious. Everywhere the old cellblock prisons were penological and financial disasters. There was nothing to be gained by forcing a convict to sit in a cell. The notion of reforming felons through forced penitence was born of morbid philanthropy at best, religious hocus-pocus at worst, and it was both cruel and inefficient. Above all, cellblock prisons were costly: the idea of engaging convicts in manufacturing had long since been laid low by the opposition of the private sector.

Industry was coming to Mississippi, and the competition of felons would not do; besides, the bulk of the state's convicts were sharecroppers and farm hands. The state should seek to enhance the agricultural skills of its convicts, like the Carolinas had done for some time. Those states were generating substantial revenues on their penal farms, and nobody was complaining about the competition of convicts. Land was land, and its yield was the same whether convicts or free labor worked it.[8]

Why was more acreage needed? Because the state's convict population had almost doubled during the past decade, and increasing migration to the cities promised further growth. Then, too, only one of the penal system's existing properties, Oakley Farm in Hinds County, was suited for large-scale agriculture. But even Oakley's soil could not support much of a cotton crop, and the other two tracts could be expected to produce nothing but truck crops.

Looking back, the purchase of those farms was probably a mistake, and perhaps a bit of political hanky-panky had figured in as well. But that was then, this was now; and those who negotiated the recent legislative package had a much broader vision than those who swung the earlier land deals. Mississippi was getting a new statehouse. Jackson was ridding itself of the old penitentiary. And the money bill authorizing the purchase of more acreage for the penal system opened the door to the acquisition of prime bottomland—cotton acreage capable of supporting large-scale agriculture. The justification offered up by the politicians was compelling.

The Purchase of Parchman Farm

The commissioners appointed to purchase additional land for the penal system acted promptly. Between December 31, 1900, and January 17, 1901, the state of Mississippi concluded fourteen separate land deals, delivering 13,789.32 acres in northern Sunflower County to its penal system. Another transaction with the Ohio Hardwood Lumber Company brought to the penal system that firm's headquarters at Gordon Station on the Yazoo and Mississippi Delta Railroad, roughly thirty miles south of Clarksdale. Gordon Station was located on the eastern fringe of the lands purchased. It boasted the rail line, a fully equipped sawmill, a headquarters building, a large hotel, a barn, a storage warehouse, several farm vehicles, numerous livestock, some twenty thousand feet of cut lumber, and other useful equipment.

Of the lands purchased, a tract of some 8,375 acres was obtained from the Iowa Land Company. Once owned by the prominent Parchman

clan of Sunflower County, it was known locally as "the Parchman place."
Soon state officials were referring to their new purchase as Parchman
Farm.[9]

All of the acreage was situated in the fertile Yazoo Delta, a low-lying
alluvial plain stretching roughly two hundred miles from Vicksburg to
Memphis and extending eastward from the Mississippi River for some
seventy-five miles to the Chickasaw Ridge, where the hill country rose
abruptly from the flatlands. Here was the heart of Mississippi's fabled
cotton belt, an expanse of land with brown, vegetation-laced topsoil
known as "buckshot" running deep.

By all appearances, the state stood poised for a grand penal experiment. Landholdings amounted to nearly 23,000 acres. These included
the huge Parchman Farm, with its 14,000–odd acres, and the three
earlier purchases: the 2,005–acre Belmont Farm, situated roughly sixty
miles north of Jackson on Honey Island in Holmes County; the
2,725–acre Oakley Farm in Hinds County, some twenty-one miles
southwest of the state capital; and the 3,207–acre Rankin County Farm,
located six miles south of Jackson.

The four tracts remained largely undeveloped, but there was every
reason to expect immediate improvement. The convict population
had grown to well over a thousand, and most of them, well over 75
percent, were African Americans. Virtually all of the black convicts,
and the vast majority of the white ones, had been raised on farms,
and as adults they had tilled the land, either as sharecroppers or as
farm laborers. They promised, therefore, to be well prepared for
penal farming, experienced not only as field hands but also as workers in the myriad vocations necessitated by large-scale plantation agriculture.

Enhancing this marriage of demand and supply were a number of
relevant provisions in Article 10 of the Mississippi Constitution of
1890. Among them was a mandate for the classification of state prisoners. Another provision called for places of worship on all state penal
farms. Still others required the implementation of a scheme for the
commutation of sentences and the establishment of a juvenile reformatory.[10] These uncommon constitutional provisions joined with the
abandonment of convict leasing to place Mississippi in the front rank
of those states pursuing penal reform as the nation entered the new
century.

Stalemate

Although a solution to the prison problem seemed at hand, state officials balked. No places of worship were built on the penal farms. No formal mechanism for the commutation of sentences was implemented. No juvenile reformatory was established. And, despite the availability of well over 20,000 acres, those who presided over the penal system continued to negotiate so-called share agreements, despatching convicts to the plantations of private planters and sharing with them the proceeds of convict labor.[11]

Meanwhile, the state penal farms remained largely undeveloped. Only a handful of convicts were despatched to Parchman; and after arriving, those few quickly discovered that not all acreage in the Yazoo Delta was equally endowed. Nearly fifty years later, after additional land deals had expanded the holdings of the penal system in Sunflower County, Senator Oscar O. Wolfe Jr., a Delta planter, remarked that Parchman was "the sorriest 17,000 acres of land in the delta area." There were, according to Wolfe, only 600 acres on the whole farm that would grow cotton.[12]

If the soil was sorry, the drainage was worse. Black Bayou, which ran squarely through Parchman Farm, meandered south through the wilderness of Washington County, eventually merging with another choked waterway, Steele's Bayou, before disgorging its silty waters into the Yazoo several miles above Vicksburg. Some forty years earlier, while attempting to get at the Confederate Gibraltar from the north, Federal military authorities had tried to navigate the narrow waterway, only to see their navy boys come back empty-handed, complaining of nasty snakes and an impenetrable jungle. The bayou was no better now, and during the rainy season its waters flooded thousands of acres, transforming the cutover flatlands into stinking mudflats.

All of this painted a rather ugly picture. The purchase of the acreage in Sunflower County had all the markings of a typical public-sector land deal after all; and if further evidence were needed, all one had to do was consider a number of shady transactions that were afoot. Private firms were exploiting the facilities at Gordon Station. Over two hundred convicts were at work on the bed of the Yazoo Delta Railroad. Others labored on nearby plantations, including properties owned by the warden's family. All the while, a large amount of agricultural pro-duce was vanishing, virtually no records were being kept, and little money was being received.

Similar activities thwarted the other state properties. Oakley was a fine farm, one with great potential, but precious few convicts were as-signed to it. Perhaps it was just as well: the sergeant worked the convicts on his own adjacent farm, presided over a number of shady deals and atrocities, and sent gifts to powerful politicians when someone blew the whistle. The sergeant at Rankin County Farm probably did better for himself, making off with wagonloads of state property on a weekly basis. Belmont Farm stood virtually dormant, manned by publicly paid em-ployees but notable for nothing except the disappearance of timber.[13]

At the root of this stalemate were the closed nominating conventions of the state's dominant Democratic Party, which for some time had en-abled the Delta political clique of Governor Anselm McLaurin to con-trol party machinery. Within McLaurin's circle, convicts were chips on the table of state politics, being doled out among favored parties for labor in the malarial swamps of Mississippi's northern river counties.[14]

In 1899 promises of convict labor had reportedly bought McLaurin's gubernatorial candidate, A. H. Longino, the support of powerful men; and in 1900 Longino had succeeded McLaurin as governor, with state convicts being divided among eleven prominent planters. Among them, McLaurin's brother, state senator Henry McLaurin, had taken his share as always, afterward putting the convicts to work at his Sandy Bayou plantation.[15]

Under Longino, as under McLaurin, these arrangements were seem-ingly beyond the reach of critics; for the board of control, which man-aged the penal system, was composed of the governor, the state attor-ney general, and the three state railroad commissioners, all of whom owed their offices to McLaurin's influence at the state nominating convention. And with the state penal farms undeveloped and undone by corruption, the profits accruing to the state through the board's "share agreements" looked good.[16] The politics of the thing seemed impossible.

The Revolt of the Rednecks

In the presidential primary elections of 1900, the executive committee of Mississippi's Democratic Party made a crucial error, breaking with precedent by failing to provide for the meeting of a state convention. That omission alienated a considerable number of local party operatives and eventually incited a political furor. Dating from the closing months of 1900, the party boss, Anselm McLaurin, was confronted by strong and mounting opposition within his own ranks, especially from the dirt farmers of the hill country beyond the Chickasaw Ridge. The rebels were ably led, and their leaders struck at the source of McLaurin's strength, advocating the abolition of the party's nominating conventions and the establishment of a statewide system of primary elections.[17]

The anti-McLaurin faction was strongest in the lower house of the state legislature, and its leaders took the offensive early in the 1901 legislative session, using as their vehicle the two joint resolutions adopted back in 1900: the one "requesting the board of control to report to the legislature a detailed statement of receipts and expenditures," the other calling for an investigation of the "management and control of the State Penitentiary." At the time they were approved, those resolutions had posed no great threat to McLaurin or the board of control. Now, with the party rank and file in the lower house of the legislature in open revolt, matters were quite different. An anti-McLaurin committee launched a vigorous investigation. When the Jackson *Clarion-Ledger* predicted in September 1901 that the investigation would place the board in a tenuous position, rumors began to fly in the capital.[18]

The committee's report, released quite early in the 1902 legislative session, included evidence of indictable transgressions by board members and employees of the penal system, and implicated by it were not only McLaurin and Longino, but also McLaurin's predecessor, former governor John M. Stone. The Vicksburg *Herald,* perhaps stretching things a bit, regarded the disclosures as the worst scandal in state history.[19]

But the combined forces of McLaurin and Longino still held sway in the senate, a fact that facilitated a number of important compromises. The investigating committee was sent back to try again, ostensibly for the purpose of clarifying its hair-raising allegations, and a second report, less critical of personages than the first, was forthcoming. Still, the second report presented a strong argument for sweeping reform, actually observing that "a dishonest Warden may, if he so chooses, safely, and without fear of detection annually rob the State of thousands of dollars."[20]

As was customary, remedial legislation defused scandal, with smiling politicians assuring the public that all was well. The statute enacted in the midst of all the political brouhaha, however, was of future importance. For after February 1902, those who presided over Mississippi's penal system were required to transfer all income into the state treasury immediately upon receipt and were allowed to disburse monies only upon the warrants of the state auditor.[21]

More significant for the future of the state penal system was a subsequent statute that at last replaced the nominating conventions of the state Democratic Party with statewide primary elections. This legislation, too, may well have been influenced by the penitentiary scandal: Governor Longino, against whom many of the charges were leveled, suddenly lent his support to the abolition of the very process that had placed him in office. Whatever the case, the 1902 session of the Mississippi legislature constituted a revolution in state politics, one that guaranteed greater influence to the small farmers of the northeastern hill country and the developing southern half of the state.[22]

Enter the "White Chief"

After the enactment of Mississippi's primary election law, the McLaurins and their political allies were backpedaling, trying to save what they could, while populism flowered on the hustings. In early twentieth-century Mississippi, of course, populists necessarily had to exploit the prejudices of white farmers. All of them did so, more or less, but none was better at it than Anselm McLaurin's greatest critic, the silver-tongued James Kimble Vardaman, who rode the vote of the "redneck" into the governor's mansion in the elections of 1903.[23]

Vardaman was a curious man. No Mississippi politician since Albert Gallatin Brown, the backwoods demagogue who led the radical Jacksonian Democrats during the antebellum era, equaled Vardaman's vicious attacks on the wealthy; perhaps no man in state history has been a more accomplished Negro-baiter on the hustings. Yet Vardaman's racism was by no means as vicious as some have represented it, and many of the causes he espoused were far to the left of the national Democratic and Republican Parties. More than one historian has labeled the so-called White Chief the most progressive Southern politician of his age.[24]

Much of Vardaman's reputation is based on his contribution to penology. None of Mississippi's governors has come to office with a firmer grasp of criminological theory than Vardaman possessed. None of them has more successfully incorporated such theory within a broader scheme of policy. And none of them has exerted greater influence on the state penal system.

Vardaman's interest in crime and punishment was long-standing. As editor of the Greenwood *Enterprise,* later the Greenwood *Common-wealth,* he had become one of the state's most passionate advocates of penal reform during the 1890s. His editorials, especially a series written in April 1894, protested brutality, reminded Mississippians of their Christian heritage, and asserted that the state penitentiary should function to prepare convicts for social respectability upon release.[25]

In 1902, upon learning of the hair-raising disclosures of the legislative committees investigating the state penal system, Vardaman had renewed the attack, claiming that avarice was destroying the moral foundations of the criminal law.[26] Now, in 1904, when as governor he assumed the chairmanship of the penal system's board of control, Vardaman invaded the closed circle of men who alone thwarted the placement of all state convicts on public lands.

The governor was uncommonly well read, and his opinions on crime and punishment were influenced, either directly or indirectly, by the recently propounded criminological theories of the Italian positivists Cesare Lombroso, Enrico Ferri, and Rafaele Garofalo. He did not believe that human beings possessed complete freedom of will, and found it "quite probable" that human behavior was "determined by countless causes over which they have no control." The biological determinism of Lombroso and the environmental determinism of Ferri were popular with Vardaman: man, he once remarked, was a "creature of heredity and environment," an animal whose acts were "often the result of influence set in motion by the unconscious deeds of some forgotten ancestor." But the governor leaned more heavily on Garofalo, whose published works attributed crime, in part at least, to "moral anomaly" among certain groups within the community. Criminals, Vardaman maintained, were "moral cripples."[27]

These opinions conditioned Vardaman's penal philosophy. He argued that the old and revered Babylonian adage of "an eye for an eye" was nonsense, a reflection of ignorance and bad breeding. Nor did the governor think that vicious punishments served the interests of the state. Legal sanctions were not "inflicted in the spirit of revenge, but rather for correction—in love rather than hate."[28]

His concept of "correction" was influenced by the fact that the vast majority of convicts reentered society. Penal discipline, Vardaman stressed, could not be allowed to embitter those being punished. The interests of the state dictated that all convicts, but especially one who was a "low-bred, vulgar creature, congenitally corrupt, [and] inured to physical and moral filth," should receive "kindly treatment, a decent bed to sleep on . . . sanitary surrounding," and management by an "upright, honorable, intelligent and just man."[29]

The governor also placed great emphasis on the tactics of convict indoctrination that were pursued by the early Victorians. Remunerative labor was an essential component of his plan, but the primary purpose of labor, he emphasized, was convict remission. The work ethic could be instilled in convicts only through a comprehensive and systematically pursued program of incentives, he thought, and other social instincts might be inculcated by the influence of Christian doctrine. Penitentiaries should be "moral hospitals," institutions that treated "patients" and released them whenever they displayed signs of complete "recovery."[30]

Vardaman considered the tribulations awaiting released convicts as well. Despite whatever constructive influence the penal system might have on an inmate, a convicted felon had a "brand" on him when he returned to society. Consequently, the opportunities offered to a released convict by illegal behavior often eclipsed those offered by legal behavior, and further criminality was normally the result. The remedy, Vardaman concluded, was to make the penitentiary a "school," an institution that provided vocational training and thus equipped convicts for successful reentry into society. A percentage of the penitentiary's profits, he added, should be allocated either to the families of convicts or to the convicts themselves at the time of their release. "I am more interested in the salvation of man," the governor assured the legislature, "than I am in hoarding gold."[31]

If evaluated in a vacuum, Vardaman's views on crime and punishment seem remarkably progressive for a Mississippi politician of his age. The governor, however, did not advance them in a vacuum. His staunch determinism considered inescapable facts peculiar to his native state, and his plan for the penal system was utterly pragmatic, a reflection of the events of his lifetime and of his broader concept of politics.

The Burden of Mississippi History

Born in 1861, Vardaman was the son of a yeoman farmer, one of the class of men that formed the heart and soul of the Confederate infantry. Vardaman grew to manhood under the influence of the legend of the Lost Cause, hearing his father and other veterans recall the Mississippi regiments in line of battle, their terrifying yell rising over the rattle of musketry and the rumble of guns on hundreds of killing fields.

This romantic legacy of defiance fell heavily on Gaelic stock and left an indelible mark on Vardaman, but certainly no more so than did the suffering of those around him. More than a third of the Mississippians who bore Confederate arms, nearly twenty-six thousand, lay buried in shallow graves far afield, and many more had been maimed: the purchase of artificial limbs consumed fully 20 percent of state tax revenues in 1866, the fifth year of Vardaman's life.[32]

The young man heard of the slaughter: of the wave after wave of butternut-clad farmers cut down before the sunken road at Shiloh; of the heroes who fell with Barksdale near the peach orchard at Gettysburg; of the starving ragamuffins who dressed their depleted ranks, stacked arms, and heard the bugle's last call near the courthouse in faraway Virginia. And all around him was the human wreckage of the war. There were the black-clad widows, their fatherless moppets in tow, struggling to eke out a living amid the postwar devastation. There were the horribly maimed veterans who sat pathetically on little benches in the town squares, whittling, dipping snuff, remembering the defining event of their lives. And, of course, there was black Republican rule.

Vardaman's father was among the surviving veterans who wandered back to flooded farmland and burnt-out homes in the wake of the war. Like so many others, he was disfranchised, forced to sell his land to meet the burden of Republican taxes, and doomed to a meager existence for the remainder of his life.[33]

No youngster could go unaffected by this, but along with it came something much worse. Vardaman saw his father and other farmers stand by helplessly as hordes of the new black freedmen, dressed in the rags of field hands, were herded to the polls by the Republican conqueror. This added insult to injury; and when the white farmers struck back against their rulers—hiding beneath the hood, conducting their reign of terror under cloak of darkness—the young Vardaman sympathized with them. Until the end of his days, he would rail against the hypocrisy of those who courted the black vote and maintain that extraordinary circumstances justified lynch law.[34]

After the hated Republicans were sent packing at last, the policies of Mississippi's "redeeming" Democrats influenced Vardaman as well; for the new regime, he thought, exploited blacks to beggar the white farmer no less than its predecessor did, and this betrayal deepened his bitterness and cynicism. These experiences molded Vardaman's general view of politics. He hated entrenched wealth and influence, attacking corporate interests and opposing America's imperialistic policies in Cuba and the Philippines as sellouts to the nation's financial elite. He regarded Mississippi's postwar rulers, Republican and Democrat alike, as carbon copies of the Yankee "robber barons." He championed the cause of the poor white man, ever seeing him as a victim of the rich. And he saw the black man as an ignorant tool of entrenched wealth and influence, a creature who, in defiance of nature, had been liberated to promote the capitalist conspiracy.[35]

The conspiracy had produced victims. Among them were those who formed Mississippi's "criminal class": "po' white trash" and "worthless niggers." These were the "moral cripples" of whom Vardaman spoke—an underclass whose members were outside the pale of civilization. Many of the state's poor whites were the surviving yeoman farmers of the old antebellum democracy, people who had been scarred, degraded, and brought to ruin by the ravages of war and the iniquities of postwar rule. Not surprisingly, they and their sons were hard, often mean-spirited characters, men consumed by hatred who were fully capable of killing without remorse. Their crimes were frequent and heinous; and yes, there was much truth in the old saying that there was "nothin' lower than po' white trash." But history, Vardaman felt, had cut these unfortunate souls adrift, and those who ran afoul of the law deserved the compassion of a Christian community.

The state's "worthless niggers" presented a far more perplexing problem, Vardaman thought, for Africans had never known civilization. Indeed, the governor viewed Mississippi's blacks as the misplaced members of a race that was "inherently immoral, ignorant and superstitious, with a congenital tendency to crime . . . [and] devoid of those qualities of mind and soul necessary to self-control." Consequently, the bulk of them were "trifling, loafing" laggards who loitered in the towns like mongrel dogs, begging for scraps of food, and even many of those who worked for a living were wastrels and public menaces. At the conclusion of the workweek, they gathered in their shabby bars, where the click of dice could be heard above even their primitive music; and as the evening progressed, the whiskey took its toll, emancipating the "savage beast." They fornicated like rabbits: nothing equaled the "brutish negro's lust." They slaughtered each other like "hogs," especially in the summer months, when the sun kindled within them "the fires of hell itself." And larceny was a way of life for the black man, as it had been in the jungle.[36]

Yet Vardaman fully appreciated the vital role of the black laborer in the state's means of production, and looked to the future with guarded optimism. Not all blacks were worthless, he stressed: quite clearly, some of them had profited by association with the white man and now worked their shares quietly and productively. Vardaman thought, moreover, that Mississippi's "worthless niggers," like its detestable "po' white trash," were the victims of history, simple people who had been placed in an impossible position by unprincipled New England merchants, grasping thousand-bale planters, Yankee guns, and postwar political hypocrisy; and that they too deserved compassion. And if white men were incapable of such compassion, he warned, they had best consider the awesome size of the black underclass.

The Agenda

The axis around which the political creed of the White Chief turned, and the source of his strength on the hustings, was a defense of white rule. Nobody believed more earnestly in the innate inferiority of Africans. No politician exploited the Negrophobia of the state's down-trodden white electorate more successfully. No man defended the racial status quo more zealously. Yet Vardaman saw widening cracks in the foundations of white rule. The huge black underclass haunted him, and the "criminal tendencies" of its members troubled him deeply. The state's jails were full of "worthless niggers," notwithstanding the frequent intervention of white planters on their behalf and the operation of a studied hands-off policy by sheriffs in cases involving black-on-black crime. This problem, moreover, promised to worsen due to potentially disastrous demographic changes. The great number of "criminal negroes" who were migrating to the state's cities,

Vardaman told Mississippi's peace officers in 1905, sought "a way to live without honest toil" and menaced "the safety of the white man's home."[37]

The question was how to counter the threat. Here, Vardaman embraced the paternalistic view of the underclass commonly expressed by the more thoughtful members of ruling oligarchies everywhere. While championing, and even wishing to expand, the numerous provisions in the state's constitutional and statutory law that impeded the advancement of blacks, Vardaman also thought that the privileged status of the white man brought with it social responsibilities. Blacks, he felt, were like children, a race doomed by genetic inferiority. He therefore wished them no harm, treated them respectfully, and actively sought to protect and improve the lot of blacks within the confines of their subordinate status.[38]

Vardaman attempted to instill his tactical paternalism in the institutions that propped the unequal social order. The church, which functioned to preserve established values, and the schools, no less valuable as tools of indoctrination, constituted the first line of defense. So while steadfastly defending white rule, Vardaman encouraged his constituents to consult their Christian principles when dealing with blacks and meddled in the state's educational system with uncommon vigor, always drawing a clear line between the types of education required for the respective races.[39]

If religion and education were proactive tools used to support the prevailing social order, criminal process was a reactive one, the last line of defense. The law was necessarily stacked against the black man, the state's entire apparatus of force necessarily vested in the hands of the white establishment; and given the pathetic history of Mississippi's misplaced Africans, it was hardly surprising that the convict population had been roughly 80 percent black since the forced termination of slavery some forty years earlier.[40] Mississippi's penal policy, therefore, was a vital component of a broader political agenda, a sphere of public administration that must be handled with great care; for the state penitentiary was essentially an institution for the wayward members of the black underclass.

What to do with them? The pivotal issue was not racial inequity; such inequity was the essence of the social system. Rather, it was one of iniquity, the manner in which the coercive power of the state should be wielded. Vardaman saw grave problems in the manner in which

McLaurin and his predecessors had employed their police powers. Their short-sighted policies, always defended by hollow appeals to the tenets of legal retributivism, had rendered legal punishment little more than an instrument of exploitation and brute force. The state had forgotten the first principle of social control and, indeed, the nexus of classical retributivism itself. The preservation of white rule necessitated policies of moral suasion and social indoctrination in all branches of public administration, but especially in the administration of legal punishment.

Vardaman essentially accepted the thesis, advanced by Marx and Engels some fifty years earlier, that law was the exclusive domain of those who controlled the means of production. He carried that thesis to its logical conclusion, rationally viewing criminal process as a mechanism of social control. And in the fashion of the eighteenth-century English aristocrats who had pioneered the penitentiary movement, he felt that the word was more effective than the sword in the management of an increasingly troublesome underclass.[41]

The governor's quest to protect white rule narrowed the scope of his penal philosophy. His political rhetoric repeatedly emphasized the absurdity of attempts to educate blacks. They were common laborers; they must never be allowed to rise above that station in life. Education could only breed rising expectations, dissatisfaction, and misery among blacks; a literate black man in white-ruled Mississippi, he once remarked, was inclined to criminality. So Vardaman steadfastly opposed education in letters at the penitentiary. Vocational training, though, especially in agriculture, promised to perpetuate the traditional role of the black man. Such training, moreover, could enhance the living conditions of the underclass, breed greater happiness among its members, and thereby strengthen the foundations of white rule.[42]

This was the agenda Vardaman brought to the governor's mansion in 1904. He was irrevocably committed to it, and he was willing to fight to achieve it. The boisterous party rank and file in the lower house of the legislature were with him, fully prepared to follow the governor into battle against McLaurin and his allies in the senate. The White Chief would emerge as the philosophical and political architect of Mississippi's twentieth-century penal system, the founding father of all that followed.

2

Dust in the Delta

Vardaman initiated his campaign for penal reform almost immediately after assuming the office of chief executive in January 1904. It began, like all successful campaigns, quietly and methodically, with emphasis on garnering pertinent facts. It proceeded to skirmishing, softening up the enemy with a number of closely calculated feints. It ended with a frontal assault, one that had far-reaching repercussions.

Often accompanied by Albert H. Whitfield, his sole ally on the bench of the state supreme court, the newly inaugurated Vardaman went for long rides before breakfast. On a number of occasions, the staff at the Rankin County Farm, which in those days housed the penal system's kennel, were snapped to attention by the unexpected appearance of the governor and the eminent jurist. Once at the farm, Vardaman and Whitfield sometimes lingered for a "hunt." Posing as foxes, convicts fled into the woods and were pursued by sniffing, slobbering bloodhounds. Vardaman, Whitfield, and the camp sergeant followed the baying hounds on horseback until their prey was duly treed, then culminated the hunt with a picnic attended by the captured convicts.[1] Vardaman exploited his visits to the Rankin County Farm to the fullest, establishing a web of personal contacts among staff members and convicts alike. From them he solicited and obtained valuable information: the Rankin County Farm was the governor's research laboratory.

Vardaman used the information so obtained to confront his colleagues on the penitentiary's board of control. He engaged them repeatedly, wresting a concession here, a concession there, undermining their position piecemeal; but on the crucial point—the removal of convicts from private lands—the governor was outvoted again and again.

Failing there, Vardaman carried his campaign to the courts of law, where he sometimes gained injunctive relief in chancery; but Whitfield was invariably outvoted by McLaurin's two appointees on the bench of the state supreme court. Even unsuccessful litigation, however, strengthened the governor's hand. Through it, he kept his adversaries on their heels, reeling from damaging allegations reported by the state's newspapers.[2]

Such tactics enhanced the principal thrust of Vardaman's campaign: a ruthless effort to tarnish the much-hyped fiscal utility of the board's "share agreements" by improving the state penal farms. The governor began with an unprecedented crusade against corruption. Vardaman dealt very harshly with graft, sacking employees at the drop of a hat, and he questioned every financial transaction, every hire, every assignment of convict labor. The word spread quickly, and the result was discernible improvement in a very short period of time.

During 1904 and 1905 Oakley became a productive ranch, raising and slaughtering livestock on an astonishing scale. Belmont, too, underwent a transformation, emerging as a considerable producer of food crops, while the Rankin County Farm, cursed by poor soil, at least stopped recording red ink. But Parchman Farm was the apple of Vardaman's eye, a place about which he spoke with almost parental devotion, and under his watchful eye it began to take shape.

During the early summer of 1904, only months after Vardaman's inauguration, Henry B. Lacey, collecting information for the state's *Statistical Register,* undertook the long trek from Jackson to Sunflower County. Amid yellow dust and sweating men at Gordon Station, Lacey observed the fruits of Vardaman's labor and concluded that Mississippi, keeping step "with the progress of advanced thought," was "evolving a system of control for its penal institution, that, whilst protecting society and punishing the criminal with hard labor, leaves open to him the door of hope."[3]

Lacey observed an awe-inspiring spectacle, but one that was only beginning to take form. Vardaman would pay scant attention to the smaller penal farms; his eyes were fixed on Parchman, and there, during 1904 and 1905, clearing operations proceeded at a lightning pace.

The sawmill at Gordon Station operated day and night, cotton acreage rolled westward daily, and locomotives, pulling cars stuffed with cotton and timber to market, disturbed the quiet lifestyles of local sharecroppers. On September 30, 1905, the state penal farms recorded a fiscal-year profit of nearly $185,000.[4]

Closing the Deal

Vardaman's successes at the state penal farms during his first two years as governor laid the foundation for a legislative offensive, which he launched in early 1906. Much of his address to the legislature of January was devoted to the evils of the penal system. He recounted historical developments, dwelling on the horrors of the state's convict lease system, pointing out that manacled men were still at the mercy of private parties whose personal interests were at odds with the moral foundations of criminal jurisprudence. He spoke of the enormous profits being earned by Henry McLaurin and others through the exploitation of the state's convict labor. He related how "distinguished gentlemen, prominent in politics," even now were buying votes with the nasty bribe of delivering manacled convicts to "some political dictator's Delta plantation." He told of acts "rivalling in brutality and fiendishness, the atrocities of . . . Torquemada."[5]

Then, following the successful tactics of earlier days, a house committee once again set out to humiliate the penitentiary board and the beneficiaries of its policies. The report of the committee was indeed humiliating, and it delivered what Vardaman wanted: recommendations for the abolition of the board of control and the placement of all convicts on state lands.[6]

The McLaurin faction had been in retreat since 1902, but the old guard, still powerful in the senate, had not struck its colors. It was now clear, however, even to the truculent and infuriated McLaurins, that eventually Vardaman would have his way, so the protectors of the status quo gave ground, bent on securing what they could. The result, effected through much logrolling, was the enactment of statutes banning "the working of the State's convicts on land other than that owned by the State of Mississippi," abolishing the board of control, and providing for a superintendent to replace the warden at Parchman.[7]

Vardaman was now virtually sovereign over state penal policy. The new superintendent was to be appointed by the governor for a four-year term; a popularly elected, three-member board of trustees was to replace the board of control; and the governor was to appoint interim trustees to serve until the elections of late 1907. In the aftermath of victory, Vardaman stacked the board with some of his most loyal lieutenants and set his political machine to work on the upcoming election of trustees. He refused to rehire Warden John J. Henry, who had close ties with the McLaurin faction, instead appointing C. H. Neyland, a farmer from Wilkinson County, to the new superintendency.

Then the governor stepped up the assault on the wilderness of Sunflower County. Nearly three-quarters of a century later, an old-timer, with eyes gleaming, spoke of the old days when he and his convicts stood waist-deep in brackish water, fought off the dreaded cottonmouth moccasin, and raised "Mr. Vardaman's farm" from the floor of the Yazoo Delta.[8]

The Blueprint

Vardaman plotted the future of the state penal system very carefully. Everything turned on his opinion that nothing would work unless the penitentiary were insulated from politics. Parchman Farm, Vardaman stressed, must be made an island, a fortress beyond the reach of influential politicians like McLaurin and altogether removed from the capricious private sector. If the penitentiary could be exploited, it would be exploited; if it were possible to return convicts to the days of penal slavery, they would become penal slaves.

Insulation required, first, a scheme capable of screening the penal farms from the many pitfalls of a large, publicly administered business. The penitentiary act of 1902 had laid a good foundation: it required administrators to transfer all revenues to the state treasurer immediately upon receipt and to disburse monies only on the warrants of the state auditor.

The statute enacted in 1906 built on that foundation. Under its provisions, the governor appointed every employee on the penal farms, the legislature held the penitentiary's purse strings, and the members of the board of trustees were popularly elected—independent of both the chief executive and the legislature. Here was a potentially effective system of checks and balances. The facts of political life would require the chief executive to share the penitentiary's patronage with both trustees and legislative leaders. The governor, the trustees, and the powerful legislators, then, would have their own people at the penitentiary, all of them keeping an eye on each other. Inevitably, Parchman would be a "snitch-run" prison—one in which informants were under every rock—and the snitching would extend from top to bottom, from the halls of the statehouse to the cotton rows of Sunflower County.

The elected penitentiary trustees were the most vital cog in Vardaman's scheme: they were the principal snitches, the watchdogs, the people on whose desks the buck would stop in the event of abuses on the penal farms. The trustees' statutory charge was to represent all facets of the penitentiary's operations. They would counterbalance the cupidity and fickleness of a republican political process serving a market economy. They would represent an otherwise unrepresented constituency of felons. They would visit the penal farms, sniffing out financial irregularities and seeking to protect convicts from the inevitable abuses of their taskmasters. No governor, no legislator, no superintendent would be beyond their reach; and in all likelihood, the trustees would police themselves. There were three of them, each representing a separate electoral district. Given Mississippi's new system of statewide primary elections, it was very unlikely that the trustees would be too chummy.

Vardaman's emphasis on political insulation also led him to stress that the penitentiary had to be at least self-sufficient, a moneymaker if possible. At all events, it could not be a financial drain, yet another public institution dependent on the wavering fiscal priorities of elected public officials. The trustees and the superintendent simply had to deal with the legislature from a position of strength: they had to come down to Jackson with black ink on the ledger.

If political insulation necessitated remunerative plantation agriculture, remunerative plantation agriculture necessitated centralization at Parchman: it was by far the largest of the state penal farms and the only one capable of producing a substantial cash crop. The Mississippi Code of 1906, reflecting the vision of the White Chief, defined the state penal system as "the plantation known as Parchman . . . in Sunflower County, and such other places . . . owned or operated by the state in the enforcement of penal servitude."[9]

At Parchman, available assets included a huge expanse of land and a large labor force consisting primarily of country folk, most of them black males. Logically, the governor embraced the same organizational scheme that had been employed on Southern plantations for well over a century.

Gordon Station would be Parchman's hub. From there a central administration would coordinate purchasing, allocate labor and other resources, receive and process raw cotton, and preside over sales. Convict laborers would be distributed among overseers on a number of "working plantations" or field camps, each allocated acreage for the production of the cash crop and raising its own food crops and livestock. The field camps would be widely dispersed over Parchman's acreage, thereby facilitating the proper classification of convict laborers and confining trouble to defensible space. Several specialized units would house carpenters, brick masons, and others capable of performing services for the whole.[10]

Implementation

Early on, during the crucial years of Parchman's development, Vardaman's system of checks and balances was ineffectual: all three members of the interim board of trustees, as well as those who were elected in late 1907, belonged to the White Chief's political faction. The lower house of the legislature was no less devoted to the governor, and Vardaman, later one of Mississippi's United States senators, would continue to exert powerful influence on state politics until 1914. A political vacuum therefore existed when the trustees got down to work, and the continuing dominance of the Vardaman faction provided them and their successors with an uncommon reprieve from many of the vicissitudes of partisan politics. The result was a rarity in American public administration: the systematic pursuit of a well-reasoned policy for a considerable number of years.

Working closely with the governor, the interim trustees got things moving during 1906 and 1907. Rankin County Farm was made the primary residence of white male convicts. Oakley Farm became the sole residence of all females, the temporary site of the penal system's major medical facility, and a holding station for convalescents. Old and infirm black male convicts were despatched to Belmont Farm. The younger and healthier black men were placed at Parchman.

During 1907 some 80 white men at Rankin County Farm raised livestock and grew truck crops while Oakley accommodated female and sickly male convicts. The women were lodged at a part of Oakley Farm known as the "Oakley Walls." There, with their virtue ostensibly protected from the nearby men by a towering fence, they produced clothing and other domestic articles for the entire penal system. Oakley's hospital, which remained a "shack" despite a number of renovations, cared for convicts from all the farms. After being released from the hospital, convicts convalesced in barracks on Oakley's farm acreage, where animal husbandry was the chief occupation. Meanwhile, some 120 black male convicts worked at Belmont Farm, no doubt thankful that poor health or advancing years screened them from the far more rigorous regimen in Sunflower County.

At Parchman the younger black men were initially distributed among nine field camps, a sawmill camp, and a carpenters' camp. Operations at the sawmill required a degree of skill not possessed by the black convicts, so 30 white men were brought up from Rankin County Farm. At Parchman's sawmill they worked alongside 6 blacks, representing the only Caucasians on the plantation except overseers and others in managerial positions. Seventeen black carpenters were on hand, however, and they manned the carpenters' camp. While the saws hummed and the carpenters transformed the raw wood into permanent buildings, some 850 black men in the field camps cleared land, hauled wood to the sawmill, prepared the alluvial soil for cultivation, and left cash crops behind them.[11]

In 1910 penal authorities increased acreage in Sunflower County with three separate acquisitions. The first, a 222–acre tract bordering Parchman to the south, was purchased in June. In September another 320 acres south of the plantation were obtained, and in October 1,358 acres adjoining Parchman to the north were added. Dating from October 1910, the holdings of the penal system in Sunflower County stood at some 15,689 acres.[12]

The inmate population grew in almost direct proportion to the demand for labor and the capacity of the penal farms to accommodate convicts. On October 1, 1907, there were 1,337 prisoners on hand. Two years later the work force stood at 1,628, and in June 1911 at 1,843. The trustees shifted a larger percentage of convicts to Parchman each year. In October 1909 some 69 percent of them were in Sunflower County; by July 1915, nearly 80 percent. The laborers were exploited to the fullest. As early as 1905, rail spurs had begun to reach into the plantation; now they reached farther, accelerating clearing operations, bringing the wilderness to heel.

Operations on the smaller farms were scaled down as the trustees diverted a greater percentage of their resources to Parchman. In 1908 the female convicts were transferred from Oakley to Sunflower County.

About three years later, when a new medical facility opened at Parchman, Oakley was reduced to a small contingent of convicts engaged in animal husbandry.[13]

The early operations of the penal farm system paid extraordinary dividends. While the produce of the satellite farms fed and clothed the convicts, Parchman's surplus lumber commanded a hefty price, and the cotton market was strong. A modest net profit of $24,606.84 was reported for fiscal year 1906–7. But during the 1907–9 biennium, profits leaped to over $176,000, and in 1913 the trustees reported an incredible profit of nearly $937,000 for the past biennium.[14]

In 1912 the members of a legislative committee visited Parchman and voiced astonishment. "Think of 16,000 acres of land stretching out before us as level as a floor and as fertile as the Valley of the Nile, in the very finest state of cultivation," the chairman wrote in his official report. The farm was "a very monument to labor that our state can boast of, and one of which we might well be proud." Indeed, it was impossible to doubt that Mississippi now had "one of the best, if not the best, Penitentiary systems in the United States."[15]

Further expansion ensued. In 1914 the board of trustees purchased two small tracts of land—one near Okalona and one near Waynesboro—and established limestone-crushing plants at both locations. Two years later the legislature created a commission and authorized it to obtain additional acreage for the penal system. The resulting acquisition of the 5,000–acre O'Keefe plantation in Quitman County—afterward dubbed "Lambert" owing to the close proximity of the Lambert community—carried the landholdings of the penal system to 28,910 acres.[16]

The Emerging Penal Farm System

By 1917 clearing operations at Parchman were virtually complete, and the farm was organized along lines that would remain largely unchanged until the eighth decade of the twentieth century. Outside the front gate were warehouses, a large gin, and a railroad depot. One crossed the tracks to approach the gate. Armed guards perfunctorily waved visitors through, and the gate seemed unnecessary because neither fences nor walls were connected to it.

Once beyond the gatekeepers, one entered old Gordon Station, which now had all the markings of a "little city." It consisted of a barnlike administration building, a guest house, a number of staff houses, a small church for employees, a post office, and the hospital. Rising above everything was a new house for the "super," a two-story mansion rendered pretentious by spindles, gables, and all the other hallmarks of Victorian architecture.[17]

Beyond Gordon Station were twelve widely spaced field camps housing male convicts, ten for blacks and two for whites; more would be established in succeeding years. The major function of the field camps was the production of cotton, but all of them were required to maintain a garden and to raise livestock for the sustenance of their staff members and inmates.

Each field camp was equipped with a long, one-story dormitory known as a cage. The windows of the cages were barred, and most of the units were subdivided into three sections—a dining room with a connected kitchen, a small room for convict trusties, and a large room for "gunmen," convicts under the gun. A corridor intersected the gunmen's room; on each side of it were approximately fifty beds several feet apart, each equipped with a foot locker. A door led from the central corridor into the dining room, in which were a number of four-by-four-foot tables. Initially the cages were made of wood, but by the thirties, convict labor had transformed most of them into brick, and all cages were equipped with electric lights, running water, and bathrooms.[18]

All field camps were commanded by a sergeant who reported directly to the superintendent. In the larger ones, the sergeant was helped by two assistant sergeants, or "drivers." Smaller camps were usually staffed with one driver, and the smallest had none. Black convicts came to call their sergeant "da Main Mos' Man," white ones simply "The Man." In both black and white camps, a driver was known as "Cap'n."

Parchman's other units had a unitary function. There was a wide range of such units on a plantation that strove for self-sufficiency, but the largest of them were the women's camp, the hospital, the brickyard, the sawmill, and the carpenters' camp.

The women's camp was equipped with sewing machines. There, like pupils aligned in desks, female convicts produced all of the bedding, curtains, and linens utilized by the entire penal system as well as the striped uniforms and the crude suits of clothing allocated to prisoners on the day of their release. Whenever the women were "caught up," they too worked the fields; and whether caught up or not, they were sent to the cotton rows whenever there was a shortage of male field hands.

Considering the small number of female convicts during the early years of the century, the women's camp was remarkably productive. In June 1917 only 26 females were under sentence, but their numbers increased over the years: between 1923 and 1933 an average of 62 women were at Parchman. Black and white women were said to share a single dormitory, subdivided into two wards, but in all probability few if any white females resided at the women's camp. There were no white women under sentence in June 1915, and records indicate that up to 1933 no more than 2 were at Parchman at one time. A small number of women, white and black, were quartered at places other than the women's camp, including the governor's mansion and state institutions for the insane and feeble-minded. Judging by the sexual and racial mores of the time, there can be little doubt that those favored few included the white women. The women's camp at Parchman, then, served principally, and probably exclusively, as a unit for black females.[19]

Parchman's hospital was divided into wards with patients segregated by race, gender, and malady as much as space would permit. Farming and the raising of livestock were conducted on a small scale so as to occupy the patients' time, to contribute to the maintenance of patients, and to discourage malingering. The brickyard produced bricks, not only for the penal farms, but also for other state institutions, and the convicts there raised food crops on roughly 60 acres of land. The sawmill was located on the northeastern part of the plantation; its crew, housed nearby at Camp Ten, was excused from farming because of the time required to produce lumber and shingles for the entire penal system. Camp Six, which housed the subunit known as the carpenters' camp, accommodated thirty carpenters who served the needs of the plantation when they were not employed in the fields.[20]

Compared to Parchman, the penal system's other units were minor operations. The only producers of revenue were Belmont and Lambert. Belmont continued to house old and infirm black males. They raised various breeds of livestock for the benefit of the other penal farms, and agriculture, most notably the growing of food crops, was conducted on a surprisingly large scale. Between 1908 and 1934 the farm had an average of about seventy convicts on hand.

With 5,000 acres of fertile, if often flooded, bottomland, Lambert was said to have great potential at the time of its purchase. In developing it, penal authorities followed the same principles of organization and management that had worked so well in the development of Parchman a decade or so earlier. In 1917, 104 convicts, including a sawmill gang and a crew of carpenters, were put to work clearing land and constructing buildings. In 1922 the farm was divided into two separate camps, and in 1930, when a third camp was added, operations were expanded. Between 1923 and 1930 an average of some 170 convicts were at Lambert, but in 1931, when a dramatic increase in commitments caused overcrowding in Parchman's cages, the plantation in Quitman County absorbed the overflow. In 1931 the convict population increased to 360, and two years later it stood at 386.

The two lime plants, Rankin County Farm, and Oakley Farm recorded financial losses each year, but they met demands that the revenue-producing units could not. The two lime plants employed from 15 to 30 convicts between them, produced lime for all the penal farms, and sold surpluses to the state's farmers at cost. Rankin County Farm was a white man's Belmont—a low-key institution for white males whose age, health, or social status disqualified them from the rigors of labor at Parchman. Fifty-seven prisoners were there in June 1917, but the population decreased steadily through the years. The farm averaged about 35 inmates during the twenties, and only 30 men were there in 1927 when the state abandoned it.

Most of Oakley's acreage stood barren. After the transfer of the women's camp and the opening of the hospital at Parchman, the unit was an unproductive farm inhabited chiefly by convalescents who raised livestock and piddled around in a vegetable garden. Housing an average of some 70 convicts, Oakley was a large and unjustifiable financial drain until 1925, when overcrowding in the two white camps at Parchman led to an accession of 75 white convicts between the ages of fourteen and twenty-one. Thereafter serving as a unit for young Caucasian felons, Oakley remained a financial drain, though perhaps a more justifiable one.[21]

The penal system also maintained a number of road camps around the state. From them ventured forth manacled men under armed guard for labor on public roads and levees. Occasionally the road camps were reinforced by gunmen from Parchman and Lambert, especially when the spring rains caused flooding in the Delta. Relatively few convicts, however, were assigned to the road camps. Fearing the private exploitation of convict labor, and ever pointing to the hefty revenues generated by penal farming, Vardaman and his allies on the board frowned on any labor that carried convicts off state lands. Mississippi thus rejected the "good roads movement" so common among other Southern states in the early twentieth century, and few of the state's convicts were links in a "chain gang."[22]

James Kimble Vardaman passed from the stage of politics virtually unnoticed, the victim of a political ideology bordering on Marxism that isolated him in the United States Senate and at last alienated his Mississippi constituents. But when the sickly old man returned to Jackson, intent on living out his days tending his radical newspapers, his blueprint for the development of the state penal system had been followed almost to the letter, and a very unique concept of convict discipline known among penologists as the "Mississippi system" was full-blown at Parchman Farm. For better or for worse, it was the greatest legacy of the White Chief.

3

The Mississippi System

The gravel road running south from Clarksdale to the state penal farm in Sunflower County invaded some of the richest cotton land in the world. Along the way one could observe the unpainted shacks of black sharecroppers and realize that here was a culture of bygone days. At journey's end was old Gordon Station, now dubbed "Front Camp" by the rough men in charge; beyond, fanning out westward toward the great river, was Parchman Farm.

Within the grounds of the penitentiary lay forty-six square miles of bottomland. It was fully six miles from Front Camp to the back side of the place, and even a cursory inspection of the sprawling acreage confirmed the accuracy of the description penned by the legislator who had visited in 1912: Parchman Farm was indeed a "monument to labor."

The Organization of Labor

By 1920 the penitentiary's regimen of life and labor was well established. The process began when the judge of a trial court notified the superintendent that a felon was lodged in a county jail awaiting his order. The superintendent, in turn, ordered the penitentiary's "traveling sergeant" to proceed to the jail, to collect the prisoner, and to transport her or him to Parchman's Front Camp. Upon arrival the convict was conveyed to the hospital, where fingerprints, photographs, and Bertillon measurements (primary physical characteristics) were taken. The convict was then given a physical examination and either assigned to the hospital for medical treatment or released for a work assignment.

After being released for labor, male convicts were issued ten-ounce duck trousers and seven-ounce duck shirts with horizontal black and white stripes, known as "ring-arounds" in prison jargon. Female convicts were given dresses with vertical stripes—"up-and-downs." Identification numbers were stamped on the front and back of uniforms. Printed copies of the rules and regulations governing the penitentiary were then distributed among the prisoners. Because few of them could read, a staff member normally explained the rules point by point.[1]

Work assignments reflected neither a convict's crime of conviction nor the mitigating or aggravating circumstances surrounding the transgression: prevailing wisdom held that the association of prisoners by "criminal tendency" could only result in the reinforcement of deviant behavior. Instead, the penitentiary's classification system was based on race, gender, healthfulness, age, and vocation. The camp structure at Parchman and the operations of the smaller farms took everyone into account except black minors, who continued to be housed with adults of their race.[2]

All of Parchman's field camps had the same goal: to squeeze the best yield from available acreage. In pursuing that goal, the penitentiary based its labor policy on the golden rule of effective management: do whatever it takes to get the most out of available labor. Neither the goal nor the means, then, differed from that governing free labor in the world outside. Getting the most out of what one had to work with was the secret to success everywhere, whether on a Southern cotton plantation or in a sweatshop up North. The difference here, at Parchman Farm, was that the laborers were felons. And because some 75 percent of the convicts sent up by Mississippi's courts of criminal jurisdiction were black, the institution's dominant cultural hallmarks, even the language of the place, were decidedly African American.[3]

In da Cage

Getting the most out of available labor required tactics that were consistent with the peculiarities of convicts. In this regard, the racial segregation of Parchman's convict laborers was quite useful to managers, enabling those presiding over field camps to operate on principles that considered the cultural traits of the two races. "Handlin' black boys and white boys was as diff'rent as day and night," stressed an old-timer.[4]

Cultural differences were accommodated by a unique concept of management. A pecking order inevitably develops within any social group, one that elevates a single member to a position of authority. In this regard, convict society is no different from that of the world outside; and during the early years of the twentieth century, a cageboss and a subordinate convict pecking order evolved in every cage at Parchman Farm.

Virtually all cagebosses were lifers well into their sentences. As veteran convicts, bosses knew the ropes and had long since adapted to prison life. As lifers, they accepted their plight and made the most of it: Parchman was their home. Bosses were therefore stabilizing influences within the cages, authority figures who did not tolerate anyone who challenged the status quo.

Sergeants and cagebosses had every reason to cooperate. A sergeant wanted a healthy, contented, cooperative labor force; a cageboss wanted his ascendancy within the cage acknowledged by the sergeant and needed his assistance in maintaining it. Conversely, a sergeant realized that his job would be extremely difficult without the support of his convicts' natural leader, quite easy with it; and a cageboss understood that his sergeant was "da Main Mos' Man," a fellow who was fully capable of causing him all manner of trouble, including reassignment to another camp.

On these terms, a degree of cooperation was inevitable, and within every cage an unofficial treaty existed between the keepers and the kept. The cageboss agreed to run his cage by the rules of the sergeant—no escapes, no killing, no maiming, nothing that might compromise labor or otherwise make the sergeant look bad in the eyes of the superintendent. In turn, the sergeant acknowledged the supremacy of the cageboss, propped his regime by granting indulgences, and did nothing that might make the cageboss look bad in the eyes of his underlings.

If there were a problem in the cage, the cageboss wanted to handle it alone: a sergeant who intruded made a cageboss look impotent. This was especially true in the black cages, and the white sergeants—fully aware of the monumental gap that separated black and white cultures— almost never intruded. Just in case, though, the sergeants had snitches in the cages. By all accounts, the cages were remarkably tranquil.[5]

In da Rows

The convicts in the field camps, both black and white, were roused by a work bell before dawn and allowed a short period to eat breakfast.

Afterward, a small number of them remained near the cage, working in the garden, while a few proceeded to the kitchen, subject to the cook's orders for the day. But at dawn's first light the great mass filed past their cageboss, formed up in the yard, and underwent something akin to a military morning call: "a hunerd tin on da line, Cap'n." Then it was off to the rows.[6]

In planting season the convicts rode mules to the fields, and upon arriving at their destination they dismounted, harnessed the beasts for the work at hand, and undertook their assigned duties as members of either the hoe gang or the plow gang. In picking season the convicts normally walked to the fields and, again divided into two groups, set about picking their daily quota. Regardless of the season, the convicts worked under the direct supervision of the drivers, and they labored in close, tight files that came to be called the "long line."

Those on the long line moved forward as one, their pace set by a "caller." The caller chanted a verse; the entire long line responded with a chorus. The practice of utilizing callers for gang labor had its roots in the slave South, and callers remained fixtures in Dixie's cotton fields until well into the twentieth century. Today, the caller survives most notably in the military, where the cadence of the march is set by the rhythmic offering of a single member of the unit and repeated by the whole.

Parchman's convicts regarded the selection of callers as serious business. Callers had to be clever: laughter was a necessity in the rows. They had to have "soul," the power to uplift the spirit with rhythm: soul was the lifeblood of the long line; an uneven pace spoiled everything. And a caller simply had to be experienced: a call that was too fast could wear a gunman down; one too slow could anger the Cap'n.[7]

Good callers were widely celebrated among black convicts, less so among white ones, and some of the chants of the black callers stood the test of time, being heard in the rows decades after the departure of their composers. Many of them, of course, dwelt on women, or "Rosie," as all women came to be known to Parchman's convicts. The callers crowned Rosie "queen of Parchman Farm." They saw her in their "midnight dreams." She was of course a sexual fantasy, sometimes a sexual memory: one caller represented her as "Big-Leg Rosie, with her big-leg drawers," who "Got me wearen these striped overalls." Other callers bemoaned life at Parchman: the early work bell, the food, the demands of The Main Mos' Man and the Cap'n, the labor in the rows. One begged the sun, "ole Hannah," for mercy: "Been a great long time since Hannah went down. Oh, Hannah, go down."[8]

A good caller helped time in the rows pass quickly. "When you listenin' how the song run, the day just go by mo faster," remembered a convict, "and befo you know it, the sergeant or the driver is hollerin' dinnertime."[9]

Normally the convicts on the long line squatted in the rows and ate their lunch with their wide-brimmed hats angled to ward off the merciless sun, and some of them learned to sleep anywhere, anytime, standing or squatting, for any period of time. A "catnap"—even one no longer than a minute—braced them for the dreaded "affanoon Hannah," which made Rosie's big legs seem less appealing. After enduring Hannah's wrath "'til she done burn up" (sunset), the spent convicts were herded back to their cages.[10]

In the yard, the Cap'n took a head count as his charges filed past their cageboss into the cage. If there had been a problem with a gunman in the fields, a word with the cageboss normally assured that all would be well tomorrow.[11]

During the hours of darkness, convicts were forbidden from venturing outside their cages. Encouraging compliance with this rule were the cagebosses, whose stock with the sergeants depended above all on their ability to maintain security. Lending a hand outside the cages were the salaried night watchmen. These "nightshooters" were normally surly, underpaid old white men, and they were authorized to open fire upon observing any movement whatsoever.[12]

Climbin' da Laddah

Labor on Mississippi's penal farms was hard, especially during the summer months. With temperatures hovering near the century mark, the drivers pushed the shuffling long line ever forward. The Delta sun bore down relentlessly as the pounding hoes raised the choking yellow dust, and the "mercy man" with his whiskey barrel full of precious water seemed to appear all too infrequently. But as the perspiring gunmen neared the limits of endurance, most of them were kept at it by a wide range of incentives.

The penitentiary's incentive program centered on its trusty system, which elevated some 14 percent of the convict population to privileged positions during the first three decades of the twentieth century. Apparently, Parchman's version of the trusty system was an outgrowth of antebellum days, when slaves generally worked in one of four capacities—as field hands, drivers, artisans, or house servants—and were allowed to improve their lot through promotion.

Like female inmates, all male trusties wore up-and-downs, but "trusty-servants" were the penitentiary's crème de la crème. The envy of other convicts, they earned and maintained their positions by good manners, docility, and superior domestic skills. They worked as domestic help in the superintendent's mansion or in the homes of other employees, as cooks and janitors, and in a variety of other positions that lightened the workload of the penitentiary's staff. Convicts panted for such assignments, for along with trusty-servant status came accessibility to the throne, so to speak; thus, assignments to the homes of the superintendent and his principal underlings, and more notably to the governor's mansion, were coveted.

This phenomenon was not unique to Parchman: it existed in prisons everywhere and exists to this day. Yet the convicts' quest for assignment to the homes of powerful men reflected a facet of legal incarceration that was, and is, identical to the institution of slavery: long and faithful service in the home of the master offered the prospect of freedom.

Parchman's employees worried about this unhappy historical parallel no more than today's prison administrators. Indeed, they clamored for trusty-servants—the more the merrier—for the number assigned to an employee was a reflection of status. In 1924 a joint legislative committee was astonished and appalled by the number of trusties assigned to the homes of Parchman's employees.[13]

Below the trusty-servants in the convict pecking order were the "trusty-artisans," a disproportionate number of them white men. Superior vocational skills often helped Caucasians escape from the field camps, as did the lingering notion among sergeants that labor in the fields was "nigger work." The best and most senior of the trusty-artisans served in middle-management positions within the penitentiary's support services, often supervising convict apprentices.

Perhaps the most notable of the trusty-artisans were those at the penitentiary's kennel. A trusty dog-handler—"da Main Mos' Dog-Boy"—was in charge; under his direct control were convict assistants, simply "dog-boys." They trained bloodhounds, German shepherds, and beagles. They followed the baying "sniff-dogs" in pursuit of escaping convicts, all the while restraining the muzzled "kill-dogs." They chaperoned the "rabbit-dogs" on hunting expeditions provided for politicians and other favored parties. Frequently they presided over dog shows, delighting the superintendent's guests. And always the dog-boys and their kill-dogs made the rounds, reminding would-be "rabbits"—escaping convicts—of the chilling fate awaiting them.[14]

Because the cotton fields went on and on, a fleeing convict never knew when he was exiting Parchman and entering an adjoining plantation. Meanwhile the sniff-dogs were closing fast, with the Main Mos' Dog-Boy and his kill-dogs right behind them. Convict lore held that a rabbit had best make his peace with the sniff-dogs before the kill-dogs arrived.[15]

The dogs, though, were a moot point for a rabbit most of the time: shooters were the more pressing concern. "Shooters" were trusty-guards who lived within the cages, and the only armed men on the penal farms. Frequently drawn from the ranks of long-term convicts, usually convicted murderers, they were appointed by camp sergeants only after years of trouble-free service. Thereafter under strict orders to avoid familiarity with gunmen, they slept apart and stood apart from their former peers, representing law and order in a society of felons.

The rooms within the cages allocated to trusty-shooters resembled the sergeant's quarters in a traditional military barrack. They contained storerooms filled with supplies; under lock and key were .30–.30 Winchester rifles and carefully rationed ammunition.

Each morning the shooters were the first to rise. Dressed in their up-and-downs, with their rifles pointed skyward from the hip, the shooters roused the sleeping gunmen with shouts, organized them for the work of the day, and reported to the arriving sergeants and drivers. As the troop of sleepy-eyed gunmen proceeded to the fields, the shooters rode ominously to the flanks, always with the Winchesters prominently displayed. As the drivers set the gunmen to work on the long line, the shooters drew the "gun line," a mark in the dirt that surrounded the working convicts. Beyond the gun line was no man's land: there, the shooters' Winchesters had license.

Such duties earned shooters both the envy and contempt of the gunmen, who labeled them "headhunters," and with good reason. The shooters were usually desperate men, men serving life sentences, and efficiency on the job alone offered them hope. They drew the gun line meticulously, afterward watching the working gunmen as a hawk views its prey. If there was a "rabbit in the row"—a gunman who dared cross the gun line—the shooter was required to shout a warning. In the absence of a response—and policy apparently said nothing about how long the shooter should wait—the shooter was under orders to open fire. The shooters were, by and large, expert marksmen, and their lethal efficiency sometimes earned the ultimate reward: shooters performing "conspicuous meritorious service" could be recommended for a discharge or a pardon. Not a few of them were deemed conspicuously meritorious after dropping a gunman in his tracks.[16]

The shooter system was the centerpiece of Parchman's incentive program. There, as in the free world, status and power had their liabilities: nothing haunted a shooter more than the prospect of running afoul of his sergeant and being returned to the ranks of the gunmen over whom he held sway. For themselves, the lowly gunmen harbored hopes of one day wearing the up-and-downs of the shooters. For with the zebralike garments came not only status and power but also greater freedom of movement, better quarters, the possibility of being reassigned to one of the cushy jobs at Front Camp, and a better chance of an early release.[17]

The efficiency of the shooter system was demonstrated graphically in the years immediately following 1922. In that year a number of reported abuses led the legislature to prohibit discharges and pardons for shooters who meritoriously slaughtered a fellow inmate. Attempted escapes more than doubled during the next three years. Governors, collaborating with penal authorities, attempted to fill the void by granting enormously increased numbers of suspended sentences, and the 1928 legislature tried to lend a hand by allowing meritorious trusties to discard their up-and-downs in favor of blue denim uniforms. But the shooters regarded mere suspensions with disdain, and the new dress code facilitated a rash of escapes. So the denim uniforms were discarded, the legislature backed off, and the old scheme was restored with a number of advertised safeguards. Thereafter, attempted escapes declined markedly.[18]

Da Way Home t' Mama

Mississippi offered its convicts many avenues to freedom during the early decades of the twentieth century. Until 1916 the only formal mechanisms for the administration of clemency were a "good-time" policy that rewarded good behavior by reducing the length of sentences, and Governor Earl Brewer's "youthful offenders program," which facilitated the early release of young felons whom the governor deemed worthy of a "second chance." Then in 1916 a statutory board of pardons was established to advise governors on clemency petitions, only to be abolished in 1924 amid allegations of inefficiency and corruption.[19]

Some eight years later, Governor Mike Conner established what he called his "mercy court." Accompanied by two colleagues, Conner traveled periodically to the state's penal farms, studying case histories, interviewing convicts, and granting pardons or suspended sentences to those he called "forgotten men."[20] The proceedings of Conner's mercy court included appearances by the spouses and other family members of convicts, and allowed both supporting and opposing letters from others. As is true today, an opposing letter from a politician, a sheriff, or a prosecutor was normally the kiss of death, whereas a supporting letter from such parties or from other respected members of free-world society usually opened the doors of the penitentiary for the convict. In the early decades of the twentieth century, of course, "respected" free-world folk were almost always Caucasians, and thus convicts—black and white alike—sent a steady stream of letters to white churchmen, businessmen, lawyers, and planters, beseeching them to come to their assistance.[21]

Conner's mercy court was quite an event at Parchman Farm. When the governor and his colleagues arrived at Front Camp, large numbers of women—virtually all of them black—awaited, "dressed to the teeth and cluckin' like hens." On such occasions electricity passed through the cages, and "the dog-boys was called out to remind everybody not to let things get out of hand."[22]

A verse from a famous song celebrates the excitement of the gunmen:

> Yonder come Miz Brodie.
> How da werl did ja know?
> By da way she wear 'er apron,
> An da clothes she wo';
> Umbrella on 'er shouldah,
> Piece ah paper in 'er han',
> She come ta see da gov'nor,
> Wants to free 'er man.[23]

More than one woman got her man; and Conner's mercy court, which functioned much like parole hearings today, was continued by his successors.[24]

Governors also freed convicts who performed meritorious public service. A notable, if somewhat troubling, example was the voluntary participation of convicts in medical experiments. In 1915 twelve inmates at the Rankin County Farm participated in a pellagra experiment, survived six months of dietary deprivation, and obtained pardons from Governor Brewer. In 1933 another ten convicts were granted executive clemency after participating in an encephalitis experiment.[25]

The whims of chief executives also were responsible for opening the doors of the penitentiary. Governors tended to be especially generous on their last day in office and on holidays, especially Christmas Day, Thanksgiving Day, New Year's Day, and the Fourth of July.

By and large, Mississippi's chief executives relied on the penitentiary's superintendents for advice on clemency, and over the years it came to be understood that the road out of Parchman Farm went through the super's office. There were practical reasons for this arrangement. A virtual free hand in the granting of clemency gave superintendents a means of controlling the size of the convict population—a flexible tool capable of countering the effects of sentences by the independent judiciary, keeping overhead expenses somewhat consistent with the appropriations of an undependable legislature, and navigating through the ebb and flow of the market economy.

For example, during 1930 and 1931 Mississippi's criminal courts manufactured unprecedented numbers of felons, Parchman's cages became overcrowded, and the tight-fisted legislature refused to increase the penitentiary's appropriation. Something had to give, and it finally did during the Christmas season of 1931, when Superintendent Jim Williamson recommended, and Governor Theodore Bilbo extended, clemency for a staggering 536 convicts at one stroke.[26]

Convict management was also enhanced by the superintendents' influence in the granting of early releases. In the hands of the supers, clemency was a carrot on a stick that they dangled just above the extended hands of the convicts, and everything suggests that it was dangled quite effectively.

Mississippi's relatively unstructured means of extending pardons and suspensions produced about the same number of early releases as

did parole boards in other states. An average of over 205 convicts—
nearly 13 percent of the population—obtained some form of executive
clemency each year between 1907 and 1933.[27]

Doan Wanna Go

Some of the convicts who were offered clemency declined it. In 1932,
for instance, one of Governor Conner's "forgotten men," John Tabor,
rejected a pardon, explaining, "You just can't beat this place for comfort." Later, when convict John Smith declined clemency and the
governor let him stay at the penitentiary, the Jackson *Clarion-Ledger*
reported: "John liked the prison. He was a hard worker, but he had a
place to sleep and plenty to eat." Murderer William Sullivan balked as
well. He was, he thought, "better off here than anywhere else" and
found his keepers "the finest people in the world." According to the
recollections of old-timers, many more convicts actively lobbied their
sergeants to screen them from release.[28]

This phenomenon may well say less about life at Parchman Farm
than it says about life on the outside. The terrible legacy of slavery,
the Civil War, and postbellum misgovernment continues to this day,
breeding chronic unemployment and almost third-world poverty among
considerable numbers of Mississippians. In the early years of the century,
and especially during the decade following the stock market crash,
however, a large number of free-world folk did well to feed and clothe
themselves. Quite clearly, life at Parchman Farm was a step up for many
of its inmates.

Also relevant is the fact that most of the convicts known to have rejected clemency were old men who had served long sentences. It is not
uncommon for long-institutionalized convicts to want to stay put, especially when they have no families waiting for them on the outside.

Whatever their reasons, many convicts liked life at Parchman Farm.
Lifer William Clark Mitchell wrote to a free-world friend: "Things here
are not as bad as they would make you believe and a man that is not
afraid to work and will attend to his own affairs can get along O.K." This
remark struck the fancy of a journalist: "A man 'not afraid to work' and
willing to 'attend to his own affairs' can 'get along O.K.' almost anywhere."[29] Clark did not tell the whole story, however: there were other
things that made him like life at the penitentiary, especially on Sundays.

Da Lawd's Day

The rigorous work schedule at Parchman Farm stole leisure six days a week, so the Sabbath, the one day of rest, was treasured by the gunmen. On Sunday mornings large numbers of prisoners attended religious services, normally presided over by a felon with evangelical talents. Within the cages, radios blared while the more energetic convicts engaged in "horsing around," to the chagrin of those trying to sleep. There was considerable interest in football, baseball, and boxing broadcasts; corn liquor was normally available; and gambling—sports betting and "rollin' bones"— emerged as perhaps the greatest hallmark of life in the cages. "Hell," remembered a former employee, "we let 'em do anything they wanted on their time so long as they did what we wanted on state time." But even on Sundays there was work to be done; and if state time were wasted by a convict's truculence or by violations of the rules, the Sabbath could be taken away by any number of disgusting work details.[30]

Camp sergeants also exploited the penitentiary's single organized recreational activity: well-behaved and productive convicts were allowed to play baseball on Sunday afternoons and on holidays. The state provided no monetary support, but as in prisons everywhere, ample numbers of bats, balls, and gloves somehow found their way into the camps. Each of the field camps had a curiously named team, and competition between the black camps was especially lively. One of Parchman's former employees, recalling the booming home runs of an otherwise forgotten inmate catcher from Drew, the flashing cleats of Snowflake Harper, and the exploits of other champions of the diamond, remembered that "the cons worked hard 'cause they knew they couldn't play ball if they didn't."[31]

The pursuit of the national pastime was no more vigorous than the pursuit of women by the inmates. The facts surrounding the advent of "conjugal visitation" at Parchman are cloudy, but it seems safe to say that the practice was not conjugally motivated. Indeed, everything suggests that penal authorities viewed sexual favors by prostitutes as a valuable tool in the management of black field hands.[32]

One old-timer, grinning sheepishly and understandably insisting on anonymity, assessed the logic behind the practice in the following manner:

Hell, nobody knows when it started. It just started. You gotta understand, mister, that back in them days niggers were pretty simple creatures.
Give a nigger some pork, some greens, some cornbread and some poon-
tang ever now and then and he would work for you. And workin' was
what it was all about back then. I never saw it, but I heard tell of truck-
loads of whores bein' brought up from Cleveland at dusk. The cons who
had a good day got to get 'em some right there between the rows. In my
day we got civilized—put 'em in little houses and told everybody that
them whores was wives. That kept the Baptists off our backs.[33]

During the thirties an employee at Parchman confirmed that sexual
privileges were restricted to black male convicts without reference to
marital status, that prostitutes were actually quartered in the central
administrative building during the day, and that they moved freely between the field camps at night. Some years later, a scholar explained
that "the white sergeants who presided over the black camps simply
'looked the other way' in accommodating what they considered to be
natural among Negroes."[34]

The sergeants did not merely look the other way: they were normally active players in the game, middlemen who facilitated prostitution. In this manner, sergeants bolstered the regimes of their cagebosses (the ascendancy of bosses depended on their ability to keep up
the flow of women), rewarded their gunmen, and often supplemented
their woefully low salaries.

Furthermore, sex is hardly an unnatural thing for white people, and
one must suspect that the prospect of a little time with Rosie might
have produced more than a few "honky high-rollers"—white 500-
pound-a-day men. Surely, then, something other than a supposed
moral superiority explains the exclusion of the white inmates, if indeed
they were excluded. Recently a former employee, drawing on the penal
farm's abundant folk wisdom, told of experiments with prostitutes in
the white cages and explained matter-of-factly that black men and white
men responded to sex differently. Black guys, he contended, "take the
stuff in stride, don't make a big deal out of it," whereas "most white
boys get all possessive and broody and fight with each other." Whatever
the reason for the supposed exclusion of the white men, the capacity to
bear unwanted children certainly explains why female convicts were
expected to remain virtuous.[35]

Nobody seems to be altogether certain who paid the prostitutes
during the early part of the century, but there was never a dearth of

money in Parchman's cages. Unlike most other American prisons, inmates were allowed to have cash, and the rules that limited the amount of it were eyewash—unenforceable and thus unenforced.

The penitentiary's visitation policy was also a managerial tool. The families of convicts were allowed to visit on the fifth Sunday of months that had more than four Sabbaths; and dating from about 1920, the lonesome wail of the fabled "Midnight Special," churning at dawn on the tracks bordering Parchman to the east, announced the eagerly anticipated arrival of loved ones.

The Midnight Special departed Jackson's depot, near the King Edward Hotel, at 12:05 on Sunday mornings. From there it proceeded northeast and then northwest on the Yellow Dog Line, winding through the little towns of the Mississippi Delta, stopping to take on passengers, and arriving at Parchman Station around dawn.

Many of the convicts could think of nothing else but these visits. They sang of their women while working in the fields, often gazing toward faraway Front Camp and the blessed depot, and many of the gunmen, especially the older ones, began to prepare for the arrival of "mama" after "weighin' up" on Saturday evening. On Saturday night they reclined listlessly in their bunks, wishing away the time. Before dawn on Sunday one could see the forms of their pathetic faces through the barred windows of the cages. And as the sun began to rise over the flat landscape of the Delta, they strained their hearing, often cupping hands over ears, trying to hear the sweet sound of the locomotive's whistle.

From Camp One—a black field camp—the convicts could see the headlight of the train approaching Parchman Station, and folklore held that those illuminated by it would be blessed by a female visitor bearing a gubernatorial pardon:

> Heah come yo' woman, a pardon in 'er han'
> Gonna say to da boss, Ah wants mah man,
> Let the Midnight Special shine its light on me.[36]

At last the train would arrive at the depot, with mama in her Sunday best, stretching and yawning amid warehouses stuffed with cotton. At Camp One much excitement ensued—"We could see ole Rosie a-comin', could smell 'er too," one former convict remembered fondly—and Parchman's celebrated grapevine soon hummed, with word of Rosie's arrival spreading like wildfire.[37]

The convict husbands who had made their quota, and who had played by the sergeant's rules, were brought up by wagon, scrubbed, grinning, full of anticipation. The convicts and their spouses reportedly shared intimate moments in designated rooms at Front Camp while others "tended the chillum." They worshiped together. They stood in long lines leading to tables heaped with fried chicken and all the trimmings. They wandered aimlessly hand in hand; they cheered wildly at the baseball games. At dusk, when the women and their children boarded the train with streaked faces, the sergeants could reasonably anticipate a manageable labor force during the weeks ahead.[38]

Da Strop

Despite the considerable number of incentives held out to them, some convicts—normally "new baws"—refused to respond. In such cases, camp sergeants were authorized to inflict corporal punishment. From the belts of the sergeants hung Black Annie, a heavy leather strap of antebellum vintage that was four inches wide, a quarter of an inch thick, and three feet long. Annie, which resembled a barber's strap and was labeled "da strop" by black inmates, was sovereign at Parchman Farm, the sole means of delivering what modern behavioral scientists label "positive punishment."[39]

Parchman's officials maintained that the character of their convict population necessitated corporal punishment. In 1910 the penitentiary's physician, Dr. A. M. M'Callum, told the American Prison Association that whipping was "the only effective method of punishing the class of criminals in the Mississippi penitentiary and keep[ing] them at the labor required of them."[40]

At the time M'Callum referred to the presence of a unique "class of criminals" at Parchman Farm, he was describing a convict population that several months later numbered 1,843 felons—509, or 28 percent, of whom had been convicted of murder; and 749, or over 40 percent, of whom had been convicted of other heinous crimes against the person. Those statistics held firm until 1929. Between 1911 and 1929 roughly 32 percent of the convicts admitted to the penal system were murderers, and some 34 percent were under sentence for other grave crimes against the person. After 1929 the penitentiary housed a steadily increasing number of property offenders, but the percentage of malefactors remained extraordinarily high.[41] Perhaps Dr.

M'Callum's assessment was correct: the Mississippi penal system had more than its share of felons whose crimes of conviction suggested dire social depravity.

There is much confusion about the terms on which flagellation was administered during the penitentiary's formative years. Certain facts, however, are clear. Throughout the history of Parchman Farm, convicts and employees alike referred to the use of Black Annie as a "whuppin'" or a "spankin'," words suggesting that the target of the strap was the buttocks, not the backs, of convicts. That was official policy at least as early as 1950, and convict testimony suggests that the same policy existed long before. During the thirties, for instance, one of them related: "They whupped us with big wide strops. They didn't whup no clothes. They whupped your naked butt."[42]

The cadence employed in the black camps whenever a convict was "whupped" is also quite revealing:

> One . . . he's gitten' de leather,
> Two . . . he don't know no better,
> Three . . . cry niggah, stick yo' finger in yo' eye,
> Four . . . niggah thought he had a knife,
> Five . . . got hit off'n his visitin' wife,
> Six . . . now he'll get time for life,
> Seven . . . lay it on trusty man!
> Eight . . . wham! wham! he gotta wu'k tomorra,
> Nine . . . he gotta chop cotton in de sun,
> Ten . . . dat's all, trusty man, you's done.

This chant describes what is regarded as a very serious offense in all prisons—getting caught with a lethal weapon—and the infliction of ten licks as punishment. It also reveals that the punishment was inflicted black-on-black—that the white sergeant delegated the chore to his black "trusty man": there were no white trusties in the black camps. This is consistent with what is known of the relationships that existed among sergeants, cagebosses, and shooters early in the century. One of Parchman's former employees explained: "Yeah . . . we mostly let the trusties be the heavies, especially in the black camps. Like on the outside, they [black convicts] had a different world, and it was good to let 'em handle their own problems. The [black] cagebosses didn't like it when their [white] sergeants came down and did their work for them. A white man actin' as the heavy made 'em look bad in the eyes of their boys."[43]

The cadence for Black Annie confirms this account: it portrays black convicts not only actively participating in the spectacle, but also reveling in it. Every camp at Parchman was unique, and surely exceptions to all general rules existed. Available evidence suggests, however, that folk wisdom, if not official policy, cautioned sergeants to allow their trusties to discipline convicts whenever possible, and always to allow black trusties to discipline black gunmen. Protecting the inmate hierarchy in the cage, it seems, was the first principle of convict management.[44]

Finally, the old cadence indicates that the convict being disciplined would work in the rows tomorrow. That revelation places Black Annie in context. The mission of Parchman Farm was to bring home the crop. That was accomplished through intensive human labor. Some convicts "turned politician," inventing ailments, discovering "new ways to limp," and going "to any length to stay out of the field," including flat refusals to work.[45] In such cases, all eyes turned toward the sergeant: incentives had failed; a power struggle was under way; the authority of The Main Mos' Man was being challenged; it was time for positive punishment.

Officially, at least, prison administrators have two options on such occasions: solitary confinement or corporal punishment. Parchman's administrators rejected solitary, regarding it as a reward for unacceptable behavior—a way for a convict to escape field work. That left the remaining option. In 1909 Superintendent Neyland emphasized that it was "absolutely necessary to whip a convict" when incentives failed to make him behave himself and "earn his salt."[46]

But an excessively disciplined convict laborer could not work, and indeed was a liability, a drain on precious resources. Hence the demands of utility, if not those of humanitarianism, impinged heavily on Parchman's sole official means of positive punishment. Those demands, to be sure, explain why a blunt leather strap—and not a bullwhip or a cat-'o-nine-tails—was utilized. "If you really wanted to hurt a man," recalls a former employee, "you could goddamn sure find a better tool than Annie." The same motive explains the logic underlying the only policy on spanking known to exist in the early years of the century: licks were restricted to a maximum of fifteen per day. "You spank a fellow right," noted a superintendent, "and he'll be able to work on."[47]

Successes and Failures

Vardaman's goals for the penal system were pursued with a remarkable degree of success between 1906 and 1934. Financial productivity easily constituted the most tangible victory. Between 1906 and 1933, while prisons elsewhere were recording mounting deficits, the receipts of Mississippi's penal farms exceeded disbursements by well over $4.2 million.[48]

The financial success of the penitentiary is easily explained. Whereas remunerative prison labor to the North, and even in other Southern states, was undone by the opposition of the private sector, Mississippi's dominant planter class never seemed to be worried about a few thousand bales being produced on the penal farms. Apparently they agreed with Governor Edmond Noel, who told the legislature in 1910 that the cotton grown at the penitentiary did not have "the slightest effect on the general market nor would any less be grown if the state would dispose of its lands to individuals." Then, too, an agrarian economy, and the virtual political disfranchisement of nearly half the state's proletariat, assured that the labor movement, with its rational opposition to competing convict labor, never got off the ground in Mississippi. Furthermore, while Vardaman's intricate system of political checks and balances did not prevent corruption, it certainly kept graft and embezzlement at manageable levels. The result was a penal system that Superintendent L. T. Fox once described quite accurately as a "profit-making machine."[49]

Other ideals of the White Chief were realized as well. Absolutely nothing about the operations of the penitentiary threatened the foundations of white rule: if a black felon got an education in letters, he got it somewhere else. Vardaman's notion that convicts should be provided vocational training was also realized. For Parchman Farm, even in its formative years, was the hub of a huge, essentially self-supporting plantation system that relied exclusively on convict labor and employed many inmates in key middle-management positions. After visiting Parchman in 1914, the editor of the Memphis *Scimitar* reported that the prison was "a school within itself."[50]

Except for only the worst years of the depression, housing, culinary arrangements, medical services, and the other essentials of life were evidently adequate by the standards of the time. The minute books of the board of trustees and the biennial penitentiary reports, which were extraordinarily candid owing to the political independence of the elected trustees, generally project a healthy convict population.

There is no reason to believe that Mississippi's convicts were subjected to any more abuse than those incarcerated in other states' prisons. By all accounts, the workload was no more demanding than that on Delta plantations employing free labor. Alan Lomax, a seemingly impartial observer who visited Parchman in the early thirties, wrote: "Only a few strands of wire separated the prison from adjoining plantations. . . . Only the sight of an occasional armed guard or a barred window in one of the farm dormitories made one realize that this was a prison. The land produced the same crop; there was the same work for the Negroes to do on both sides of the fence."[51] The writer David Cohn, in his account of growing up in Mississippi, noted that the regimen at Parchman Farm was a simple extension of a black person's normal lifestyle: "They do the same work, eat the same food, sing the same songs, play the same games of dice and cards, fraternize with their fellows, attend religious services on Sunday mornings and receive visitors on Sunday afternoons." Cohn quoted a giggling black woman about to be conveyed from a jail to Parchman: "It ain't no diffunce, white folks. I'm got to work wherever I'm is."[52]

Likewise, available evidence suggests that the manner in which corporal punishment was inflicted at Parchman during the early years of the century was relatively tame by the penological standards of the day. Only one scandal alleging excessive flagellation occurred during the first three decades of the twentieth century. It came in 1914, amid the political jockeying that accompanied the demise of the Vardaman faction, and was apparently a component of a much more pervasive campaign to discredit the old guard. "Whenever the boys down in Jackson went at each other," remembered an employee of the penitentiary, "they had to have some dirt to sling, and it was amazin' how often they looked for it up here."[53]

No doubt Parchman, like all prisons, had its share of human abuse during the first decades of the twentieth century, but Black Annie was evidently not responsible for much of it. On May 7, 1936, the Jackson *Clarion-Ledger* noted quite accurately that "flogging abuses have been rarely reported from the Mississippi penitentiary."

Nor, conversely, did conservative "get-tough-on-crime" advocates have reason to be displeased. Security at Parchman Farm was adequate, indeed quite good if compared to other American prisons of the period. Felons were punished by the denial of freedom and by an exacting regimen of discipline; and the hallmarks of convict life were unpleasant enough to discourage recidivism in rational beings. While records are scanty for the early years of the century, available commentary suggests that few convicts offered themselves for recommitment.[54]

Credit for most of the early successes of the penal farm system must be assigned to Vardaman himself. He continued to keep an eye on things, visiting the farms regularly, studying the appointment of every employee closely, and his measured philosophy was realized in many instances. The historian Albert D. Kirwan rightly observes that Vardaman generally appointed able and humane administrators "who seemed to see the penal institution as a hospital for the morally sick."[55]

Vardaman's political successors assured that his principles enjoyed many successes after he had passed from the stage of politics. Governor Noel, who succeeded the White Chief, displayed great interest in the penal farms and consistently advocated better arrangements for minors and the creation of a formal mechanism for early releases. Governor Brewer also showed great interest in the plight of young felons and rooted out graft at the penitentiary with a vigilance that alienated all political factions. Governor Henry L. Whitfield, one of Vardaman's most intimate friends, sought to bolster the "moral hospital" and reminded an obstinate legislature that the White Chief had hoped to make the agricultural operations of the penitentiary a model for the state's farmers. Bilbo, who rode the old Vardaman horse to two terms in the governor's mansion and to a seat in the United States Senate, regarded Parchman as "the greatest of the State's institutions" and pursued most of his colleague's principles throughout a long career.[56]

The minute books of the penitentiary's board of trustees suggest that Vardaman's philosophy prevailed among many of its elected members as well. Lawrence Yerger, who served as president of the board until 1914, was a steady advocate of benevolent convict discipline. James F. Thames, a future superintendent who was president of the board during the twenties, often propounded an almost philanthropic concept of penology. Colonel Will Montgomery, who sat on the board for the central district until his death in the mid-twenties, was a close friend of Vardaman and his personal representative among the trustees.[57]

Montgomery's efforts on behalf of the convicts were eclipsed by those of his widow, Betsy, who was appointed to the board of trustees to complete her deceased husband's unexpired term. She was elected trustee in her own right in both 1927 and 1931, and served as president of the board between 1932 and 1936. According to one observer, "Miss Betsy's" terms displayed "a record of . . . endeavor to make life for the state's unfortunates just a little of brightness in knowing someone was interested in them as human beings."[58]

Mrs. Montgomery was fully cognizant that she was a "bleeding heart" in a sphere of public administration where few hearts bled. She was, moreover, no blushing belle in temperament and regarded her office as a sacred trust. The penitentiary was "one institution that should not be run in the dark," she stressed. "The authority to rule over human beings placed absolutely under their control" often led even competent penal authorities "to blow up completely." More than a few employees of the penal system felt Miss Betsy's lash, and the minute books of the trustees abound with examples of her efforts to improve the lot of the convicts.[59]

There is also much reason to conclude that superintendents followed Vardamanite principles of convict discipline until the early 1930s. The precedents established during the long, successful tenure of the benevolent planter C. H. Neyland, Vardaman's handpicked super, were apparently enduring. Jim Williamson, who served as superintendent during both of Bilbo's stints as chief executive, was a stout defender of his convicts and a consistent advocate of formal religious programming. Superintendent Fox, who presided during the twenties, scolded the legislature with reckless abandon and lobbied passionately for rehabilitative services that went far beyond those championed by Vardaman himself.[60]

The penitentiary had failures, of course. A widely publicized scandal transpired during 1913–14, when several highly placed penal authorities, among them Trustee Yerger and another of Vardaman's faction, were convicted on charges ranging from embezzlement to the misappropriation of public funds. Shortly thereafter, "gross negligence" by Superintendent J. C. Gathings resulted in a fire at Oakley in which thirty-five convicts, trapped on the upper floor of a burning building, perished in screaming agony.[61]

The minute books of the board of trustees confirm the dismissal of a number of employees for unacceptable behavior. The trusty-shooter system bred abuses flagrant enough to occasion repeated remonstrances. And despite the evident vigilance of the board, surely there were unreported iniquities. All prisons have them, some more, some less; and one feels somewhat confident in speculating that a remote penitentiary housing a predominantly black convict population, employing white overseers of modest class origins, and operating in the heyday of Jim Crow, had its share.[62]

Other failures of the penitentiary were rooted in the inability of

Vardaman and his disciples to impose their views on the legislature, where there was truculence even during the gubernatorial term of the White Chief. Vardaman did not like the trusty-shooter system, which he thought tempted a man "to do wrong to his fellow prisoner," and he was extremely reluctant to grant executive clemency for the lethal "meritorious service" of shooters, but his passionate pleas for the employment of civilian guards failed to inspire the legislature. Nor was Vardaman successful in his attempt to establish separate institutions for young convicts of both races. In 1906 a journalist found children, black and white, "crowded in with the old and hardened criminals." Three years later, a scheme segregating youthful white convicts at Oakley was implemented but quickly discontinued. In 1916 an industrial training school for delinquent white youth was established near Columbia, and in 1925 youthful white felons were again segregated at Oakley. Yet the legislature, apparently agreeing with former governor Anselm McLaurin that there was "no use trying to reform a negro," did not provide for black minors. In 1929, when 302 youngsters were housed with adults in the black camps, critics labeled the penitentiary a "school for vice."[63]

Apparently a great deal of vice resulted from the presence of women at the penitentiary as well, notwithstanding their separate camp. In 1925 Trustee Thames told delegates to the annual meeting of the American Prison Association that the women's camp was a "little bit closer" to the men's quarters than was desirable. It was, in fact, "not more than three or four hundred yards from one of the men's rooms." The transfer of the women's camp to a more isolated part of the plantation followed shortly, but the presence of women remained a source of difficulty. According to a former employee, the male and female convicts "stopped at nothing in trying to get at each other." Sometimes, he recalled, "we would just turn our heads and pray for all that sowing of oats to end up with a crop failure."[64]

The weakening hold of the Vardaman faction on state politics assured further compromises of the philosophy that launched the penal farm system. There were spirited religious services in Parchman's black camps featuring much "howling and squealing," but the ideal of a "moral hospital" was crippled by the absence of places of worship for convicts on the penal farms.[65]

Vardaman's recommendation that a percentage of the penitentiary's profits be allocated to convicts and their spouses was also rejected by the legislature. One prison official thought that paying wages to convicts would be counterproductive: the wives of shiftless black men, he speculated, would scheme to get their spouses in the penitentiary so as to make them breadwinners. Racial considerations aside, however, it is safe to say that opposition to paying wages came primarily from the legislature's reluctance to increase the overhead expenses of the penal system.[66]

The fact is that virtually every facet of the penitentiary's operations deteriorated more or less after about 1914, when the Vardaman faction was eclipsed in the state political arena. The conviction of two Vardamanite penal authorities on charges of embezzlement in 1914, and the subsequent sentence of one of them to an extraordinary five-year term, coincided with the political demise of the White Chief and was accompanied by attacks on other vestiges of his rule. The purchase of the O'Keefe plantation in Quitman County—a suspicious land deal flagrantly violating Vardaman's principle of centralization at Parchman—followed in 1916, and thereafter the structure of penal administration that Vardaman willed Mississippi rendered the penitentiary a bleeding sore on the body politic.[67]

The front line of conflict pitted the elected trustees against the lower house of the legislature, which controlled the penitentiary's purse strings. But skirmishes, often rising to the size of pitched battles, erupted between chief executives and trustees as well, and frequent fights between governors and legislators and among the trustees themselves were no less hot. Such conflict, of course, was the inevitable result of a functional system of checks and balances. However, the allure of convict labor, the profitability of penal farming, and the coveted patronage of the penitentiary carried tensions to alarming levels.

To some extent, the problem stemmed from a fundamental flaw in Vardaman's system of checks and balances. Trustees, like chief executives, were required to stand election every four years. After Vardaman's day, that statutory requirement—so harmless during the reign of a political strongman—occasioned vicious in-fighting and assured that the entire staff of the penitentiary normally turned over every four years.[68]

The result was fluctuating priorities, inconsistent farm management, and declining revenues. Declining revenues, in turn, led to smaller legislative appropriations, and dating from about 1917 the penitentiary operated with insufficient capital. Afterward, as the physical plant and the general standard of living on the penal farms degenerated, governors, trustees, and superintendents virtually begged the legislature for catch-up funds. Sufficient monies were not forthcoming, however, and the standoff between the trustees and the legislators at last culminated amid the litter of the Great Depression. By late 1933 the convicts were living in squalor, deficits were mounting, and a majority of Mississippi's legislators had decided that Mr. Vardaman's old scheme had run its course.[69]

"The Walls": The Mississippi State Penitentiary at Jackson, ca. 1880. Courtesy of the Mississippi Department of Corrections (hereafter cited as MDOC).

Roster of convicts delivered under the French-Jobes lease, 1875. Courtesy of Lonnie L. Herring, Jr. (hereafter cited as LLH).

Ethelbert Barksdale, editor of the Jackson *Clarion* and a leading opponent of Mississippi's convict lease system. Courtesy of the Mississippi Department of Archives and History (hereafter cited as MDAH).

Governor James Kimble Vardaman, principal architect of the Mississippi penal farm system. MDAH.

Superintendent's home at Parchman, ca. 1916. MDAH.

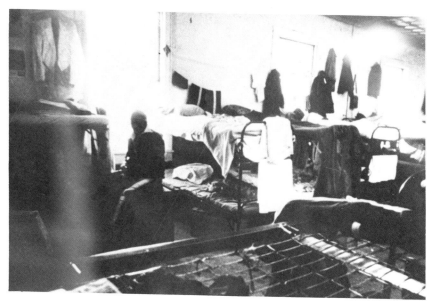

Interior of a Negro cage, ca. 1940. LLH.

Sewing room at Parchman, ca. 1950. LLH.

Laundry day at a Negro camp, ca. 1940. LLH.

Negro gunmen preparing to ride to the fields, ca. 1920. MDAH.

The long line, ca. 1940. LLH.

A mercy man and his wagon, preparing to transport water to the long line, ca. 1950. LLH.

Convict dog-handlers, ca. 1940. LLH.

Trusty-shooters in their up-and-downs, ca. 1940. LLH.

Convict baseball team, ca. 1950. LLH.

Black Annie and ring-arounds in a sadistic display, 1967. LLH.

Mrs. W. A. "Betsy" Montgomery, chairwoman of the penitentiary board of trustees, 1932–36. MDAH.

Part II

All Things to All People 1934–1952

We regard it as good business, good management, good penology, and not at all incompatible with the reform and rehabilitation of criminals, to work the convicts under humane conditions so that, under efficient management, their labor returns a profit to the state above the cost of their keep.

—Jackson *Clarion-Ledger,* January 31, 1947

4

The Magnolia New Deal

In January 1934 the state of Mississippi was in the worst throes of the Great Depression. Nowhere were the ramifications of the crash more evident than at the penitentiary. The convict population had climbed to above 2,600, but for two years the legislature had failed to allocate a cent for permanent improvements, and a spartan appropriation for mere maintenance had amounted to only $32.21 per inmate during 1932 and 1933. The physical plant was a wreck. The convicts in the overcrowded cages were hungry, sickly, and in rags. Medical services were virtually nonexistent. Farm operations were at a low ebb.[1]

The financial accounts included in the biennial penitentiary report released in early 1934 confirmed that the problems were of long duration, merely brought to a head by the current economic dilemma. About 40 percent of the net profits reported for the period 1906–33 had been generated between 1906 and 1913, when Vardaman's political machine had held sway. After July 1, 1913, and continuing until June 30, 1933, the business affairs of the penitentiary had degenerated steadily. A deficit of over $707,000 had been recorded between 1929 and 1933.[2]

Governor Mike Conner thought the penitentiary could do better if the institution could be emancipated from the awkward system of checks and balances imposed by Vardaman some twenty-eight years earlier. Since coming to office in 1932, Conner had been engaged in an increasingly bitter struggle for the patronage of the penal system with Betsy Montgomery, president of the board of trustees, and her ally, Trustee Thad Ellzey of the southern district. Mounting difficulties at Parchman had placed the trustees in a no-win situation, and the governor had maneuvered to exploit their vulnerability. Now, in early 1934, Conner garnered support in the legislature and "attacked from ambush." In February a legislative committee reported "evidence of a lack of business judgment and economy" among the trustees, and in March the legislature stunned political observers by rushing through a sweeping reform package purporting to place the penal system on a "practical business basis."[3]

The Penitentiary Act of 1934

The penitentiary act of 1934 abolished the elected board of trustees effective January 1, 1936, and created a board of commissioners composed of three gubernatorial appointees.[4] At a stroke, the watchdogs of Vardaman's old scheme were gone.

The announced goal of the reformers was retrenchment. The statute declared that the penitentiary would punish felons at no cost to the state, at a profit if possible. That priority led not only to political consolidation but to physical consolidation as well. The offices of the new board of commissioners would be at Parchman, not in Jackson, as had been the case with the meddling trustees. Oakley Farm and the lime plant at Okalona would be leased to private parties. Five thousand acres adjoining Lambert would be purchased.

A number of the statute's provisions brought its sponsors crucial support in the legislature. The old administrative structure had divided patronage among trustees and governors, thereby spreading the spoils so thin that powerful elements in the statehouse had been frustrated. Now, legislative leaders got their share. Concentrated in the hands of chief executives, the patronage of the penal system became a much more useful tool in the governor's necessary task of legislative management, and Conner soon exploited it.[5]

Apparently the mandate to lease Oakley and purchase land adjoining Lambert was also part of the deal. For years Lambert had been plagued by chronic flooding. Yet nobody asked questions when Trustee Montgomery expressed doubt about the motives behind the purchase of additional land in what she described quite accurately as "an overflow drainage district." Nor did anybody respond to Montgomery's queries about the curious decision to lease Oakley Farm. Soon the 2,725–acre tract was delivered to a private party for $651.25 per annum.[6]

The governor and a considerable number of interested parties also had reason to be pleased by a provision of the act that required "annually all of the able-bodied male convicts over the age of 21 years and under the age of 50 years . . . to work for a period of six days on the public roads in the counties in which the . . . farms are situated." That provision facilitated two practices of consequence. First, it assured that chief executives could please politicians in the Delta, the cradle of political power in Mississippi, by delivering them convicts for labor on public works. Second, it opened the door to the private exploitation of convict labor. Long experience confirmed that the employment of convicts outside the penitentiary led inevitably to cupidity. Now, in the absence of independent inspectors, convicts could be distributed far and wide.

Other than Montgomery and Ellzey, a handful of legislators, and fifty or so deposed employees at the penitentiary, everyone seemed pleased with the new arrangements. Conner came calling at Parchman in July, slapping backs at Front Camp, touring the wretched cages with his hand-picked superintendent, Oliver Tann, a former camp sergeant and the brother of the governor's campaign manager. Two weeks later Conner entertained over five hundred legislators, county agents, and other public officials at a barbeque on the grounds of the penitentiary.[7] All in all, it was a masterpiece of political maneuver.

The New Context of Penitentiary Politics

The demise of the board of trustees removed one of three players from the game of penitentiary politics. Remaining were the chief executive and the legislature. The governor now held all the patronage; the legislature continued to hold the purse strings. Penitentiary politics, therefore, revolved around the ability of chief executives to manage the legislature.

There were three common denominators for success. First, governors had to assure that their principal appointees at Parchman were loyal, trustworthy, politically adept, prudent, and cooperative. Under the provisions of the new statute, the primary function of the commissioners was to look after the political interests of chief executives. They were brokers for the spoils of the penitentiary, men who negotiated contracts with the private sector and distributed staff positions, commodities, and convict labor. One imprudent appointment to the board could undo a governor.

So could the wrong superintendent. Chief executives and commissioners had to balance the demands of politics with the essential interests of penal farming, which were defined by superintendents. In the absence of a politically independent board of inspectors, superintendents held great authority and responsibility. They were, in fact, virtual feudal barons who enjoyed sovereignty in the day-to-day operations of the penitentiary. The convicts were at their mercy. Commissioners merely rubber-stamped their purchase requisitions. In most cases it was necessary to heed the advice of superintendents in every staff appointment, in negotiating every contract. Perhaps no appointment in state government demanded more gubernatorial scrutiny. Chief executives simply had to employ superintendents possessed of great expertise in large-scale agriculture, considerable managerial skills, and a degree of political savvy and influence.

Second, the cotton market had to improve. Cotton was almost worthless in 1934, and Parchman's warehouses were stuffed with dusty bales. No matter how expertly a superintendent managed farm operations, and no matter how shrewdly patronage might be distributed, continuing deficits would upset the political applecart.

Finally, a smokescreen had to envelop the penal farms. Control of the penitentiary brought governors incalculable political sweets, but control had its liabilities. State history confirmed that the penal system provided political detractors with a splendid avenue of attack, and Conner's own success in deposing the board of trustees was a recent case study of this phenomenon.

Conner and his immediate successors understood these facts of political life and successfully exploited their opportunities. Loyal, discreet chums of governors manned the board of commissioners and conducted their wheeling and dealing without fanfare. A new breed of superintendent also emerged. Until 1934 Parchman's superintendents had been farmers—men on the right side of politics, to be sure, but not one of whom had enjoyed a statewide political reputation. After the departure of Oliver Tann in early 1936, planter-politicians found their way to the superintendency.

Tann was a dray, a loyal workhorse appointed as a component of Conner's attack on the board of trustees, and he was retained in the wake of victory to look after things until Montgomery and Ellzey vanished from the political scene some twenty-two months later. He was succeeded in early 1936 by Governor Hugh White's appointee, James

F. Thames of Mendenhall, formerly chancery clerk of Simpson County, penitentiary trustee for the southern district from 1913 to 1930, and afterward state highway commissioner.

There followed the instructive eight-month superintendency of J. H. Reed, a Delta planter with but modest political influence who resigned after finding himself incapable of combatting the currents around him. In November 1940 an embarrassed Governor Paul B. Johnson replaced Reed with his hometown crony, Lowery Love of Hattiesburg. Love was a planter, a former state senator, an unsuccessful candidate for lieutenant governor, and a leading figure in the powerful Mississippi Baptist Convention. He moved on to the secretaryship of the state eleemosynary board in the spring of 1944 and was succeeded by Marvin E. Wiggins. Like his predecessor, Wiggins was an experienced planter, a former state senator, and an unsuccessful candidate for lieutenant governor.

The selection of such chief administrators put the first piece of the political puzzle in place, but neither governors nor superintendents could control the state of the cotton market. Here, Lady Luck came to the rescue. In 1936 the penitentiary sold cotton at prices ranging from about 12 to 14 cents per pound, and a year later one consignment drew only 8.43 cents per pound. But mobilization in Europe led to a steady appreciation in the value of cotton dating from 1938, and prices mounted substantially between 1940 and 1945 due to the war. Then, following a brief postwar slump, the value of cotton rose to unprecedented heights. By October 1950 it was selling at over 40 cents per pound on the New York market.[8]

Governors were also quite successful in screening the penal farms from political detractors. In January 1936 a curtain fell around a penitentiary that was a pork barrel of gubernatorial patronage, and one that was fraught with potential for graft and human abuse. The federal government posed no threat, for the doctrine of states' rights extended to the administration of criminal justice, and the federal judiciary studiously avoided involvement in state penal institutions. The same was true of the state judiciary: never did the Mississippi bench do anything that might have compromised the sovereignty of chief executives or their appointees at the penitentiary.[9]

The legislative branch of state government was equally pliable. The distribution of the penitentiary's patronage among the oligarchy of the Delta bought the support of all the right men in the statehouse.

The penitentiary committees of the house and senate, whose members conducted inspections and penned potentially damaging reports each year, were courted by governors, and superintendents entertained the committeemen lavishly at Parchman.

Feasts were laid out on the dining tables of the guest house or, in fair weather, on tables placed on the front lawn of the superintendents' mansion. Grinning, shuffling trusties served prime beef and mounds of vegetables on massive platters, told of their contentment, and wondered if they would be remembered by the governor. At the kennel, politicians marveled as the dogs performed. A dove hunt, with convicts substituting for retrievers, was often on the agenda, as in the days of Vardaman. Later the politicians conducted a cursory inspection of the superintendent's favorite units, where the convicts virtually stood on their heads to display productivity and delight with their taskmasters. And then it was back to Front Camp, where a generous superintendent distributed the penitentiary's fruits among the supposed inquisitors.[10]

The commissioners, operating from Front Camp, neutralized potential threats posed by local politicians. Among the local folk requiring constant attention were the members of the Sunflower County Board of Supervisors, who found their way to Parchman frequently, and the county district attorney, whose grand juries held jurisdiction over the penitentiary. The supervisors were content so long as they were given a little produce, allowed to place a worthless nephew or a "kissin' cousin" on the payroll from time to time, and allocated a few convict laborers for both public and private work projects. District attorneys, too, took their share of the penitentiary's fruits, and the members of the grand jury enjoyed themselves immensely during their cursory inspections of the penitentiary, departing with everything from bags of vegetables to choice cuts of beef.[11]

Only the general public and journalists threatened to rock the boat. The public was uninformed and generally indifferent. Hazy accounts of back-breaking labor, of Black Annie, and of the deadly shooters circulated among Mississippians, but the penal farms were well off the beaten path and shrouded in mystery. In 1934 Trustee Montgomery found it "surprising to know how few people understand, or in fact, have ever thought about . . . what the penitentiary is, or how it is operated."[12]

The "team" running the penitentiary made great efforts to assure that the mystery lingered. The tone of the biennial penitentiary reports changed dramatically. Earlier reports—those penned by the politically independent board of trustees—had been remarkably candid. After 1936 there was a degree of candor, but only when superintendents and commissioners tried to justify larger appropriations.

Governors and superintendents engaged in fulsome mutual flattery. Conner and Tann, ever dwelling on the proverbial "bottom line," could not say enough nice things about each other. Thames was a capable superintendent, but not the wizard Governor White said he was. Love talked frequently about the big money he was generating, always taking care to mention the many paths of righteousness he was blazing at the penitentiary, and Governor Johnson, a great fan of the gridiron, once told the press that Love was a "triple-threat back doing three things at once: managing a big farm, managing a big business, and . . . [being] warden for 2,600 convicts." Three successive gubernatorial administrations described Wiggins as God's gift to Mississippi.[13]

A trusting press printed all the platitudes and defended the penitentiary passionately. On July 17, 1932, at a time when convict life on the penal farms was galling, the Jackson *Daily Clarion-Ledger* argued, "Very few states give their prisoners more humane treatment or keep them in healthier environment." Official reports of overcrowding, starvation, and sickness failed to alter that editorial opinion. "The more we study conditions elsewhere," another staff writer observed on October 29, 1933, "the greater is our respect for the Mississippi system." The executive branch of government managed the press very effectively in later years. None of the state's leading newspapers questioned the operations of the penitentiary with any consistency until well into the 1940s.

Two instances illustrate the almost inevitable result of the strong-governor scheme of penal administration. In early 1935 Trustee Montgomery charged that convicts had been denied the essentials of life and worked on private plantations in violation of the law. Those allegations, lodged by the most experienced penal administrator in Mississippi, were ignored by the legislature, the grand jury, and the press. Roughly five years later, when the besieged Superintendent Reed made a number of unsettling public statements about the penitentiary, Governor Johnson denied any knowledge of the problem. Then, after a legislative committee confirmed inexplicable financial losses and open warfare between factions at Parchman, the governor defused the budding scandal by simply changing superintendents. And then, when the new superintendent, Lowery Love, reported that everything at the penitentiary was "proceeding smoothly" owing to "splendid organization," everyone was quite satisfied.[14] Such was the nature of penitentiary politics in the absence of Vardaman's watchdogs.

Riding Mr. Conner's Horse

Operating behind closed doors and blessed with a rallying cotton market, superintendents Tann, Thames, and Love carried the penitentiary out of the bog of the Great Depression between 1934 and 1944. Tann's official report for fiscal year 1934–35 would have one believe that he presided over a renaissance at the penitentiary. Nothing resembling a renaissance transpired, but the superintendent did renovate the sawmill and the brickyard, keep the convicts busy, and begin a campaign to refurbish the physical plant.

Otherwise Tann's time was devoted to politics. He simply had to show a profit, and somehow, by hook or by crook, he did. Cotton acreage was expanded, and observers noted that farm buildings were being erected as fast as the sawmill could produce lumber. Tann sold the increased yield of his cash crop, along with the hundreds of bales that had been produced and stored by his predecessor, in the glutted market. He also reduced operating expenses, most notably in the line items of kitchen supplies, medical services, and electricity. And in preparing his financial statement for the fiscal year, the superintendent deferred payment on a number of expenses, thereby willing red ink to his successor.[15]

These tactics enabled the superintendent to show a misleading but politically fortuitous "profit" of nearly $142,000. "Waving a typed statement triumphantly at a press conference" on January 30, 1935, Governor Conner represented the penitentiary's financial recovery as "just another example of savings that can be realized through a reorganization of government along business lines." The grand jury of Sunflower County said much the same thing in its presentment of March. Later in the year, Tann's contribution to the biennial report hailed the superior wisdom of the governor and his legislative allies.[16]

A substantial deficit for the 1935–36 fiscal year made all the boasting seem ridiculous, but Conner and Tann were long gone by the time the bad news broke. On January 1, 1936, they had the satisfaction of witnessing the statutory death of the board of trustees. Conner turned the executive office over to his successor, Hugh White, boasting to the end that his administration had placed the penitentiary on a sound financial footing, and Tann resigned in triumph.[17]

The superintendency of Jim Thames produced more substantive results. Thames increased brick production and, capitalizing on Tann's renovations at Parchman's sawmill, led the carpenters and bricklayers to impressive levels of production. Between 1937 and 1941 the convicts produced 650,000 bricks and 1,350,000 feet of rough lumber. Those materials were used to renovate cages and other buildings and to construct an enlarged cold storage plant, an ice plant, a bigger woodworking shop, a small canning factory, a mattress factory, and a new sewing room for the female convicts.[18]

Animal husbandry improved with the expansion of the corn and oat crops, milk and meat production mounted steadily, and by 1941 the dairy and beef herds had been restored to pre-Depression levels. Cotton production also increased. In March 1937 the grand jury noted that the superintendent's "scheme of soil fertilization and improvement as well as conservation is among the best . . . in Mississippi." There was a 25 percent increase in the 1936 cotton yield to 4,324 bales, and the 1937 crop yielded 5,863 bales. The next two years brought further increases, and the steady appreciation in cotton prices enabled the superintendent to turn very real profits. For the four-year period that began on July 1, 1936, and ended on June 30, 1940, the penitentiary reported net profits of almost $400,000. Thames boasted of his accomplishments a great deal, and with some justification: when he left Sunflower County in the spring of 1940, Parchman was reportedly "the only profit-making prison in the country."[19]

Following J. H. Reed's brief, unhappy superintendency, and a substantial deficit for fiscal year 1940, the energetic Lowery Love arrived at Parchman with a number of his friends from south Mississippi in tow. After reflecting on the rising value of cotton and the cost of provisions in the inflationary economy, the new superintendent launched a campaign to render the penitentiary entirely self-sufficient. He promptly reduced cotton acreage and increased acreage in food and feed crops in a like amount. Several months later Love released word that the penitentiary had produced enough meat, vegetables, and feed to supply itself during the winter of 1941. There would be a profit of "about $325,000" for fiscal year 1941, he reckoned; returns would be better if only the penitentiary had access to more operating capital.[20]

Love's tactics produced grumbling among a number of Delta politicians, but nobody could doubt his success. The Jackson press described the superintendent's accomplishments as a model for the state's farmers. Governor Johnson hailed his superintendent as a magician. The 1941 legislature hesitated but eventually approved an increase of nearly 61 percent in the penitentiary's appropriation.[21]

The following year brought the two master strokes of Love's administration—the construction of a new canning factory and the establishment of a centralized dairy. During 1942 some 100,000 gallons of vegetables were canned. The dairy began operations with 275 cows, grew rapidly, and so impressed the governor that he represented it to the press as a major accomplishment of his administration.[22]

Superintendent Love's successes unfolded almost daily. Cotton sales for fiscal year 1941 totaled nearly $500,000, and the next year cotton and cottonseed sales catapulted to over $885,000.[23] Love continued to exploit the inflationary economy, capitalizing on rising cotton prices while simultaneously reducing the penitentiary's dependence on the private sector. But Love was doing considerably more than manipulating the wave of inflation: he was getting much greater production from much less acreage. According to his press release of December 1943, 5,700 bales had been ginned, and a net profit of some $358,000 could be expected for fiscal year 1943. The superintendent, though, was far more pleased with other statistics. Between July and December 1943 the penitentiary had canned 80,000 gallons of vegetables and stored large amounts of food and feed. The livestock inventory listed 3,800 hogs, 250 milk cows, 850 head of beef cattle, and 825 mules and horses. Meat consumption, the superintendent added, had been almost halved to twenty thousand pounds per month; the penitentiary had not been forced to purchase beef from the private sector in two years.[24]

In June 1944 the penitentiary recorded in excess of $586,000 in cotton sales, nearly $118,000 in cottonseed sales, and well over $595,000 through the sale of surplus food and feed crops, thereby concluding a three-year financial recovery that produced an impressive net profit of $1,123,223.58. More important for the future, however, were Superintendent Love's additions to the penitentiary's physical plant. By the summer of 1944 the "triple-threat back" had begun construction on a machine shop, a shoe shop, a modern slaughter house, a large implement shed, and an addition to the cold storage plant that would double its capacity.[25]

By 1944 Mike Conner's goals had been realized. Parchman was operating on a "practical business basis," pumping exorbitant revenues into the state treasury, and figuring ever more prominently in the distribution of sweets among those on the right side of politics.

A Fly in the Ointment

There was, however, a problem that Governor Conner had not foreseen: a number of Mississippians thought the state penitentiary should do a great deal more than make money and feed the state's political spoils system. Vardaman had been largely forgotten amid the clatter of construction that characterized Lowery Love's Parchman, but the correction-oriented penal philosophy of the White Chief, if not the political motives underlying it, emerged anew during the late thirties and early forties. This time the notion that the state penitentiary should seek to redress the underlying causes of criminality emanated from the North, arising from realities peculiar to that section of the country.

The dire social manifestations of urbanization and of a maturing market economy manufactured convicts at an alarming rate in the industrialized Northern states, and the increasing strength of organized labor continued to erode productive work by convicts. Seeing nothing but evil in their explosive, overcrowded cellblock prisons, Northern liberals soured on the old penology and began to seek solutions to a problem of serious and worsening dimensions. In time they came to see much virtue in the theories of social and behavioral scientists who argued that it no longer sufficed merely to deter crime through the certainty of punishment afforded by evenly applied custodial sentences.

The old guard fell back before the onslaught. The advent of probation and parole, which reflected a headlong retreat from the thought that had launched the penitentiary movement over a century earlier, altered the profiles of prison populations substantially. Those felons remaining behind bars came under the scrutiny of experts who attempted to "diagnose" and "treat" the factors that "determined" criminality. Earlier emphasis on incapacitation, deterrence, and retributive punishment faded. The new rage, propelled by behaviorism and an undertow of redeeming Christian theology, became convict rehabilitation.[26]

Such thought was generally confined to the wealthier states of the North until the thirties. But the leveling influence of the Great Depression, and the pragmatic federalism born of it, opened the floodgates.

The Federal Bureau of Prisons, motivated by chronic overcrowding, undertook a massive campaign designed to reduce its convict population and to provide better organization and management in its penal institutions. In 1930 the federal parole system was created. Four years later the federal penal system initiated a comprehensive program of inmate classification. "Scientific" research was conducted on behalf of each commitment by classification committees. Personality traits, work skills, and educational needs were tabulated by the committees for the purpose of determining the type of penal environment to which convicts should be assigned. Options for commitment included the old cellblock prisons of the federal system, which were labeled "maximum security," and a number of recently acquired buildings and camps, which were designated as "medium security" and "minimum security" institutions.

These changes were advertised as progressive steps toward the individualization of convict treatment, and the example of the bureau of prisons was embraced by many state penal systems, including those of Georgia, North Carolina, and Texas. Soon a rebirth of idealism, fed by the pervasive spirit of the New Deal and the influential dogma of First Lady Eleanor Roosevelt, came to characterize an increasing number of penal administrators across the nation.[27]

Meanwhile, Mississippi was headed in the other direction, back to the "sound business principles" of early nineteenth-century penology. In both 1929 and 1933 penologists surveying the penal systems of the separate states commented on the total absence of the "paraphernalia of reform" in Sunflower County, and the program of development pursued at the penitentiary during the following decade altogether eschewed the Yankee innovations.[28]

The status quo was defended zealously. On March, 3, 1934, the Jackson *Daily Clarion-Ledger* warned that it was "dangerous for society to fall into the error [of thinking] that science can, through a little remodeling, make model citizens of all hardened criminals." That opinion commanded almost universal support in Mississippi. Seldom did the Jackson press fail to defend the increasingly peculiar hallmarks of the state penal system.[29]

Yet new ideas began to infiltrate Mississippi during the late thirties, most notably among the emerging middle classes of Jackson and the relatively cosmopolitan coastal counties. Slowly, the leading features of Parchman's system became ever more contentious, notwithstanding the cloak of mystery that shrouded the penitentiary.

Black Annie, of course, was an Achilles' heel: despite official policy, the characters of the inmates and their keepers rendered a degree of abuse inevitable, and at all events the strap was a public relations nightmare. In March 1937 the penitentiary received bad press when an escapee, apprehended in Virginia, fought extradition and charged that he and five other convicts had been given "80 lashes on their bare backs for failing to give alarm when another prisoner escaped." The allegations were fended off by Governor White and Superintendent Thames, but similar reports surfaced more frequently in future years.[30]

The trusty-shooter system was also a liability. The shooters had been controversial since Vardaman's day, but rarely had the abuses of the now-legendary headhunters been assessed with any specificity by journalists, grand jury presentments, or the reports of legislative committees. During the late thirties, however, chilling stories relating the efficiency of Parchman's convict constabulary began to appear in the state's newspapers.

While dead rabbits in the penitentiary's cotton rows alarmed many free-world folk, others were flabbergasted and chagrined by the degree of freedom afforded trusties. Indeed, in 1938 the senate penitentiary committee censured the entire trusty system. Parchman's trusties, the astonished politicians reported, were "free to roam as they please"; they had been observed "in public places with women and whiskey"; and penitentiary officials were guilty of the "promiscuous use of trusties in civilian clothes as chauffeurs."[31]

All that was quite true, and it reflected the extent to which the remote penal farm in Sunflower County had become an outpost of civilization, a subculture that defied the prejudices and expectations of the broader political society. Further evidence of this conflict, moreover, surfaced in 1940, when a legislative probe inspired by Superintendent Reed's difficulties at Parchman resulted in an official report revealing ruinous factionalism among staff members, inexplicable financial irregularities, and a great deal of socially unacceptable behavior in the cages.[32]

By the late thirties and early forties, a number of journalists, professional organizations, and influential public figures were ruminating on all the unsettling disclosures about the penitentiary, expressing moral indignation, and advocating reforms that would bring Parchman Farm into the mainstream of the national movement for penal reform. In September 1938 an editorial in the Jackson *Daily Clarion-Ledger* argued that "the cost of maintaining prisons is a great waste unless some of the money spent is devoted to the rehabilitation of the inmates." By 1940 the state bar association was coming around to a reformative concept of penology, and in early 1941 the Mississippi Conference on Social Work endorsed a resolution declaring that convict rehabilitation was the sole purpose of legal incarceration.[33]

Such views found support among a handful of legislators. Their leader was state representative Howard A. McDonnell of Biloxi, a gutsy New Deal Democrat who was beginning a long career in the statehouse that would earn him respect among even Mississippi's conservative majority. McDonnell's attacks were radical. In 1941 he laid out his creed in the house of representatives: "The sooner the public realizes that crime and criminals are the natural results of a given cause, rather than a vicious and willful surrendering to the evil, the sooner will safe and humane legislation be enacted to cope with the problem scientifically, rather than vindictively."[34]

McDonnell's language was far too extreme for the average Mississippian: somehow it seemed ridiculous to believe that the age-old concept of criminal guilt should be thrown over so unceremoniously, and the black complexion of the state's convict population did nothing to promote the idea among old-timers. But the times were changing, and by the early forties the notion of reforming "fallen" men and women at the penitentiary, if not that of reforming society itself, had a nice ring to it.

The first statutory manifestations of changing criminological thought in Mississippi came in 1940, when the gallows were abolished in favor of the "more humane" electric chair, and in 1942, when the legislature at last provided for the establishment of an institution for delinquent and dependent black children at old Oakley Farm.[35] Those reforms had no great impact on the penitentiary, but they reflected important shifts in public opinion and portended of things to come.

The concept of parole was the first great cause of those who advocated reforms in the adult penal system. As early as 1936 a bill calling for a politically independent board of pardons and paroles drew surprising support. Similar measures were introduced and debated extensively during subsequent legislative sessions, and in late 1939 Superintendent Thames endorsed parole in his biennial report. In the spring of 1940 Howard McDonnell hosted the annual meeting of the Southeastern States Probation and Parole Conference in Biloxi. There, a number of eminent persons joined the crusade for parole, and thereafter the reformers lobbied extensively among state legislators.[36]

Still, the idea of an independent parole board remained unpopular in the statehouse. For the old suspension system had been a vital cog in the wheels of the penitentiary for many years; it continued to work perfectly well, said its defenders; and legislators, always suspicious of heady abstractions emanating from the North, saw no reason to fix something that was not broken.

A Crippled Chief Executive

Something finally broke. In the summer of 1940 Governor Johnson grew quite ill, remained more or less incapacitated until his death in December 1943, and in the process demonstrated a number of liabilities within the state's system of penal administration.

From the first, Johnson had guarded his clemency powers very closely, exercising them only after careful deliberation, and thereby breaking with the long-standing precedent that gave Parchman's superintendents a virtual free hand in awarding pardons and suspended sentences to their charges. Superintendent Love was perfectly content with the governor's desire to assure fair play, and even applauded his vigilance, but illness progressively forced Johnson to cut back in clemency proceedings. For some reason, Acting Governor Dennis Murphree refused to pick up the slack, and he was none too eager to allow Love greater latitude. The result was unfortunate: daily, the incentives that motivated senior trusties at the penitentiary were compromised.[37]

Swamped with applications for executive clemency, and responding to Love's pleas for assistance, Johnson and Murphree supported the establishment of "some kind of investigating agency, parole board, or pardon board to assist the governor in determining which of these cases are meritorious." Such talk opened the door to reform and sent McDonnell's hopes soaring, but the 1942 legislature stopped short of embracing parole, instead resurrecting the old board of pardons. That compromise equipped the chief executive with a three-member advisory body, but Johnson's continuing sickness and Murphree's curious lethargy handcuffed the new board, creating a large backlog of petitions and breeding truculence among trusties at Parchman.[38]

By 1943 the situation had Love in a box. The inmates did not like the superintendent. His first principle of management was that a tired convict was a manageable convict, and he admittedly worked his charges to the limits of physical endurance. Love had also launched a campaign to stop all the whoring and gambling at the penitentiary, and that departure from traditional policy had alienated his veteran sergeants and the convict hierarchy in the cages. Now the trusties, especially the shooters, were upset by the interrupted flow of suspensions and pardons, and the superintendent was experiencing terrible problems. As early as February 1942 Love told a reporter that the situation at Parchman was grave, and that the attitude of the convicts had him "sitting on a keg of dynamite." By 1943 he was frantic.[39]

Love's anxiety was compounded by political problems. The strong-governor scheme of penal administration assured that Governor Johnson's extended illness created a vacuum in penitentiary politics. The vacuum appeared, moreover, at a time when Parchman was producing massive profits, and a number of state legislators and local politicians, all jockeying for a greater share of the spoils, posed a problem of no small proportions. Superintendent Reed's difficulties in 1940 had been the first manifestation of the problem: "eaten alive" by Delta politics and failing to get the support he thought he needed from the chief executive, he resigned. Love had tougher skin than his predecessor and was much better equipped for a knock-down Delta brawl, but he was forced to go toe to toe with political detractors from the day he arrived at Parchman, and by 1943 he was overmatched.

The superintendent's woes were rooted in political geography. He, like Governor Johnson, was from south Mississippi. That fact in itself was offensive to the closed society of the Delta, and the Deltans were all the more outraged by the inevitable result of the political spoils system, which had fashioned a staff at the penitentiary composed of south Mississippi "rednecks" to the virtual exclusion of the local folk. Nor did Love fawn in the presence of the local aristocracy: he was an outsider, and he despised the Delta nabobs no less than they despised him.

The superintendent's crusade for self-sufficiency at the penitentiary, which cut out local contractors, also caused resentment, as did his decision to sell huge amounts of surplus food crops and other produce on the open market. And Love simply refused to sanction the graft and other illegalities that kept the local boys happy: on one occasion a well-connected bumpkin threatened "to git yo' goddamn job" when the superintendent refused to give him his standard ration of beef.[40] All this, combined with the complaints of overworked, sex-starved, dice-robbed gunmen and the truculence of uninspired trusties, added up to trouble.

As early as 1941 the grand jury of Sunflower County, traditionally Parchman's stoutest defender, reported evidence of excessive flagellation at Camp Five, and further criticism of Love's regime was forthcoming the next year. The district attorney, it seems, was on the warpath, and the 1943 presentment of the grand jury went so far as to assert that convict welfare was being sacrificed to moneymaking. The dying governor emphatically denied the charge, assuring everyone that he was "more concerned with the welfare of the inmates than with making a lot of money" at Parchman. Love, resisting the temptation to publicly lambast local politicians, also refuted the findings of the grand jury. Feeling a tightening noose, however, the superintendent broke for daylight, advocating the abolition of the trusty-shooter system, the hiring of civilian guards, and the construction of a maximum security unit. To make his point, Love put his convicts to work on a special camp for "hardened criminals" almost immediately. Later he endorsed parole and a "very definite and well balanced Rehabilitation Program" as the only solution to his problems.[41]

The attack on the superintendent continued. Two Delta senators with enormous influence, Oscar Wolfe Jr. and Fred Jones, expressed grave, if remarkably well-timed, concern about conditions at Parchman. They were supported by McDonnell and his small band of followers in the legislature, and in January 1944, to the surprise of nobody, the newly inaugurated governor, Tom Bailey, called for sweeping reforms at the penitentiary. Meanwhile, speculation was rampant at Parchman Farm. Clearly, the penitentiary stood on the threshold of a new era.

5

A Little of This, a Little of That

Governor Bailey's inaugural address to the legislature expressed his displeasure with the penitentiary, advocated new programs for the reformation of convicts, and endorsed a parole system patterned after "that adopted by the Federal government and most of the states of the Union." Shortly thereafter a special legislative committee headed by Senator Wolfe and including Senator Jones departed for Parchman. Meanwhile, a bill calling for an independent parole board was introduced in the senate and assigned to the judiciary committee. While Bailey and the beleaguered Love gave the bill public support, William Keady of Greenville, chairman of the senate judiciary committee and a man destined for bigger things, guided the legislation through stormy sessions.[1]

The Compromises of 1944

Senator Wolfe's committee report, which included many tales of woe emanating from convicts, was released with great effect in the midst of the debates on parole. It was a remarkable document, one that criticized almost every facet of operations at the penitentiary without directly censuring Superintendent Love.

The committee endorsed a politically independent parole board and in effect called for the repeal of Mike Conner's strong-governor scheme of penal administration. Discovering conflict between farm operations and convict welfare, the committeemen advocated the creation

90

of a powerful, independent board of commissioners and a division of the penitentiary's operations between two administrators: a superintendent or manager with expertise in agriculture and a warden educated and experienced in penology, both to report as equals to the board.[2] Here, as early as 1944, was an unsettling legislative opinion that Mississippi's attempt to unite penology and remunerative plantation agriculture in a single scheme of public policy was becoming ever more problematic.

On February 21, 1944, two days after the committee's report was made public, the senate voted 38–5 to abolish the board of pardons and to create a parole board patterned after that employed by the federal penal system, and the lower house followed suit in mid-March. Legislation designed to implement the Wolfe committee's other recommendations, however, ran into "well-organized and persistent opposition" on the floor of the senate. Fully fifty amendments were proposed before the senators could reach agreement, and then the lower house did not like the senate bill. While the two chambers maneuvered to reach accord, a Jackson newsman, apparently understanding the currents beneath all the political rhetoric, bemoaned the "farcical and hypocritical" behavior of the politicians and contended that the public demanded better care, recreation, religious instruction, and "rehabilitation" for the convicts.[3] At last a heavily compromised reform package limped through the legislature.

The statute added the chief executive, sitting in an ex officio capacity, to the three gubernatorial appointees who already constituted the board of commissioners and made the board sovereign over all purchases exceeding $100. It also stipulated that the commissioners, not the governor, would employ the superintendent, the physician, the dentist, and the head bookkeeper. With the concurrence of the commissioners, the superintendent was to make all other appointments, including those who would occupy the new positions of farm manager, husbandman, and assistant chaplain.[4]

There was not much reform here. The strong-governor scheme remained intact, and now the chief executive was to attend the meetings of the board. Despite all the sound and fury about convict rehabilitation, the legislature mandated nothing resembling such a program, instead focusing on staff positions and money bills capable of enhancing agriculture.

In the final analysis, only one change of any consequence was effected by the 1944 legislature. The creation of a parole board, positioned squarely between the governor and the superintendent, stripped the penitentiary's chief administrator of his traditional influence in the granting of early releases. That reform ended the superintendent's ability to control the size and makeup of the convict population, threatened the trusty system around which middle management and security turned, and compromised the most vital component of the penitentiary's internal incentive program.

Thus fell the second major facet of Governor Vardaman's old scheme. The 1934 legislature had opened the door to countless abuses by abolishing the independent board of trustees. Now, in 1944, political jockeying and legislative compromise penetrated the heart of Parchman's system. Nobody paid much attention to the minority report submitted by the five senators who voted against the parole bill. They represented the old suspension system as the axis around which the penitentiary's operations turned and predicted that parole would cause insurmountable problems. Howard McDonnell quite agreed. Raising the bloody stick, he represented the triumph of parole as the entering wedge of a penal reform movement that would eventually terminate the reign of "the old antiquated maxim of 'an eye for an eye and a tooth for a tooth'" and usher in the scientific methodology of the new "corrections."[5]

When the smoke generated by the stormy legislative session of 1944 cleared, Governor Bailey reflected on the problems of the penitentiary and took stock of his resources. His predecessors had laid a foundation for bigger and better agricultural operations. The 1944 legislature had bestowed on the penitentiary a biennial appropriation of some $1.2 million as well as a hefty special appropriation earmarked for the renovation of the physical plant. Concluding that he had the resources to please everyone if only he could bring proper leadership to the penitentiary, Bailey stacked the board with his most trusted supporters, moved Superintendent Love to the state eleemosynary board, and appointed Marvin Wiggins to the superintendency.[6]

The governor displayed uncommonly good judgment in selecting Wiggins. The new superintendent was the consummate farmer, a man who brought with him the dirty fingernails of thirty years' experience in large-scale Delta agriculture. Wiggins also had considerable powers of judgment and good business sense, and he was adept at surrounding himself with competent underlings. He was not afraid to delegate responsibilities to his staff, he fought hard for their welfare, and he got production from them.[7]

He got production from the convicts as well. In managing them, the superintendent was a hard man but, by most accounts, a fair one. Wiggins understood convicts, convicts understood Wiggins. All agreed that convicts were convicts and that Wiggins was boss.[8]

There was something unsettling about the superintendent. Like most Mississippians of his generation, he had known hard times, and hard times had left their mark. He could smile, jaw, and slap backs with the best of the Delta boys, but beneath it all, one sensed, was the temperament of a rattlesnake. Neutralizing the serpent, in the best of Southern tradition, was wife Pauline, a sweet, caring woman whose presence softened the superintendent. Pauline, however, knew her place: the word in Jackson was that a prudent man would keep out of Marvin's way.[9]

Whenever Wiggins's powers of intimidation failed him, he could turn for support to the ruling oligarchy of the Mississippi Delta, in whose company he had moved for years. Fred Jones was his ally. So was Oscar Wolfe Jr. Allied with his native shrewdness and years of experience in Magnolia politics, those connections made the superintendent an extraordinarily gifted political navigator.

Wiggins would carry Parchman to what old-timers remember as its "golden age," all the while attempting to reconcile the old and the new at the penitentiary. And with detractors biting at his heels every step of the way, he would hold the line until advancing years and the politics of civil rights at last banished him to the obscurity of retirement.

The Postwar Surge

Wiggins profited from the strength of Mississippi's postwar economy. The cotton market was strong, the state treasurer raked in huge tax revenues, and the future looked rosy. Often in the company of the governor, and always with his political cronies from the Delta in tow, the superintendent made the rounds in Jackson, lobbying in his quiet, almost sinister manner and heading back to Sunflower County with more than his share.[10]

He exploited it to the fullest. Wiggins's first hire was a good one: C. E. Breazeale, an old friend of the superintendent, agreed to fill the new position of farm manager. Breazeale was an accomplished farmer, a planner of the first rank, and a man with whom Wiggins could work. They worked, worked feverishly, and soon the superintendent had a blueprint—a comprehensive scheme for the enhancement of agriculture.

Afterward, the dust of construction always hovered over Wiggins's penitentiary. A new gin, new farm buildings, new staff cottages, new cages, a slaughter house, a lard plant, a machine shop, a shoe shop, and an addition to the cold storage plant appeared very quickly. New wells began to cough up more of the precious, rust-colored water. Brick water towers soon rose over the various camps.

Wiggins's emphasis on the production of food and feed crops and his success in improving the beef, swine, and dairy herds made the penitentiary a horn of plenty. Parchman's dairy herd, in fact, became the talk of the Delta, Wiggins's pride and joy, but improvements at the canning plant, which enabled the penitentiary to ship large consignments of canned goods to other state institutions, towered over his earliest political triumphs.[11]

Wiggins also laid the foundation for greater cotton production. Supported by experts on loan from the Cooperative Extension Service of Mississippi State College, he slowly introduced scientific techniques of farming. Legislators lent a hand, providing funds for the purchase of tractors, combines, and other machinery. Soon Wiggins assaulted the tangled swamps flanking Black Bayou, the key to Parchman's drainage system, and upgraded the penitentiary's sadly deficient twenty-mile road net.[12]

Within three years, Wiggins had transformed the penitentiary. Everyone still called the place Parchman Farm, but quite clearly it was now a plantation, one of the largest in the Mississippi Delta.

Gotta Correct 'Em, Too

From day one, Superintendent Wiggins was diverted by pressure to implement programs designed to "correct" convicts. To some extent, this point of view reflected the nation's continuing redefinition of penal goals, which shortly would lead the American Prison Association to change its name to the American Correctional Association. More significant, though, were developments in Mississippi.

Beginning in the early forties, mechanization had begun to drive appreciable numbers of the state's sharecroppers and farm laborers off the land. This phenomenon gained pace during the latter stages of World War II, leading to slow but steady growth in Mississippi's urban population. After the war, when the soldiers returned home, the depopulation of rural areas picked up steam, unemployment became a problem in the towns, and a "baby boom" promised more of it in the years ahead. These changes had dire criminological implications: dating from about the time Wiggins became superintendent, there was an upsurge in crime and delinquency in Mississippi, especially in Jackson.

The state's old guard, of course, responded to the "crime wave" with traditional "get tough on crime" rhetoric, but many among the professional classes came to believe that new developments required new policies. Throughout the late forties and fifties, the causes of, and cures for, crime and delinquency were hashed and rehashed by journalists. Few subjects, in fact, commanded more attention in the capital press.[13]

All the clamor led to a strong movement for reform in Mississippi's processes of criminal and juvenile justice. The reformers, with whom Governor Bailey sympathized more or less, kept a close eye on the penitentiary after Wiggins's arrival, and attacked under the banner of Howard McDonnell, now a member of the state senate.

McDonnell headed the Mississippi Association of Crime and Delinquency, an organization boasting an impressive roster of members, principally judges, defense attorneys, journalists, and criminal and juvenile justice practitioners. Their primary goal was to identify and resolve problems within the state's processes of criminal and juvenile justice.

The activities of the association were anchored on specially appointed committees chaired by eminent personages. The various committees visited institutions, collected evidence supporting a preconceived hypothesis, prepared printed reports, and distributed them widely on the eves of legislative sessions. During Wiggins's early years, the association conducted studies of the abuses inherent in "the patronage system of the state penitentiary appointments," the omissions of the penal system in convict rehabilitation, and the need for a system of adult probation. Meanwhile, McDonnell railed against capital punishment in the senate and drew surprising support in an attempt to outlaw Black Annie.[14]

Wiggins did not like the criticism, thought many of the proposals for reform "downright stupid," and despised the snooping committees that popped up at Parchman. Yet the mounting strength of McDonnell and his collaborators impressed the superintendent, and he tried to make the most of it. Wiggins frankly admitted the penitentiary's shortcomings, pleaded for patience, and encouraged the reformers to lobby legislators for funds and staff positions commensurate with their goals.[15]

The superintendent's sympathy with the reformers was partly tactical: he was always on the lookout for political allies and never opposed anybody who wanted to throw money at his penitentiary. Strategic considerations, however, also made Wiggins warm up to talk of convict rehabilitation: he thought that the likely effects of the recently enacted parole statute necessitated reforms at Parchman.

The new, politically independent parole board, Wiggins perceived, was a two-edged sword. On the one hand, it was a buffer, a political entity that took heat off both the governor and Parchman's superintendent. On the other hand, the board posed a threat to the super's traditional sovereignty over the various forms of clemency. Lowery Love, Wiggins knew, had been undone by such encroachment. Governor Johnson's illness had stripped him of the incentives around which Parchman's entire system of management revolved, and Love had lost control.

Wiggins worried a great deal about this divorce of authority and responsibility. All of the governor's appointees on the parole board were politically well connected. All of them could be expected to have their own agendas. None of them knew a thing about Parchman. If they refused to work with the super, they could have a disastrous effect on the penitentiary.

Wiggins worked hard to get along with the members of the new parole board. The political appointees who manned the board, however, did not always bend to his point of view, and in a number of cases, Wiggins thought, they displayed appalling disregard for the facts of prison life. The only solution, the superintendent decided, was to bolster the penitentiary's system of internal incentives. The implementation of new programs might or might not atone for the negative effects of parole. But programs that were appealing to convicts would equip staff members with new managerial tools, plums that could be given and taken away. They might also bolster convict morale. And, if nothing else, they would make for good public relations.[16] For these reasons, Marvin Wiggins became a reformer.

Shortly after arriving at Parchman, the superintendent made plans to attend the annual meeting of the American Prison Association in New York City, and in the autumn of 1944 he probably squirmed uncomfortably as he was introduced to the litany of the new "corrections" in the Big Apple.[17] As time would tell, however, Wiggins took notes. Within days of his return to Mississippi, the popular Methodist minister A. R. Beasley arrived at Parchman and, in the capacity of chaplain, began to formulate plans for a "rehabilitation program" with the help of his assistant, George H. Skutt.

The program was launched late in the year, when Beasley initiated a modest elementary education program in "the three R's" for a handful of convicts. It was a trial run, everything went well, and an expanded version of the program, formulated with the assistance of the state department of education, was put into effect on September 26, 1946. The expanded program was much more ambitious, being designed to provide adult elementary education to the roughly 900 convicts who had less than a fourth-grade education. Classes were taught by literate convicts. The chaplain and his assistant provided supervision. Consultants included the superintendents of two local school districts.[18]

One-hour classes were offered during the lunch break three times each week, and supervised study periods were held every evening after the convicts returned from the fields. The racial segregation of the education program produced interesting comparisons. An unidentified convict-teacher spoke of the "enthusiasm and quickness" with which his Caucasian pupils learned; by January 1947 one class was reportedly clamoring for a course in algebra. The teacher of the black participants, life-term preacher Marion Enochs, found no clamor for the higher mathematics among his students and taught them nothing but the multiplication tables. The way he did it, though, was remarkable, his success even more so. A visiting journalist reported: "Negroes in prison stripes chanting the multiplication tables in the rhythm of their beloved spirituals heralds a new policy trend. . . . 'Five times five is twenty-five, five times six is thirty, five times seven is thirty-five and five times eight is forty', they sing-song as they tend to their fields under the sole guard of 'trusties.'"[19]

It was indeed a new policy trend, a stunning departure from the traditional racial parameters of state penal policy. But Wiggins brushed aside the arguments of critics, supporting the classes as boosters of morale, and an amused reporter observed that the prisoners "read with obvious pride in their new ability to pronounce the printed words." An inmate ridiculed that view of the education program, remembering instead that none of his peers "gave a damn about education" but participated "because we had to and because we wanted out of the joint." Whatever the case, by June 30, 1947, a reported 600 convicts had enrolled in the program, and it was said that over half of them learned to read and write.[20]

Chaplain Beasley also implemented a comprehensive religious program. In 1945 the board of commissioners authorized religious services in the camp dining halls, approved the purchase of a number of pianos, and mandated that all convicts attend Sunday morning services. Thereby blessed with a captive flock, and advising the parole board on all petitions, Beasley held the cards necessary for success. Soon a multitude of preachers representing various denominations descended on Parchman. Often they delivered sermons that inspired the black convicts to the point of either real or calculated delirium. The chaplain was impressed; the camp sergeants were not. The inmates, according to witnesses, enjoyed the singing, pleased the chaplain with frequent "amens," and hoped for parole.[21]

In January 1946 Beasley organized the "Inmates' Gospel Service of Camp 6," a group of evangelical convicts bound together by a written constitution. The pious members of the group, who numbered fifty-three by August, held spirited services on Sunday mornings. A visitor found the spectacle amusing. "There is no church or chapel and guards stand by with guns, but the spirit of the service is good," he wrote. "The leader, a prisoner, is an ordained Baptist minister, and a rather forceful, spirited preacher, oddly enough."

Beasley convinced Dr. D. A. McCall, the executive secretary of the board of the Mississippi Baptist Convention, to stage a revival at Parchman in May 1946. McCall stayed a week, preaching fire and brimstone whenever Wiggins could spare a detachment of field hands, and in the end seven convicts claimed to be converted. Several months later Dr. McCall was authorized by Jackson's Calvary Baptist Church to return to Parchman and baptize the seven convicts, along with one more who had come to see the light since the evangelist's departure. The eight men, dressed in their ring-arounds, waded into a small stock pond and were dunked in its muddy waters under the watchful eyes of Winchester-brandishing shooters.[22]

By June 1947 Chaplain Beasley had established Sunday schools at every camp; conducted 949 services, attended by a total of 37,622 convicts and visitors; and accumulated a massive amount of religious literature. "If part of our job is to rehabilitate the prisoners for a return to the outside world, it seems to me we ought to try to educate them," Beasley told a reporter. Such talk made for good press, but there is reason to believe that not all the inmates profited. "C'mon man, you don't really believe that any of us read that Jesus shit?" asked a beneficiary of Beasley's reading program.[23]

If the inmates were unimpressed by the advent of educational and religious programming at Parchman, they were surely pleased with the many indulgences held out by Wiggins. In December 1944 the superintendent initiated the nation's first furlough program, one allowing well-behaved convicts to leave the penitentiary for a period of ten days during the Christmas season. This, Wiggins knew, was powerful incentive for good behavior, a tool that might help him partially atone for his diminished influence in the granting of early releases. The same motive led the superintendent to alter the penitentiary's long-standing visitation policy. After March 1946 the immediate family members of convicts were allowed to visit every Sunday for two hours, and for the entire afternoon every third Sunday, while other relatives and friends could visit once every six months. Another innovation designed to inspire good behavior among convicts was the introduction of motion pictures: in 1947 penal administrators purchased a portable projector and began showing movies at each camp twice monthly. Wiggins also implemented a system that allowed convicts to bypass their sergeants and to "convey suggestions and express grievances [directly] to the prison administration."[24]

The Unholy Alliance

Despite these innovations, Wiggins's worst fears were realized between 1945 and 1948: his penitentiary was progressively undermined by the advent of parole. After a number of early problems, the parole board began to process applications very rapidly in 1946, and the board's success in identifying and paroling the best of the penitentiary's long-term convicts was confirmed the next year, when Mississippi achieved the lowest parole revocation rate in the thirteen-state Southeastern States Probation and Parole Conference.[25]

The effects began to be felt at the penitentiary in early 1946, when a large group of trusties, manageable old-timers all, bid adieu at Front Camp. Their departure signaled the first stage of the erosion of middle management and security at Parchman. In March a troubled board of commissioners compounded the penitentiary's problems by overreacting, adopting policies upgrading the qualifications for trusty status and restricting the mobility of all trusties.[26]

By early 1947 the ranks of Wiggins's veteran trusties had thinned appreciably, management and security in the cages were compromised, and the demise of the penitentiary's well-oiled scheme of behavioral reinforcement was breeding increasing truculence among the gunmen. The camp sergeants fell back on their last line of defense, employing Black Annie on the recalcitrants, but some of them apparently went too far, for a widely reported scandal alleging excessive flagellation erupted in May. Wiggins moved decisively to mend his fences, and a period of relative tranquility ensued. In December, though, trusty Edmund Perryman ran amok, stabbed the wife of a nightshooter, fatally wounded a camp sergeant, and then committed suicide.[27]

The widening cracks in Parchman's foundations suggested that perhaps the state had been a little hasty in abandoning the old suspension system, which after all had been the fulcrum of the penitentiary's scheme of convict management. But there was also the argument, propounded by Senator McDonnell and his noisy followers, that the parole statute had been merely the first act of the piece, and that difficulties would continue so long as the state operated a labor-intensive cotton plantation with little or no regard for the ideals of modern corrections.

McDonnell's notion of corrections translated into more staff positions and larger appropriations for the penitentiary. That, if not his medical model for Parchman, found support among Delta politicians, who sensed—as they did in 1944—an opportunity to increase the flow of money to their section of the state. For his part, Wiggins thought McDonnell's views hilarious, and doubled up with laughter at the thought of his gunmen being diagnosed and treated by a battery of psychiatrists. But he too sensed opportunity and was willing enough to play along.[28]

The unholy alliance was promoted by gubernatorial politics. Governor Bailey's death in November 1946 had elevated his lieutenant governor, Fielding L. Wright, to the office of chief executive. An ambitious man who coveted the governorship in the upcoming election, Wright sorely needed to broaden his political base within the state. By all appearances he broadened it, in part at least, by supporting far-reaching changes at the penitentiary. At all events, Wright's successful gubernatorial campaign attracted support among key Delta politicians, and once elected he emerged as an ardent supporter of a sweeping penal reform package that, while pleasing McDonnell and his corrections lobby, promised to deliver a huge increase in jobs and money to Sunflower County.[29]

A great deal of behind-the-scenes jockeying concerning the terms of a comprehensive penal reform package transpired during the early months of the 1948 legislative session, but the magnitude of the measure promoted by the governor and the senate leadership kept the issue in doubt until the early spring. In March, however, the penitentiary's most celebrated inmate, the charming murderer Kennie Wagner, walked out Parchman's front gate with a .45–caliber machine gun and successfully evaded the bloodhounds he had trained as the Main Mos' Dog-Boy.

"The notorious Kennie Wagner 'walk-away' from the Mississippi penitentiary," noted an editorialist, "could not have been timed better to increase legislative support of pending bills instituting reforms in prison administration." So it would appear. One legislator remarked that parole allowed "the cream of the crop" to leave the penitentiary. Another observed that parole had spread the trusty-shooter system "as thinly as warm butter may be spread on a crisp cracker." In bed with the reformers, Wiggins stoked the fire, stressing that he and his staff were incapable of combating the effects of parole and lobbying successfully for a legislative package of unprecedented scope.[30]

The Penitentiary Act of 1948

The penitentiary act of 1948 authorized the employment of fifty civilian guards, thereby increasing the Sunflower County tax base by some $120,000 per annum, pleasing those who sought to terminate the trusty-shooter system, enhancing the governor's patronage, and adding to the size of Wiggins's staff. The same interests were promoted by provisions that added an educational director, a vocational director, a classification officer, and a classification records clerk to Wiggins's stable and granted across-the-board salary increases to all existing employees.

The statute also reflected a number of tradeoffs. One of them, a token concession to be sure, authorized the superintendent to spend up to $3,000 annually on psychiatric treatment for convicts. Another, which repealed a plum bestowed on local government by the penitentiary act of 1934, banned convict labor on the roads of Sunflower and Quitman Counties. Yet another authorized an almost predictable land deal—the sale of half Lambert's acreage—but nobody complained about the curious decision to unload the same floodplain that Mike Conner's cronies had hyped as an agricultural bonanza only fourteen years earlier. The central thrust of the penitentiary act of 1948, though, was a new commitment to remunerative plantation agriculture and the delivery of immense resources to Wiggins's farm manager.[31]

The justification for, if not the motives underlying, the statute was offered up by McDonnell's surly Delta ally, Senator Fred Jones—who, not incidentally, represented Sunflower County. There was a pressing need to supplement the convict constabulary with civilian guards, he pointed out. Across-the-board salary increases would attract "higher-type" employees, he theorized optimistically, ignoring the political context of all penitentiary appointments. And since the absence of a modern classification system was "one of the worst evils of our present penal system," the addition of classification specialists would solve a maze of problems, allowing the penitentiary to segregate convicts "according to criminal tendencies."

Jones also found great wisdom in mitigating the "back-breaking" labor required of convicts: it "degraded" and made them despair, he observed sympathetically. So it was time to withdraw at least half the gunmen from the fields, to replace them with machines, and to embrace the scientific methods of modern agriculture. Hence Wiggins would be provided with a professional agronomist, bigger and better machinery, the assistance of publicly paid technicians, and seed money to finance major farm improvements.

All this was consistent not only with the principles of business but also with those of modern correctional administration, Jones emphasized. For increased mechanization and the advent of scientific farming techniques would allow Mississippi to pursue the correctional philosophy of the Federal Bureau of Prisons. The penitentiary would establish industries, employ the displaced gunmen within them, produce goods that could be distributed among public institutions via a state-use system, and thereby provide vocational training for convicts while also promoting the public interest. Thus came the justification for a vocational director.

Vocational training, however, could not possibly occupy all the time of the convicts if intensive human labor were to be reduced by 50 percent. Hence the need for an educational director: education, Senator Jones explained, was the very essence of convict rehabilitation. All the philosophy confused Superintendent Wiggins, but the politics of the thing were impeccable, and he thought he could pull it off so long as the politicians kept the money coming. The key to everything, he felt, was the mechanization of farm operations.[32]

Toward the "Golden Age"

The penitentiary act of 1948 came at the outset of Governor Wright's own term of office. Perhaps no chief executive in state history has enjoyed a more tranquil administration. Wright became the darling of white Mississippians when Southern Democrats, incensed by the civil rights platform of Harry Truman and the national Democratic Party, forged the Dixiecrat Party and nominated him as Strom Thurmond's running mate in the presidential election. The failure of the Dixiecrats had no apparent effect on the governor's statewide popularity, for Germany, Japan, and Italy lay in ruins, and in Mississippi, as elsewhere in the country, peace had brought prosperity.

The cotton market, yet to feel the pinch of the new synthetic fibers, boomed. State tax revenues, still dependent on the produce of planters, soared. Enjoying a happy relationship with legislative leaders, Governor Wright smiled a great deal, said all the right things, and appeared to get along with everyone. In this climate, Marvin Wiggins carried Parchman to its zenith.

The superintendent's chums in the legislature made it all possible. In the smoky antechambers of the statehouse, they had bought Wiggins's support for the recently enacted penitentiary bill with a number of promises. The provisions of the statute that banned convict labor on the roads of Sunflower and Quitman Counties ended countless problems with local politicians. The sale of roughly half of Lambert's flooded acreage removed an albatross from Wiggins's back.[33]

The politicians had also promised heftier appropriations. Now they delivered. During fiscal year 1948 Parchman got a new administration building, a new hospital, a new and "splendidly equipped" canning plant, forty new cottages for employees, and a number of new barns. The following biennium brought the construction of a tuberculosis unit, a new steam laundry replacing "the old wash-tub method," a new dairy, and a "pure dairy barn" to house Wiggins's prized herd.[34]

During fiscal year 1947 the penitentiary produced 600,000 pounds of beef and pork, and soon a poultry unit was added. D. L. Edson, the agronomist Wiggins hired in 1948, immediately undertook soil surveys in league with experts from the Mississippi Cooperative Extension Service. The next year, after Wiggins's dragline had transformed Black Bayou's tangled, snake-infested waters into a placid irrigation canal, Edson's scheme of land use enabled the farm manager to exploit the new drainage system and all available farm machinery. By June 1951 the penitentiary boasted a fleet of thirty-four all-purpose tractors, more on order, and a modern machine shop to maintain them.[35]

Soon Parchman's fields flowered as never before. Food crop production was prodigious, easily doubling the needs of the penitentiary. By July 1949 the new canning plant was producing between 3,000 and 5,000 gallons of canned goods daily. Production increased later in the year when an artesian well was dug, and the penitentiary's shipments of canned goods to other state institutions reached new heights.[36] Meanwhile, truck after truck conveyed raw cotton to Front Camp. The gin hummed, buyers gathered around the administration building, and stuffed boxcars swayed as they lumbered toward the processing plants of Memphis, New Orleans, and the Mississippi Delta.

The convicts, along with the state treasury, profited from the penitentiary's mounting prosperity. In February 1944, shortly before Wiggins arrived at Parchman, a number of convicts had complained about a daily ration that consisted of $\frac{3}{10}$ ounce of coffee, $\frac{9}{10}$ ounce of sugar, over $1\frac{1}{2}$ ounces of lard, a bountiful serving of vegetables, and 3.2 ounces of meat.[37] Compared to the diets of most free Mississippians, that ration was hardly mean, but the penitentiary's culinary arrangements improved dramatically after Wiggins took the helm.

As early as April 1945 every convict received a daily ration of a quart of milk and an ounce of butter, and afterward a much wider variety of dairy products appeared on the menu. By the summer of 1949 convicts were gobbling down all the fruit and vegetables they wanted, and later in the year their meat ration was increased to a half-pound daily.

The meals enjoyed by the inmates on holidays, especially on Christmas Day, were nothing short of feasts, and after 1948 a professional dietitian coordinated all culinary arrangements at Parchman.[38]

Ever-improving food services were complemented by ever-improving health care. The new hospital was said to be "commodious; well planned and a credit to the State." The superintendent experienced difficulty in hiring and retaining competent medical personnel, but between 1948 and 1952, when the inmate population averaged about 2,000, only a reported 10 or so convicts died each year. In January 1951 the chaplain contended that "the physical care provided for inmates at Parchman equals, if indeed it does not exceed, that to which the average Mississippian has access."[39]

The improvement of the physical plant also accrued to the advantage of the convicts. One member of Wiggins's staff insisted that the brick cages were infinitely superior to those housing enlisted personnel in the United States armed forces. Furthermore, if the coming of parole diminished the incentives inherent in trusty status, working conditions in the penitentiary's many new shops partially compensated. Convicts competed vigorously for the more favorable assignments—the shoe shop, the dairy camp, and the new steam laundry.[40]

Wiggins also sought to bolster the penitentiary's sagging system of internal incentives by holding out a number of new indulgences to the convicts. Journalism made its debut at Parchman in 1949 when a shoddy, mimeographed inmate publication dubbed *Inside World* was distributed among the camps. The quality of the little magazine improved with the purchase of an electric mimeograph machine in 1950, and in its second year of operation *Inside World* received awards from the National Association of the Penal Press for being the most improved prison newspaper and for having the best inside coverage.[41]

Organized musical activities got under way about the same time. In early 1951 Chaplain S. B. Harrington procured musical instruments, opened a "music school," and formed a fifteen-piece orchestra. The black convicts tended to hang back, preferring instead their own sessions in and near their cages.[42] But Harrington's program started organized music at Parchman; the black musicians would come around later.

Following the terms of the agreement he struck with legislative leaders in 1948, Wiggins withdrew increasing numbers of gunmen from the fields and engaged them in "rehabilitation programs" as more and more farm machinery arrived. In May 1948 one W. R. Burrus of Greenwood, a veteran rehabilitation counselor for the state department of education, was appointed educational director. His school graduated 308 convicts on March 31, 1949, and Burrus reported that the average convict-student had advanced from a first-grade to a fifth-grade level during the term.[43]

The energetic R. L. Patterson, who replaced Burrus as educational director in the summer of 1950, carried Parchman's education program to new heights in a very short period of time. During biennium 1949–51 the penitentiary maintained elementary schools in eighteen camps, employing 112 convict-teachers and serving 1,142 convict-students. Of that number, only 81 failed to complete their classes, and 78 pupils earned fourth-grade certificates. In addition, Patterson organized a special advanced class providing instruction through the twelfth grade for 26 convicts and a typing class utilizing reconditioned typewriters obtained from the Veterans Administration. Supported by the chaplain's distribution of some forty thousand pieces of literature between 1949 and 1951, the adult education program had progressed to a point far beyond the most optimistic projections of its founders by the summer of 1952.[44]

The classification of convicts "by criminal tendencies" began in July 1948, when W. D. Durrett was appointed classification officer. Durrett replaced Parchman's "outmoded method of registrar's records" with what he described as "a modern and adequate system." By the summer of 1949 two camps had been designated for inmates who were physically or mentally incapable of regular duties—Camp Four for white men and the old hospital for black men. Collaboration between the classification officer and the educational director had led to reported improvement in the penitentiary's rehabilitation program by the summer of 1951. Work assignments and placement in the educational program were being determined by a block of tests, and ongoing study was resulting in a considerable number of reassignments.[45]

Durrett described the classification system as "a model of efficient organization," but the camp sergeants were displeased. "Wiggins let the convicts run the farm," remembered one malcontent. "I suppose he had to please McDonnell and the other shysters in the legislature, but he sho' did it at our expense. Any con who could convince the chaplain he had found religion, or convince that damned Durrett he was too good for nigger work, got re-classified." A black convict agreed. "Sure," he recalled, "we did whatever it took to get outta dem cotton fields. Wouldn't you?"[46]

Less dependent on field hands owing to farm mechanization, Wiggins issued a new policy in 1951 allowing two-hour lunch breaks Monday through Friday and terminating all labor at noon on Saturdays. So as to occupy the increasingly idle convicts, the superintendent established an intercamp basketball program and allocated state monies for the purchase of sports equipment.[47]

All the while, the Christmas furlough program begun in 1944 was expanded. By January 1951 well over 2,000 convicts had spent a part of the Christmas season in the company of their families, with only 12 failing to abide by the rules.[48]

Perhaps the superintendent's crusade to bolster convict morale explains the penitentiary's ever-diminishing escape rate; certainly that was the official explanation. Or perhaps would-be escapees were deterred by Wiggins's extraordinary improvements in security, especially his shooter system and legendary bloodhounds. Whatever the case, attempted escapes, which had averaged slightly more than 73 annually during Love's superintendency, decreased to 36 during Wiggins's first year and averaged under 16 per annum between 1948 and 1952.[49]

By midcentury Parchman Farm was at high tide, a curious admixture of plantation agriculture and penology, and there was ample reason to say that the institution was successful as both a plantation and a prison. In 1947 a journalist had said just that, pronouncing Parchman's system "good business, good management, good penology, and not at all incompatible with the reform and rehabilitation of criminals."[50] Now, some four years later, business was better, management was better, and hard statistics confirmed uncommon penological triumphs.

6

High Tide

By the early fifties, Parchman Farm was among the most famous penal institutions in the United States, and most of the credit or blame for whatever the prison was, and whatever it was not, could be assigned to its superintendent. Marvin Wiggins was in charge, and had been since the day of his appointment in 1944. Governors Bailey and Wright had practically abdicated the penitentiary to him, and Wiggins had remade it in his own image.

The old system of convict management essentially remained intact: Wiggins believed in going with the flow, in accepting things that had evolved naturally through trial and error. But the superintendent had his own agenda, and, building on the old, had presided over a number of significant modifications. Some things, though, had not changed; and through the years the marriage of the old and the new had made the penitentiary a profoundly complex place, a subculture that was of great celebrity among those in the world outside. Free-worlders talked about it, wrote about it, sang about it; but few of them understood it. There was no other prison quite like Parchman Farm.

The Super as Protector

Up at Front Camp, "Mr. Marvin" lived in "The Big House," attended by "Miss Pauline" and the luckiest of trusties. Now, however, The Big House was strikingly different. Gone were the spindles and gables. Gone was the air of antebellum splendor. Not one magnolia, not one moonbeam, was discernible around the super's new ranch-style home. The old Victorian mansion had gone with the wind, the victim of utility.

Yet folks still called the super's low-slung abode The Big House, and from it every morning emerged Mr. Marvin. Sometimes he paused in the yard, seemingly surveying his domain, perhaps pondering his crowded itinerary. More frequently he proceeded directly toward the administration building, his gait familiar to all.

As Wiggins walked down the corridors, staff members and trusties nodded respectfully. All of them knew from long experience never to get pushy, never to get in Mr. Marvin's face. The super, though, was pleasant enough as he passed them, and his faint, all-knowing smile could make one's day.

Upon entering his office, Wiggins seated himself at a huge desk, loosened his suspenders, literally rolled up his sleeves, and got to work. The governor, the attorney general, the director of the state building commission, or a penitentiary commissioner might telephone; if so, all else went on hold. All else, that is, except visits and telephone calls from members of the legislative delegation of the Yazoo Delta. These men and women were the super's chips in the game of state politics, the people whose support was as essential as the spring rains. For years senators Fred Jones and Oscar Wolfe Jr. had stirred the drink, whipping together a united voting bloc and bringing its power to bear in Jackson. Without them, Wiggins knew, he and his penitentiary would be in big trouble.

Then there were the cotton buyers who loitered outside the super's office, glad hands in their pockets. Wiggins often kept them waiting for extended periods, but they never went away. In the end, his daily political jockeying complete, the super always saw them.

Wiggins could wheel and deal with the best of them, politicos and cotton buyers alike, and his attitude toward such folk was already legendary. They were outsiders. They were on the make. But they were necessary evils, and insiders had to get along with them. Getting along required giving and taking, trading off, but an insider could never lose sight of the farm, could never compromise that which was beyond negotiation.

Wiggins personified Vardaman's notion of the ideal superintendent. He viewed the penitentiary as a vulnerable fortress, one always besieged by the capricious world outside, and he saw himself as its protector. Parchman was Wiggins's farm.[1]

Employees accepted the superintendent's authority or were soon gone, eased out of the picture without fanfare, and all of them were subject to two general rules. First, nobody was to assume that he understood the big picture. That was the super's domain, his alone, and he could not afford to have staff members go off half-cocked. "Take care of your own business, and let me take care of all of you," he told employees on more than one occasion. The second rule was that nobody could lose sight of Parchman's vulnerability, of the vultures who circled outside, especially politicians.

To ward off this threat, Wiggins gently discouraged social intercourse between Parchman's employees and outsiders, promoted an us-against-the-world attitude among his staff, and insisted that employees have no connections with politicians. Mr. Marvin, and Mr. Marvin alone, handled the vultures.[2]

The Super as Political Economist

Wiggins was the consummate Delta politician, and even today his wheeling and dealing is a major focus of Parchman lore. By all accounts, his concept of political economy was profoundly different from those who preceded and followed him.

The super was, for example, extremely reluctant to pay his political debts with jobs. The staff was too small as it was, and every one of them had to perform. Above all, though, Wiggins did not want a "politician's snitch" within his inner circle.

Nor was he willing to part with his cash crop. The white stuff, he knew, was the bottom line, the litmus test for his mettle among the power brokers down in Jackson, so not many of the penitentiary's legendary "walking cotton bales" walked very much during Wiggins's superintendency. Likewise, the super frowned on sweetheart contracts. If things were roughly equal, he might play along; if not, no deal.

Still, the politics of the thing demanded tradeoffs, and Wiggins of course made them, albeit on terms that were compatible with what he defined as the essential interests of his penitentiary. By some accounts the super paid many of his political debts with beef; if so, that probably explains his otherwise curious reluctance to centralize Parchman's beef herd. Others tell of "gap-acreage on the back side of the farm," contending that Wiggins allowed private planters to make seasonal intrusions into the penitentiary's ill-defined boundaries. These, however, were "chicken shit, no more than several hundred acres," according to one party, who stressed that such transactions "gave Mr. Marvin a slush fund that helped a lot of folks out in their hour of need."[3]

The superintendent was also willing enough, some say, to allocate convict labor to private parties, although he never did so when labor was needed at the penitentiary and always insisted that the convicts be tended by his drivers and paid a modest wage under the table. During Wiggins's years, Parchman's crop was normally among the first in the Delta to be "laid by," and several former staff members and convicts alike recall that once the picking at the penitentiary was done, gunmen were normally put to work on private plantations. They also tell of great competition among convicts for such assignments, explaining that the money they earned "greased the cage economy."[4]

Wiggins's notion of political ethics was extraordinary, and it earned him the respect of even those politicians who came up empty. The word in political circles was that the super was a stickler on the subject of finance, that he guarded Parchman "like Beauregard guarded Charleston," and that "players had to play by Wiggins's rules." This, surely, was what Governor Hugh White had in mind when he told the press in 1952 that the super was "honest, conscientious, and competent."[5]

The Super and the Legend

Wiggins was always troubled by what he regarded as a dangerous conflict in the expectations of the public. On the one hand, a prison administrator was expected to preside over a horrible place, a place of suffering secured by brute force and capable of intimidating would-be felons in the free world. Here, the prototype was Alcatraz, the federal prison situated in San Francisco Bay. It was an ominous joint housing the worst of the bad boys, and the propaganda of J. Edgar Hoover and his friends over at the bureau of prisons had made Alcatraz a legend, an institution that frightened little boys and girls across the nation.

Many of the separate states had followed the federal example. There was Sing-Sing in New York, Rahway in New Jersey, Angola in Louisiana, and many others, all of them distinguished by the horror stories that were told of life behind their foreboding gates.

On the other hand, there was something about such prisons that conflicted with the peculiar American ideal of freedom, perhaps with American religiosity as well, and in recent years there had been a great deal of public concern for the plight of convicts and a pervasive crusade to improve their lot. The result was much confusion about what a penal institution should be, and it forced a prison man to walk a thin line, to project his joint as a chamber of horrors and a Sunday school all rolled into one.[6]

Wiggins had little difficulty in projecting Parchman Farm as a chamber of horrors, for in 1944 he had inherited a prison that was already a legend, and the message conveyed by the legend was quite simple: do not run afoul of the law in Mississippi.

Some of the legend was rooted in the rare glimpses Mississippians got of their remote penitentiary. For decades, early-rising hunters and fishermen, unhappily trapped at railroad crossings, had seen the forlorn faces of black women as they boarded the Midnight Special in the lazy little towns of the Delta. Occasional convict labor outside the penitentiary had fed the fire. Motorists grimaced as they passed the sweating road gangs in their striped overalls, always attended by the stalking shooters. Convicts working on the levees had also contributed: almost everybody in the Delta told stories of manacled convicts, guarded by hard men with shotguns, singing their soulful blues as they tried to hold back the waters of the Mississippi and its tributaries during the rainy season.

There were also those who had observed the lethal efficiency of Kennie Wagner and "Hog-Jaw" Mullins, Parchman's past and present Main Mos' Dog-Boys, as they directed their sniff-dogs and kill-dogs in pursuit of fleeing convicts. The state's journalists found that such stories sold newspapers, and for years they had reported them with great zeal, representing Parchman's sergeants and veteran trusties as the toughest customers this side of Alcatraz.[7]

The published works of novelists, too, had pumped the legend. William Faulkner's *The Mansion*, for example, related the "doom" of the murderer Mink Snopes, who did not "even count off the years as they accomplished" on Parchman Farm. Snopes trod the passing days "behind him into oblivion beneath the heavy brogan shoes in the cotton middles behind the mule which drew the plow and then the sweep, then with the chopping and thinning hoe and at last with the long dragging sack." This, though, was only one of many Parchman stories in the works of the great novelist: Faulkner made reference to the state penitentiary frequently enough to justify a doctoral dissertation assessing the role of prisons and prisoners in his published works.[8]

All of this had contributed, no doubt; yet the legend of Parchman Farm was primarily the work of black people—the blues artists of the

Yazoo Delta. Many of them served time at the penitentiary: Eddie "Son" House; Huddie "Leadbelly" Ledbetter; McKinley Morganfield, better known as "Muddy Waters"; and Washington "Bukka" White are the most famous of the lot. Two of the songs—"Parchman Farm Blues" and "The Midnight Special"—were the heart of the legend. Yet there were many others, some published, some not, that helped paint the ominous picture.

Above all, the music warned of the plight that awaited felons on Parchman Farm. A verse of "The Midnight Special" began with a reference to a man's girlfriend, a lonely "widow-woman," and then proceeded:

> Well, ya bedder do 'er right;
> Ya bedder not gamble,
> And ya bedder not fight;
> Well, da sheriff he'll grab ya,
> An' da baws'll bring ya down;
> Da nex thang ya know, baw,
> Ya Parchman bound.

Bukka White's recorded version of "Parchman Farm Blues" (1940) contained a verse that told of the first stage of a convict's trek to the wilds of Sunflower County:

> Judge gave me life this morning:
> down on Parchman Farm.
> I wouldn't hate it so bad:
> but I left my wife and my home.
> Oh goodbye wife:
> all you have done gone.
> But I hope some day:
> you will hear my lonesome song.

The arrival at the jail of Parchman's traveling sergeant, who through the years had come to be known as the ogre "Long-Chain Charlie," was told in song as well:

> I looked out the window,
> saw the long-chain man,
> saw the long-chain man,
> Oh, he's comin' to call us boys, name by name. . . .[9]

References to the most odious facets of life on Parchman Farm also appeared in the songs. An early work bell and a sparse breakfast were lamented in "The Midnight Special":

> Well, ya wake up in da mawnin'.
> An' ya heah da werk-bell ring.
> An' dey march ya to da table.
> Ya see da same ole thang.
> Ain't no food up on da table.
> Ain't no poke up in da pan.
> Butcha bedda not complain, baw.
> Ya get in trouble widda Man.

And of course there were many songs that bemoaned forced labor in the cotton fields, such as Mose Allison's 1950s version of "Parchman Farm Blues":

> Well, I'm sitting over here on the Parchman Farm,
> And I ain't never done no man no harm,
> Well, I'm puttin' that cotton in a 'leven foot sack,
> With a twelve-gauge shotgun at my back.

Bukka White's "Parchman Farm Blues" summed everything up:

> Oh listen men: I didn't mean no harm.
> If you want to do good . . . stay off
> the Parchman Farm.

The legend fed by these musicians was bigger than life itself, a mesh of fact and fiction containing a hefty dose of maudlin sentiment, and it was promoted by the scare tactics of judges, law enforcement officials, and parents. In Greenwood, a troubled father and a judge once colluded, trying to reform a mischievous white youngster. "Next time," promised the judge, "you'll be hoeing cotton at Camp Five with a Winchester at your back. Now let's talk about Parchman Farm a little bit." Black parents employed similar tactics, telling their offspring hair-raising tales about murderous trusty-shooters and burly white sergeants who whipped "bad li'l niggahs" on the cold floors of the cages. The same message was conveyed in the public schools by the "baw-you-in-big-trouble" speeches delivered by visiting police officers. The devil lived on Parchman Farm.[10]

Along the way, much unfounded rumor had found its way into the legend. For instance, during the first half of the century, no less than today, people whispered about the unmarked graves near the penitentiary's orchard, suggesting that convicts were murdered wholesale by their hard-hearted keepers. Such stuff made for a good story, and it certainly carried the legend to impressive levels, but it was hardly based on fact: Parchman, like all prisons, had its share of inmates whose remains went unclaimed, and the penitentiary's graveyard, which was in fact located near the orchard, had to be located somewhere.[11]

Like the stories told of Count Dracula over the years, the legend of Parchman Farm had come to rouse cold fear in most Mississippians, especially the members of the state's black community. Planters whose properties abutted Parchman complained that their laborers refused to work the acreage near "the line." "Them black folks was scared to death of the farm," remembered an employee of the penitentiary.[12]

Throughout the first half of the twentieth century, Mississippi's public officials had hardly been displeased by the legend that surrounded their penitentiary. As one of Parchman's employees put it: "Most of their stories were bull shit, but I reckon that's what a prison is all about."[13] This was to say that public officials thought it essential that a prison's image should cause would-be felons among the general population to pause and reflect before acting, and for years Parchman's superintendents had done nothing to dispel the myth. By Superintendent Wiggins's day, however, the Alcatraz model was beginning to fall on hard times, and the legend that surrounded Parchman Farm was becoming a bit of a liability, just like Alcatraz itself was becoming a public relations problem for the bureau of prisons.

Personally, Wiggins was not well equipped to meet the demands of conscience-stricken reformers. His appearance alone hurt him. He resembled, an admiring employee remembered, an "old gunslinger: a man with cold eyes and gaunt face, kinda stiff and formal most of the time and with an air about him that made you think he knew somethin' you didn't; you know, the kind of fella you just didn't mess with." Nor was Wiggins sympathetic with those who thought felons were sick, in need of treatment, and deserving of benefits that were denied law-abiding citizens. To the contrary, he thought convicts were as rational as folks in the free world, if perhaps a bit less intelligent; that the bulk of them had either rolled the dice and lost or fallen prey to their own passions; and that prisons existed to instill what mom and dad, the schools, and the churches had failed to instill earlier. Hence the super liked the old Alcatraz model, thought the grim legend of Parchman Farm quite useful, and on several occasions contributed to it.[14]

One such occasion was the day in 1950 that a black man—an ill-informed fellow from up North—attempted to enter the penitentiary without authorization and was turned away by a salaried white guard. The would-be visitor got pushy, the guard despatched him roughly, the black man filed a complaint with the United States Department of Justice, and a scandal broke. Wiggins's public response was quick and to the point: "He was lucky that a white paid guard was at hand. One of our Negro trusties would have shot him at once."[15]

Over the years Wiggins came to understand the necessity of toning down Parchman's grim reputation, the importance of the press in image building, and his own liabilities in dealing with journalists. So he entrusted the difficult task of balancing the penitentiary's public image to Bob Patterson, his director of education. Patterson was everything Mr. Marvin was not, a squeaky-clean type of guy with boyish enthusiasm who thought an open-door policy toward journalists was advisable. Initially Wiggins was none too keen on the idea, but he increasingly accepted Patterson's judgment. By the early fifties, journalists were calling on a regular basis, even being allowed to poke about on their own.[16]

Patterson was extremely good at managing the flow of information to the outside world, and saw to it that the state's newspapers were never without happy accounts of life on Parchman Farm. Some of his news releases were exaggerated, some of them quite true, but at all events they mitigated the mounting liability of the penitentiary's legend. The picture of Parchman painted by the state's newspapers, especially by Patterson's favorite, the Jackson *Clarion-Ledger,* portrayed something akin to a Sunday school, one practicing the no-nonsense theology of the Mosaic Code.

The Super as Father

Safe and secure within the grounds of the penitentiary, Mr. Marvin was extremely paternalistic toward his own, always referring to members of the staff as "my people" and to convicts as "my boys." He was also capable of uncommon kindness. A tragedy affecting the family of a staff member "brought Mr. Marvin and Miss Pauline a-callin', both of 'em more upset than anybody, offerin' help and all." The birth of a child brought them a-callin' as well. On one occasion, "Mr. Marvin held the little thing, tears almost wellin' up in those hard eyes of his, talking about how we had birthed a fine chile that was gonna be a sergeant, maybe even super, someday."[17]

Wiggins often displayed similar compassion for troubled convicts. One employee remembers:

> There was this Nigra trusty—I forget his name—who turned rabbit. Mr. Marvin was rough on rabbits, had their butts beat numb, but this time, when he heard that the guy's mother was dyin', he checked it out and had him brought up to Front Camp, right to his office. Get the picture: a stinkin' shooter fresh from the rows in the boss's office! Anyhow, the shooter was half scared to death, wouldn't bring his eyes up off the floor, and Mr. Marvin asked him why he had turned rabbit. 'Cause ma mammy is gonna die, suh, and ah wants to hold her hand one last time afo she go,' the guy says. Well, I had never seen Mr. Marvin get a lump in his throat like that. Shit, within an hour the shooter was all cleaned up, holdin' a furlough, and on his way home with me doin' the drivin', and Mr. Marvin told me to leave the boy alone—to let him hold his mammy's hand as much as he wanted. And he give me a few bucks right out of his own pocket—told me to take the boy by a florist and let him buy some flowers for his mammy. All this shocked all hell out of me at the time, 'cause Mr. Marvin was one bad ass, but I seen plenty more of it over the years.[18]

This story, along with countless others, sheds light on Wiggins's capacity for compassion. But it also says something about the racial views of a white man who was virtually sovereign over some 1,500 black convicts.

Wiggins's attitude toward the black man was evidently no different from that exhibited by thousands of other white Mississippians of his generation. The last of the Confederate veterans were dying off, carrying the worst scars of the Civil War and its terrible aftermath to the grave, and with their passing the old hatred toward blacks was ebbing. Po' white trash were still abundant, of course, and they continued to affect the old rancor toward black people, desperately trying to convince someone, perhaps themselves, that they were better than somebody. But all across Dixie the reign of lynching had virtually ended, and most white folk had settled into a comfortable, if cloudy and unequal, relationship with black folk.[19]

Later, the civil rights movement, driven forward by federal bayonets, would reopen old wounds deep in the psyche of Mississippi's native sons, temporarily rekindling the fire of their pathetic ancestors. In the early 1950s, however, racial hatred among white people was the stuff of the "redneck," and those of Marvin Wiggins's class wanted nothing to do with it.

This is not to say that the superintendent was a champion of racial equality. He "believed that God had made black folks and white folks different."[20] He was no liberal when it came to talk of racial integration. Yet within Wiggins was none of the vicious racism that uninformed outsiders often assign to all white Mississippians of his time.

As a young man he had worked with African Americans, straddling the cloudy line that separated the races. As a planter he had employed black men in managerial positions, had worked the fields with them, and had shared many facets of life with them, always grappling, no doubt, with that cloudy line. As Parchman's superintendent, he continued to grapple with it, yet certain facts are clear.

Wiggins regarded black felons, no less than white felons, as "my boys." He looked out for the welfare of both. He allowed for racial peculiarities in the penitentiary's segregated camps, just as he allowed for peculiarities of gender in the male and female camps; but he held out the same basic rules to all convicts, black and white, male and female. There is absolutely no evidence even hinting that racial hatred on the superintendent's part led to the abuse of one black convict.

On the contrary, available evidence suggests that, if anything, Wiggins was partial to his African American convicts, a pioneer in what is nowadays called "reverse discrimination." According to one of his longtime employees, the superintendent "expected a lot from the white boys, feelin' there wasn't no excuse for them, and a lot less from the black ones, sayin' not many of them had a chance in life." Wiggins got more from his black convicts, too. They "normally outworked white boys two, three to one, made trusty much faster, and went home much quicker." Indeed, black convicts "used their heads" while many whites "bit off their noses to spite their faces." Wiggins once told a journalist that the only troublemakers at Parchman were white convicts, and everything suggests that they, not blacks, were the principal victims of the sergeants' straps during Wiggins's long superintendency.

The Super as Penologist

Superintendent Wiggins's penal philosophy was simple and straightforward. Parchman's statutory mission was to punish convicts at no cost to the state, at a profit if possible. That was easy enough, Wiggins thought, for the demands of agriculture and those of penology were entirely consistent. But agriculture was the dog, penology the tail; and failure was inevitable if the tail were allowed to wag the dog. Parchman needed to be run like any other plantation, the super insisted. If it were, penology would take care of itself.[21]

Above all else, Wiggins wanted a contented labor force. From the day he arrived at Parchman, he stressed that there must be good food, and lots of it. Like successful prison men everywhere, he understood the peculiar status of food within the convict subculture.[22]

From the beginning, too, the superintendent understood that idle convicts were the greatest single threat to effective prison administration. Not just convicts, but all people, he thought, were at their best when they were productively employed. In a prison, though, a rigorous regimen of manual labor was essential: it diminished the "piss and vinegar" of young men, putting them to sleep at an early hour, and thus promoted order during the dangerous hours of darkness.

Too much of a good thing, however, could have a negative effect, Wiggins thought, and from the first he fretted because his gunmen's workday was too long, threatening heatstroke and guaranteeing foul tempers, especially among the growing number of city boys who were unaccustomed to the rigors of field work. The super therefore extended the lunch break in the fields and lowered his gunmen's daily quota of cotton to two hundred pounds a day, hardly an excessive pick, even for a city boy. Afterward he always emphasized the necessity of mechanized agriculture, pointing out that more machinery would facilitate the realization of the penitentiary's mission. Mechanization would enhance profits and make for good politics. But it would also reduce human labor to a reasonable level, improve the morale of convicts, allow penal authorities to bolster Parchman's incentive program, and thereby enhance management and security.[23]

Incentives, Wiggins thought, made the world go around; in that regard, convict laborers and free laborers were no different. Consequently, the super was generally pleased with the scheme of behavioral reinforcement he inherited at Parchman and made improvements that carried it to a high level of sophistication.

There was nothing novel about the logic underlying the scheme. Today behavioral scientists term it "social learning theory," but its origins date back to the eighteenth century, its utilization within prisons to the mid-nineteenth.

The basic idea is that the behavior of human beings is determined by the experienced and observed results of behavior. To mold behavior, then, one must hold out explicit rules, simplistic positive and negative stimuli, and a reasonable schedule of behavioral consequences, all the while providing living examples of the results of positive and negative behavior. In penological terms, these principles call for prisons to have clear, simple rules, a related and uniformly followed schedule of rewards and punishments, stages offering progressively improved living conditions, and convicts personifying the pleasures of conformity and the pains of nonconformity.

Essentially, the psychology underlying this scheme was advanced in the "hedonic calculus" of the English philosopher Jeremy Bentham, and the concept of prison discipline that stemmed from it was first introduced in the mid-nineteenth century by the Scottish penologist Alexander Maconochie. Later, the concept was implemented on a grand scale by Sir Walter Crofton, director of Queen Victoria's Irish prisons, and still later in the century it was embraced, for the most part, by the famous American penologist Zebulon Brockway at New York's Elmira Reformatory. Afterward, the concept figured prominently in the American reformatory movement, and during the 1930s it was lent powerful support by the operant learning theory of the eminent psychologist B. F. Skinner.[24]

By the early 1950s, stages, progressive promotion, and accompanying positive and negative stimuli were beau ideals of penologists throughout the Western world. No prison, however, had more successfully instituted the concept than Marvin Wiggins's Parchman.

All convicts began their sentences in the cotton rows, the penitentiary's penal stage. There, the rules were simple and explicit, and a gunman who observed them earned immediate rewards. Most of the rewards—sex, whiskey, gambling, baseball, visitation—had evolved long before Wiggins's arrival at Parchman, and initially the super was not overly pleased by the presence of vice in the cages. But a remarkably contented population of veteran convicts made Wiggins loathe to tamper with existing arrangements. It would be ill advised, he decided, to take away what long had been bestowed.[25]

To the traditional incentives Wiggins added more during his early years: the education program, the "picture shows," the Christmas furloughs, the extended visitation privileges, the basketball games—all of them managerial tools for his sergeants. The super's system of promotion, which provided his lowly gunmen with living examples of the rewards attending good behavior, was even more effective. Most of it predated Wiggins, but here too he brought improvement.

As always, gunmen could be elevated to trusty-shooter, gaining status, increased mobility and other liberties, and sleeping quarters apart from the convict herd, while also improving their chances for further promotion.

Gunmen could also, as always, be elevated to the status of trusty-artisan, and among trusty-artisans there was a pecking order based on where one worked. Assignments to the kennel, the laundry, and the dairy were coveted, but the highest of the high worked at Front Camp, where there were women.

As always, the best convicts could become trusty-servants, and they too had a pecking order. At the bottom were those who worked in a driver's shack. Assignment to a sergeant's cottage was a step up. Higher still were those who worked in the cottages of the agronomist, the chaplain, the classification officer, the farm manager, the assistant superintendent, and others high in administration. On the farm, though, the "Main Mos' Trusties" worked for Mr. Marvin and Miss Pauline at The Big House, enjoying privileges that were perhaps unique among American convicts. And there were the lucky few who were elevated to the governor's mansion in Jackson. "Oh, sweet Jesus," an old man who "served unner Mr. Marvin" remembered, "dem was da ones in high cotton."[26]

Wiggins's innovations added new positions for trusties. The most popular were those on the staff of *Inside World*, the prison's newspaper. Less so, but still reckoned to be "pretty lucky dudes," were the trusties on the "picture show" staff, who were afforded remarkable mobility. Both groups were "in the know," the roots of Parchman's convict grapevine.[27]

All of these promotions led gunmen out of the cotton rows. By October 1953, less than 62 percent of Parchman's convicts would remain in the fields, and all of them could reasonably anticipate promotion if they played by the rules.[28]

So much for positive incentives—things that encouraged specified behaviors. Just as important in Parchman's scheme of things were negative incentives—those that discouraged specified behaviors. Again, the bulk of them were inherited by Wiggins, but he introduced a number of new ones and made significant modifications in those that existed.

What went up at Parchman could come down: one slip, one violation of rules, could send a trusty back down the ladder, sometimes all
the way down to where he had started—to the ranks of the sweating
gunmen—either temporarily or permanently. Demotion in rank not
only amounted to more work and fewer indulgences; it was also a social stigma, especially for those near the top of the trusty pecking order.

Wiggins's Parchman had occasional problems with trusties, several
of them quite serious, but a careful researcher finds few cases of trusties
offering themselves for demotion during the super's first nine years on
the job. "Only idiots risked their up-and-downs," recalled one of Mr.
Marvin's convicts.[29]

Wiggins complemented his incentive program with policies designed
to head off trouble in the field camps. Either a sergeant or a driver had
to attend the convicts on the long line at all times. There had to be six
trusty-shooters for every hundred convicts on the line. No shooter
could allow a gunman within twenty feet of him. Some of the shooters
were armed with twelve-gauge shotguns. The "scatter guns," not the
Winchesters, were turned on escaping convicts whenever possible,
peppering the rows, scaring all hell out of the rabbit, but bloodying
rather than killing him.[30]

At the cages, Wiggins reinforced nightshooters with "shackshooters," trusties charged with guarding the doors of the cages at all
times, and ordered the dog-boys to continue to make their rounds,
exhibiting their kill-dogs and thus reminding the gunmen of the perils
attending escapes.[31]

The super made it perfectly clear that the incentives held out to
shooters did not include a ticket back to the free world, and he let it be
known that he would "have the asses" of those who abused their privileged status. He demanded a full report from the attending sergeant
or driver whenever a shooter's firearm was discharged. He held out incentives other than clemency to shooters who meritoriously performed
their duties. And, true to his word, he came down hard on those who
abused their powers, ordering them returned to the ranks of the gunmen and "lettin' nature take its course in the cages." In the spring of
1952, a journalist found the shooter system remarkably effective and
observed correctly that the "old system or custom under which an
armed trusty who killed an escaping convict qualified for a pardon was
abandoned some years ago."[32]

Wiggins remained a staunch advocate of Black Annie until the end of his days, but thought the threat of removing pleasures would normally get the job done. Hence his tolerance of vice in the cages and his campaign to hold out new indulgences: all of them were carrots on a stick.

But specified transgressions by convicts always brought a spanking: insubordination that was in any way threatening to staff, assaults on other convicts, stealing state property, getting caught with a weapon, turning rabbit. The number of licks administered was determined by the track records of convicts and the gravity of offenses. Normally, a first offender guilty of a petty transgression was merely introduced to Annie—one to five pops—and the same was true of minor offenses such as simple theft and minor insubordination. Surviving rabbits were given considerably more than an introduction to Annie, and a convict who laid a hand on his sergeant or driver, remembers an employee, "got 'is ass wo' out."[33]

If, on the other hand, two convicts wanted to engage in what the law terms "mutual combat"—a fistfight between consenting parties—the sergeants and drivers were under orders to "let 'em go at it." The logic here was simple: "Hell, it was better to let 'em resolve it in the open than in the cage—less heat on the cageboss that way."[34]

Wiggins introduced a new policy for gunmen who "bucked the line"—those who refused to work the rows—and for those who worked them poorly. The attending sergeant or driver would separate the recalcitrant gunman from the others and leave him sitting in the rows alone, well away from the water barrel. If he refused to rejoin the line, the same procedure would be followed the next day. Meanwhile, the sergeant would seek the assistance of the cageboss in bringing the gunman around while at the same time withdrawing indulgences. Failing that, Black Annie would be employed.[35]

Fixed rules governed the use of the strap. Black Annie could be applied to nothing but a convict's buttocks, never drawing blood. If a convict turned up in the hospital, the sergeant would "have all hell to pay," and then the cageboss and his boys paid in turn. "The idea is to change bad attitudes, not to incapacitate a man," the superintendent often reminded his underlings.[36]

The infliction of corporal punishment at Wiggins's Parchman was observed by journalist Gene Roper. Convict Ronnie Pitts, a young white man from Jackson, was caught stealing drugs from the hospital. This was a crime worthy of a sergeant's direct intervention, so Pitts's Main Mos'

Man "took him into central dining hall where all the convicts could see from the various blocks, stripped down Ronnie's pants and applied the lash to his buttocks. But the lash in such cases," Roper emphasized, "is nothing like what you see in the superhuman movies when pirates or other criminals get huge whelps across their backs until they drop unconscious." On the contrary, sergeants were prohibited from drawing blood, convicts suffered "only stings," and the greatest damage inflicted was embarrassment, both for the victim and the convicts who observed the spectacle. The convict spectators, Roper reported, "usually walk away, go outside on the porch or turn their backs."[37]

Behavioral reinforcement pervaded every facet of convict life at Marvin Wiggins's Parchman. Bob Patterson explained the simplicity of the thing to a civic group: "It is altogether in the individual's attitude that you will find the indication as to how he or she will get along at Parchman. Anyone who comes there ready to travel the path of good behavior will get along all right—will never have any trouble."[38]

Apparently the "path of good behavior" was appealing to, and followed by, most convicts. Investigative reporter Roper, who was allowed to interview convicts apart from staff members during the early fifties, found great contentment among them. Young Ronnie Pitts—the same convict who had been spanked in Roper's presence—told him that he had "no special complaint with treatment," and that his keepers were "as fair as could be expected." Roper heard similar talk at the women's camp, where inmates were allowed to "loll outside on a bench when they're not sewing uniforms." Convict Evelyn Stevens described her life as "really just like home." "Under the circumstances," agreed Ruth Dickens, "we're pretty well off here." While conducting the interviews, Roper noted Wiggins's new shackshooters. About fifty feet away from the white female convicts was "a brick guardhouse where a white woman trusty has a rifle over her arm." Likewise, across the way in the segregated unit for black females were "negro women trusties armed with rifles."[39]

The Super and the Prison Economy

Like all prisons, Mr. Marvin's Parchman had an institutional economy through which convict-entrepreneurs and staff members cooperated to deliver goods and services to the general inmate population. Like all prison economies, a number of the goods and services delivered were illegal. Like staff members in all prisons, many of Parchman's supplemented their incomes in this manner, operating as middlemen in a black market. Unlike most other prison economies, however, Parchman's enjoyed the support of the super.

In 1944, when Wiggins arrived at the penitentiary, graft among staff was rampant, and sergeants had a long history of being at odds with superintendents who looked too closely at their camps. This, Wiggins knew, would not do. One source of the problem, he thought, was the woeful salary structure of the penitentiary. So he set out to make amends, lobbying for across-the-board salary increases, and getting them in 1948. Still, the salaries of Parchman's employees remained terribly low. As late as 1955, six civilian guards were hired at a monthly salary of $200, and a year later the annual salary of Wiggins' chaplain was $3,390.[40]

Under these conditions, Wiggins concluded, a degree of graft was inevitable at the penitentiary, for convicts had the same needs and wants as free-world folk. Some of those needs and wants were immoral, some illegal, and some were at odds with Parchman's essential interests. But regardless of official policy, most of the needs and wants of the convicts would be satisfied through a black market, just like in the free world.

In the free world, Wiggins knew, successful black markets required a degree of collusion by public officials: everybody, for instance, knew that Mississippi's sheriffs were players in syndicated gambling operations and in the illicit alcohol business. In a prison, a black market was even more dependent on public officials: on staff members serving as middlemen in commercial transactions between convict-entrepreneurs and free-world business contacts. Given the restricted freedom of the convicts and the low salaries of the staff, such arrangements were inevitable; and like middlemen everywhere, staff members exacted commissions.

These arrangements had both an upside and a downside. The upside was that petty graft corrected a diseconomy—unrealistically low staff salaries—while also establishing a mutually beneficial business relationship between staff members and the brightest convicts. And where a mutually beneficial relationship existed, tradeoffs were possible.

The free world worked the same way. The sheriffs who were players in illegal alcohol and gambling operations traded off with criminal elements, often promoting law and order on other fronts. But sheriffs were by no means the only public officials in the free world who were players.

Since the days of Reconstruction, the inability of the average citizen of Mississippi to pay taxes had resulted in an extremely weak tax base, low salaries for all public officials, and an almost universally accepted notion that the salaries of those who worked in the public sector had to be supplemented under the table. County supervisors, for example, were paid virtually nothing, and everyone knew that the contracts they negotiated included a little personal garnish. It was six of one, a half-dozen of the other, claimed defenders: raise taxes for everybody and pay public officials legally, or keep existing arrangements, letting the people with money pay them illegally.

The downside of all this was rooted in the hypocrisy and ignorance of free-world folk. They were hypocrites because they liked a good moral crusade, supporting legal proscriptions on the very same goods and services they coveted and consumed. They were ignorant because they actually thought a $200–a-month guard at Parchman could be expected to enforce notions of morality inside the joint that could not be enforced on the outside.

No matter how hypocritical or ignorant free-worlders might be, however, their expectations were politically threatening. Furthermore, they placed Parchman's superintendent between a rock and a hard place. As Lowery Love's superintendency confirmed, a crusade against graft and immorality in the cages pitted a super against market forces and led to no good. The laws of supply and demand were invincible: one way or another, the convict market would be supplied. More important, if a crusade against graft and immorality were undertaken, the inevitable result would not do. The demands of the convicts would be satisfied directly by free-world business contacts, thereby compromising security, and staff members would no longer be middlemen: indeed, an adversarial relationship would exist between "honest" staff and the brightest convicts. In the end, an important, even essential tool in controlling convicts—a medium for giving and taking—would be lost.[41]

There is no reason to think that Wiggins ever lined his own pockets. But he certainly conceded to economic reality and attempted to make it a managerial tool. Marvin Wiggins knew when to attack a problem head-on. He knew when to turn his head. And he knew how to give and take, how to sacrifice lesser things to gain greater ones. In the case of petty graft at Parchman, he attacked when necessary, turned his head when he could, and otherwise traded off.

The Super as Convict Manager

Wiggins's unwritten policy on institutional graft considered the penitentiary's long-standing chain of command and the social structures and processes he inherited. The mission of his assistant superintendent—the "li'l super"—was to keep his ear to the ground, informing Wiggins of what was up in the far-flung field camps. Otherwise camp sergeants ran Parchman. "In most cases," Wiggins maintained, "a sergeant knows best."[42]

So it would seem. A number of his sergeants were the sons of former sergeants, men who had been born and reared on Parchman Farm, brought up through the ranks, and allowed to succeed their fathers. Not one of them had much formal education; not one of them had either training in, or much use for, conventional principles of penology. Yet the sergeants were the old guard, experts on the closed world of Parchman Farm; and in managing their convicts, they drew on long-standing folk wisdom.[43]

Sergeants were still known to their convicts as "The Main Mos' Man" or "The Man." All of them, however, had long since moved up to modest cottages at Front Camp. Occupying their old shacks near the cages were the drivers, still known as "Cap'n" to the convicts.

Unlike former times, the drivers, not the sergeants, presided over the convicts who labored in the fields under the guns of the shooters. Occasionally, a sergeant would appear in the cotton rows astride his horse and have a word or two with his Cap'n and his shooters, but he never hung around very long. Sometimes a sergeant would drop by the cage, dismount, enter, and linger for several minutes, talking the talk with his gunmen and always concluding his visit off to the side, privately conversing with a graying convict. Such visits, however, were infrequent. By all appearances, sergeants were figureheads, good ole boys feeding at the public trough.

Appearances were deceiving: Parchman's sergeants were very much in charge. In the fields, the Cap'n did his sergeant's bidding, receiving daily work orders and following them. The shooters who assisted the Cap'n in the fields were also the sergeant's boys: veteran convicts who had been elevated from the cotton rows at his sole discretion, and who could be returned to the ranks of the gunmen at his whim. The result was interesting. The Cap'n, who presided over the shooters, reported to the sergeant. But the shooters reported to the sergeant independently, and they kept an eye on the Cap'n.[44]

A similar system of checks and balances allowed sergeants to manage their cages. As in Vardaman's day, dominant convicts served as cagebosses with the blessings of the camp sergeants. Over the years, however, a very sophisticated convict hierarchy had evolved in every cage. Now below the cageboss was an heir apparent and a number of subordinates who acted on orders from above. At the bottom were the most recent commitments, gunmen in the male camps, "virgin Rosies" in the female.

Through the years Parchman's superintendents had grappled with two questions. The first was whether to accept the convict hierarchy or to oppose it. The second arose if the camp hierarchy were accepted: to what extent should the cagebosses and their boys be monitored by sergeants and drivers?

Policies opposing the convict hierarchy and those tying the hands of the sergeants and their drivers accounted for much of the turmoil at the penitentiary in past years. But meddling superintendents had come and gone, and the sergeants had continued to work with their cagebosses. Since 1944, however, Wiggins's appreciation of such arrangements and his studied tolerance of petty graft had formalized and extended the old system of cage management.

The cagebosses were still responsible for cage security, for protecting the lives and limbs of their underlings, and for assuring that every gunman remained fit for field work. Likewise, the sergeants and drivers still acknowledged the sovereignty of cagebosses and—understanding that the appearance of "po-lice" undermined the bosses' authority—generally stayed away from the cages unless summoned. How a cageboss fulfilled his end of the bargain was his business; if he failed, however, it was time to move him out, time to reassign him to another camp.

Now, though, sergeants and cagebosses were allied as never before. For The Main Mos' Man not only acknowledged the supremacy of the boss but also propped his regime with greatly increased indulgences, the most notable being those that fed the cageboss's syndicated activities: prostitution, bootlegging, gambling, moneylending, trafficking in "tame" narcotic drugs, and, in some cases, influence in the delivery of furloughs, paroles, and pardons. Arrangements differed from cage to cage, but all of them operated on mutual back-scratching.

Under the cageboss were his lieutenants. Every cage had a "bank" and a "money-man" who presided over gambling and moneylending. Every cage had a pimp—a convict who coordinated the delivery of prostitutes to the gunmen. Most cages had a still run by a "hooch-man" and a gaggle of "hooch-boys," all of whom took great pride in the quality of their mash liquor.

High in the hierarchy of the cage were the boss's goons, tough guys who kept the gunmen in line. Sometimes a nudge from the cook—"no poke up in da pan"—was enough. Sometimes assignment to a cleaning detail—normally reserved for the newest commitments—sufficed. Sometimes recalcitrants were forced to stand on soft-drink crates, balancing themselves for considerable periods of time. And if all else failed, the boss's goons could always rough a fellow up a little, although never enough to interfere with the next day's field work.[45]

Every cage also had its canteen-man, who like the cageboss was appointed by the sergeant. His official job was to sell commodities to the gunmen—tobacco products, candy, and the like. His unofficial job was "hip boy" for The Main Mos' Man—the guy who served as middleman between the sergeant and the prison economy.

Arrangements differed from camp to camp. In some of them, the sergeant was the player. In others, it was the Cap'n. And in still others, according to one source, The Main Mos' Man and the Cap'n "were as honest as the Pope." But business in most camps was big. The best canteen-men had connections with their peers in other cages and with the right trusties at the canning plant, the dairy, the hospital, and every other unit at Parchman. Like cagebosses, canteen-men had convict underlings who assisted their far-flung business operations, and at least one of them had a "director of procurement" whose job was to handle "da stuff dat fell offen da backs of da trucks."[46]

The cage economy was often lubricated by considerable amounts of money. Some of it was smuggled into the cages, mostly by visiting wives and prostitutes, and an influx of cash also came when convicts worked private plantations. Barter, though, was the principal means of exchange among the convicts. "A toothbrush fer some writin' paper, hooch fer fags; y' know how it goes," one former convict explained. And another, a delightfully frank old Rosie who worked at the hospital during Wiggins's superintendency, tells of "bendin' over in da love closet at da hospital, lettin' him [a convict-worker] pound away fer a minute or two," and making off "wid a *fine* li'l radio."[47]

The super, the sergeants, and the drivers were aware of virtually everything that went on in the cages, if not in the hospital's love closet: the number of convicts who wore "snitch jackets" boggles the mind. The canteen-man was the sergeant's "Main Mos' Snitch," with his canteen-boys snitching on his behalf, and The Main Mos' Man counted on him to keep an eye on the cageboss. Meanwhile, the cage-boss snitched on the canteen-man for the sergeant, and the shooters snitched on both the cageboss and the canteen-man.

Not to be left out, the Cap'n normally had a snitch or two of his own in the cage, and more than one Cap'n served as snitch for the li'l super, tattling on The Main Mos' Man. But the li'l super did not en-tirely rely on the reports of the Cap'n, so sometimes he had his own snitch in the cage. And Mr. Marvin, who was hardly a trusting fellow, sometimes had a snitch in the cage as well.[48]

All prisons have snitches. But Vardaman's old system of checks and balances, which originally pitted governors, legislators, and trustees against each other, had bred snitching from top to bottom at Parch-man Farm, and by Wiggins's day the institution may well have been the best supervised prison in history. "I reckon I knew who snored, who had gas, which ones gang-banged which Rosies, and how well they did it," claims a former driver.[49]

The setup worked pretty well, thanks to the connections and sanc-tions of The Main Mos' Man. The favored positions of the cageboss and canteen-man atop the convict hierarchy were no more secure than their ability to deliver desired goods and services to their underlings in the cages, and to do this they needed the assistance of the sergeant and driver. For their part, most sergeants and drivers turned their heads when necessary, facilitated the activities of their cagebosses and canteen-men, and discreetly took their commissions.

So everybody was about as happy as possible. The Main Mos' Man and the Cap'n supplemented their meager salaries, thereby allowing the state of Mississippi to pay them next to nothing. The natural lead-ers of the convicts presided in the cages, allied with penal authorities and enforcing their rules. And the arrangements were safeguarded by an astonishing system of surveillance that had almost everybody in a snitch jacket.

Meanwhile, most convicts were remarkably content. "The camps was wide open," remembered one of them. "You could get everything you ever wanted. . . . The trusties ran the drugs, there was ladies on the weekends, and dice rollin' all the time."[50] Contented convicts, in turn, pleased the sergeants and drivers. Every workday, as constant as ole Hannah, the Cap'n led his gunmen to the rows, brought home his quota, and gave Mr. Marvin the leverage he had to have in dealing with the folks down in Jackson.

Beneath the Calm Exterior

While few people in the free world understood the mechanics of it all, the politicians were at least pleased with what seemed to be a calm, secure, and productive prison. The greatest of the state's penal reformers, Senator McDonnell, told a reporter that no superintendent had "made more physical improvements and other progress" than Wiggins. The rotund Hugh White, who was beginning his second term in the governor's mansion, went further, telling journalists in early 1952 that Wiggins was "one of the most valuable men who ever worked for the state."[51]

Mr. Marvin accepted the accolades magnanimously, always putting on a confident face in public. But as the winter of 1951 drew to a close, more and more of his nights were sleepless, and during them he walked The Big House, pondering the future with grave concern. Down in Jackson, unsettling political currents were developing. The population of the state was shifting ever more to the east and south, and a new breed of politician, one with language and priorities strikingly different from those of the old Delta boys, would soon settle into the statehouse. The complexion of the state bar was also altered, and journalists seemed to be worshiping new gods as well. Already these influences were creating fissures, even in the Delta, and the results of a number of elections near home troubled Wiggins.

So did other changes. The shift of the state's population from farm to city continued with all its troubling social manifestations, and the ledgers of Parchman's registrar indicated that the penitentiary was receiving more Caucasian felons every day. Most of them were "lazy, smart-assed city boys who respected nothin' or nobody," and none of them knew a sweep from a broom. "When you start bringing a boy up on concrete," a penitentiary official once remarked, "you're going to wear out more than toenails."[52]

The wear was painfully obvious in the white camps, but Wiggins was more troubled by a change among the African Americans being brought up by his traveling sergeant. It was slight, and as yet not a serious problem, but an increasing number of the blacks also hailed from the state's emerging cities. They were younger, the sons of sharecroppers who recalled their days in the cotton rows with disgust, and the old folk wisdom of yesteryear—the principles on which blacks had been managed since the days of Vardaman—now seemed less effective.

Meanwhile, parole continued to steal the best of Wiggins's long-timers: the old gray-headed cagebosses were a disappearing breed; the shooters were younger; even The Main Mos' Trusties who tended The Big House seemed like puppies compared to those of yesteryear. And Howard McDonnell just would not shut up. By all appearances, he would eventually get his probation bill through the legislature, thereby diverting the best of the state's felons from the penitentiary. By all appearances, too, he would eventually succeed in getting his statutory ban on Black Annie, thereby stripping the sergeants of a crucial sanction at a time when convicts were becoming ever more unmanageable.

If all this was not bad enough, the farm was being raided by G-men. Recently, at the order of President Truman, unsmiling agents of the Federal Bureau of Investigation had begun to poke around, looking into allegations of what they called "civil rights violations."

The world was changing. Mississippi was changing with it. But Wiggins was no longer a young man, and he had no idea how his fine-tuned prison could continue to be all things to all people. How long, the aging superintendent wondered, could his veteran sergeants hold the line?

Part III

Mississippi v. Mississippi 1952–1972

I think most of us meant well. But the changes that hit Mississippi between about 1950 and the early seventies—especially the collapse of the cotton market and the civil rights movement—made fools of a lot of us. There were just too many currents—some of them bound up in our history, some of them in the new stuff—and none of us could agree on how to handle them. So we didn't take care of business and the feds took care of it for us. It always works that way nowadays: look at education. Anyway, that's how old Parchman Farm went down, and it was a goddamn shame.

—A former member of the Mississippi legislature,
November 28, 1996

7

Parchman under Siege

On January 16, 1952, William B. Alexander, the newly appointed chairman of the senate penitentiary committee, delivered a stinging denunciation of Parchman Farm on the floor of the Mississippi senate.[1] Alexander was a native of Cleveland, a little town just down the road from the old penal farm, and his spirited speech displayed alarming divisions in the legislative delegation of the Mississippi Delta.

Marvin Wiggins mounted his warhorse, rallying support to the old standard, and found that the lower chamber of the legislature remained firm. In the senate, however, his flank was in the air, left unprotected by the retirement of traditional allies and the appearance of newcomers who did not seem to understand the ground rules of penitentiary politics.

Alexander's attack signaled the opening round of Mississippi's penitentiary wars, a twenty-year conflict that would lead to the courtroom of United States District Judge William C. Keady.

The "Scalawags" and Their Agenda

Senator Alexander did not get along with Superintendent Wiggins, and rumor held that his reforming zeal was born of rancor. But his hostile view of the penitentiary, while perhaps conditioned by personal feelings and the vicissitudes of Delta politics, was inspired primarily by the gathering storm clouds of the national civil rights movement.[2]

Difficulties had begun to unfold in 1950. First there had been serious problems with the state of California over the extradition of an escaped black convict. Then several reports of racial abuse at the penitentiary had popped up, and the appearance of FBI agents at Parchman

135

had sparked unsettling speculation. Late in the year, a terrible indictment of the penitentiary written by former Jackson newsman Craddock Goins had appeared in *True Detective* magazine.[3]

All this had occasioned outrage among most white Mississippians,
but Alexander, an experienced attorney, perceived a dangerous undertow, a broadening of the traditional scope of penitentiary politics. The
federal agents who snooped around the black camps, the senator warned
privately, were the advance elements of an army of conquest, one
threatening the entire superstructure of Mississippi's racial caste system.
Parchman Farm might well be a great prison, but that really did not
matter: the place was a political liability of unspeakable dimensions,
and it could never withstand what was coming, especially with the likes
of Marvin Wiggins at the helm.

Bill Alexander was among the first of a new breed of state politician,
a breed of tactical reformers who saw the writing on the wall and advocated remedial measures. One conservative, recalling those native sons
who had cooperated with the hated Republicans during the Reconstruction era, labeled Alexander and those of his ilk "scalawags."[4]

Alexander emerged as an outspoken critic of the penitentiary during
the 1952 legislative session. Referring repeatedly to the results of his
recently concluded survey of 250 "correctional experts" across the nation, he belittled the professional qualifications of Wiggins and wanted
to clip the superintendent's wings through the creation of a Jackson-
based department of corrections. Alexander also advocated an adult
probation system, pointing out that Mississippi was one of only three
states without this "progressive correctional tool," and he wanted rehabilitation programs to supplant farming at the penitentiary. With
"better corrective measures," he insisted, "we could greatly cut down
on repeaters, and the savings would be equal [to] or better [than] the
financial gains of the state by the forced labor system."[5]

Although he appreciated the many triumphs of Wiggins's administration, Howard McDonnell found much virtue in Alexander's view of
affairs. In late February the two senators sponsored a bill calling for
25 percent of the penitentiary's annual profits to be set side for "the
correction, welfare, rehabilitation, recreation and health of the inmates including vocational training." The measure stipulated further
that 10 percent of annual profits would go to the development of a
religious program, and that the remaining 65 percent would be earmarked for construction and mechanization.[6]

The revolutionary bill failed, but the reformers certainly had their say, and their attacks went to the very core of existing policy. The "present set-up gave nothing to the convict who did not come from a farming area," McDonnell argued, and such a convict was "not a bit better able to make an honest living when he gets out of the penitentiary [than] he was before his conviction and incarceration." It was "a well established fact among penologists that no correctional institution should operate for profit."[7]

Whoa: this was an incredible point of view, one redefining the penitentiary as an eleemosynary institution, a place like the state mental hospital where sick folk were treated at public expense, and it was accompanied by other criticism that struck at Mississippi's traditional definition of a penal institution. Exploiting the debilitating effects of parole on middle management and security, Alexander and McDonnell reopened the debate on the trusty-shooters. There had been "suspicions of certain unnecessary shootings" for several years, Alexander contended, and in the spring and early summer he protested vehemently when several prisoners crossed the gun line and fell prey to Wiggins's shooters.[8]

The reformers were even more adamant in their attacks on Black Annie. Alexander printed a booklet decrying the evils of the lash, distributed it among legislators and journalists, and actually carried one of the sergeant's straps into the senate chambers, waving it with great effect in the faces of his detractors. He continued to hit hard throughout the 1952 legislative session, all the while utilizing the considerable skills he had acquired in a successful career as a trial lawyer. On one occasion he asked: "If a man were spread-eagle[d], stripped and placed stomach down on the cold concrete floor, with four other prisoners holding him fast as the lash was applied, slave-fashion, and Jesus walked in, do you think he would approve?"[9]

The senator and his supporters offered alternatives. The strap and the shooters would be unnecessary, they stressed, if only a maximum security unit could be made available to penal administrators. "Progressive correctional experts" everywhere, said Alexander, favored solitary confinement over corporal punishment.[10]

The reformers gained ground during 1952. The upper house of the legislature was especially sympathetic. There the concept of an adult probation system was popular, and a bill calling for the abolition of corporal punishment at the penitentiary cleared the senate by an astonishing 30–6 vote, only to be killed by Wiggins's allies in the lower chamber of the legislature.[11] The notion of reforming the penitentiary also attracted powerful support outside the statehouse. The Mississippi Bar Association was somehow brought around to liberal views, and several influential journalists joined the attack. Oliver Emmerich, editor of the McComb *Enterprise-Journal* and an active member of the Mississippi Association of Crime and Delinquency, lent his considerable influence to the cause of penal reform. Hodding Carter, the Pulitzer Prize–winning owner of the Greenville *Delta Democrat-Times,* began to train his guns on the penitentiary. Even Jackson's powerful Hederman press moved to the left.

Mr. Marvin at Bay

Marvin Wiggins observed these developments with consternation. The prospect of having the penitentiary administered from Jackson by a bureau within state government was unthinkable. There were already too many political chefs in the penitentiary's kitchen; the addition of a group of Jackson bureaucrats would be downright intolerable. A probation system was no less threatening. Parole was stealing the best of the penitentiary's long-timers, probation promised to remove the best of the short-timers, and Wiggins was haunted by the prospect. Nor could the superintendent think about the demise of his shooters or the abolition of the strap without despair. The new civilian guards were woefully incompetent, the shooters alone held the lid on the penitentiary, and Black Annie was his sergeants' sole means of maintaining order in the camps. The advertised panacea of a maximum security unit, Wiggins remarked privately, sounded like something a "shyster lawyer" would propose.[12]

Since becoming superintendent in 1944, Wiggins had played politics behind closed doors, prudently avoiding public combat with legislators who attacked his penitentiary. Now, however, it was becoming increasingly clear that his detractors were scoring points, so in early February he publicly refuted Alexander. Well might solitary confinement suit the failed cellblock prisons of the North, but it was anathema to the successful, labor-intensive Mississippi penitentiary, he told a journalist. It allowed inmates to malinger, thereby threatening the very existence of penal farming. Besides, placing a human being in a dark hole was inhumane, notwithstanding the notions of "progressive" wardens in other parts of the country. The convicts themselves preferred the strap, he asserted.[13]

The superintendent "called in all his political debts and played all his political chips" in contesting the proposed reforms. Alexander and McDonnell were opposed stoutly in the legislature, Wiggins's staff supported their boss, and "numerous prisoners" interviewed by lawmakers endorsed the superintendent's negative view of solitary confinement. Alexander and his supporters were beaten back in the statehouse, but the reformers would not go away.[14]

The veteran superintendent grew depressed. Parchman Farm faced unprecedented challenges. Yet Oscar Wolfe was gone, Fred Jones was on the way out, and Alexander, McDonnell, Keady, and their supporters in the senate threatened the penitentiary's existence. Especially galling to Wiggins was the notion that a prison had to lose money to be effective: that was absurd Yankee talk born of failure, he thought, and any Mississippian who bought it was a damn fool.

Much the same was true of the campaign to abolish Black Annie, Wiggins stressed. Even the threat of spankings was a remarkably effective tool, especially among Parchman's ever-growing white convict population. Indeed, nothing but the threat of embarrassment conveyed by the presence of the strap prevented open rebellion in the white camps.

Image was everything to these white boys. They "had to have their tattoos and duck-tail haircuts." They had to pose as bad guys, so more and more weapons were appearing in their cages. Old-fashioned shanks were below their supposed dignity: "they had to have switchblades, and those with the new crabapple switch-knives thought themselves the cat's canary." Their heroes were thugs. James Dean, their fellow rebel without a cause, headed the list; but closer to home, they admired no one more than the escaped murderer Kennie Wagner, who remained at large, thumbing his nose at the law.

The white boys also regarded labor in the fields as "nigger work," and increasing numbers of them were refusing to work. In former times, "th' old men in the cages," the veteran cagebosses, had handled such problems. But now most of the old men were gone, set free by the parole board, and their places were being taken by fellows who were less cooperative. There were, in fact, signs that men with gangland connections were rising to the top in the white cages. At any rate, more white cons were assaulting their peers, more of them were sabotaging farm machinery, and more of them were turning rabbit. In the face of these problems, Alexander and his allies, who were safe and secure on the outside, wanted to emasculate the sergeants, disarm the shooters, and build a unit in which these thugs could rest.[15]

If trouble in the white cages bothered Wiggins, he was becoming frantic about the business affairs of his penitentiary. Inflation had been rampant since the war; reforms had necessitated the purchase of much expensive equipment and the hiring of many new employees; annual operating expenses had increased from $374,288 in fiscal year 1942–43 to $1,005,377 in fiscal year 1952–53.[16] The superintendent was painfully aware that the financial health of his penitentiary demanded ever-increasing cash crop production and the maintenance of high cotton prices. He was aware, too, that Parchman's political well-being depended on a black bottom line. Heretofore fortune had smiled on Wiggins, but now the introduction of synthetic fibers was beginning to be felt in the cotton market, and in May a terrible drought struck the Delta. By the early summer of 1952, the super could see that his sparkling record of production was in dire jeopardy.

Wiggins was having trouble enough coping with the crippling effects of earlier reforms. Now it seemed clear that eventually the legislature would "put the cart before the horse." Governor White was sympathetic but none too eager to do battle with the senate, so on August 23, 1952, Wiggins abruptly resigned the superintendency. The governor summoned his troubled superintendent to Jackson, encouraged reconsideration, and apparently made a number of promises. Reluctantly, Mr. Marvin agreed to stay on.[17]

The Politics of Appeasement

Wiggins was besieged on all fronts in the months that followed. The long drought of 1952 was among the worst in Mississippi history. Black Bayou ran "flat dry," the penitentiary's wells coughed up diminishing amounts of the precious water, and every attempt to irrigate the vast acreage failed. Through it all, the farm manager slept on his feet, attempting to save what he could, while Wiggins, bareheaded, perspiring profusely, and with sleeves rolled above the elbow, joined his sergeants and their gunmen in the fields.[18]

Governor White attempted to reduce overhead expenses by granting large numbers of suspensions and pardons while Wiggins and his
staff tried to cope with the worsening problems spawned by Parchman's sagging security system. Both efforts came to naught. In April
1953 the governor suffered a torrent of abuse from conservatives for
turning malefactors loose on society.[19] Several days later, a youthful
white gunman had his throat cut in the rows.

Hodding Carter's Greenville *Delta Democrat-Times,* which learned
of the homicide before penal authorities released official word of it, accused the superintendent of a cover-up and demanded official inquiry.
Such "irresponsible" reporting made Wiggins furious. He commenced
sulking, his mood worsening as the newspaper continued its sniping,
and in June he got a measure of revenge by denying Tom Karsell, Carter's managing editor, passage through Parchman's front gate. Karsell
screamed to the heavens through the medium of his newspaper, alleging in the process that Governor White had not been to the penitentiary since coming to office. White told reporters "off the record" that
Karsell was a "dirty liar," but the Associated Press printed the comment anyway. The war of words offended Senator McDonnell, who
only recently had been one of Wiggins's strongest supporters. In an
abrupt about-face, McDonnell called for the super to be replaced by a
"trained prison administrator." Meanwhile Senator Alexander kept up
the attack, criticizing Wiggins's failure to hire a psychiatrist and a black
chaplain, and pledging that he would personally escort journalists to
the penitentiary.[20]

Word broke almost simultaneously that the long drought had proved
more damaging than expected. With gross income diminished by some
$328,000, the penitentiary recorded a deficit of over $295,000 for
fiscal year 1952–53.[21] The deficit was a bitter disappointment for Wiggins. It was his first.

Then the Mississippi Bar Association adopted a resolution calling
for the employment of trained "correctional administrators" and a
"qualified" superintendent. This was too much. Governor White an-
grily called a press conference at which he defended farmer Wiggins.
The bar was unaware of the type of convicts who were incarcerated
at Parchman, he told newsmen. "I don't understand what those fellows could be thinking about. When the day comes that we have to
go around powder-puffing hardened criminals, then God help the
country."[22]

   Yet the appearance of such powerful opposition made White reconsider. He closeted with Wiggins, emphasized the necessity of compromise, and afterward endorsed a probation system, a maximum security
unit, and a new policy on the use of the strap. Wiggins jockeyed behind
the scenes to head off a probation statute but otherwise followed the
governor's plan of appeasement. He told journalists that henceforth
Black Annie would be utilized only as a "last resort" in disciplining unruly convicts and begrudgingly accepted the maximum security unit.
Ninety percent of his difficulties at Parchman were attributable to some
two hundred white prisoners, he explained to a journalist. A maximum
security unit was not the solution. Indeed, the construction of such a
facility would be a "mistake." For that reason he had discontinued
construction on Superintendent Love's unit for troublesome inmates,
but he would not actively oppose the resumption of the project.[23]

   Governor White attempted to bolster his position at a press conference, where he outlined his super's virtues and accomplishments,
refuted the "gross misrepresentations" of the *Delta Democrat-Times*,
and invited journalists to inspect the penitentiary. Soon a number of
newsmen were knocking at Parchman's front gate. Among them were
Kenneth Toler of the Memphis *Commercial Appeal* and Wilbur Minor
of the New Orleans *Times-Picayune*. They were greeted by a congenial
Wiggins, who "literally handed the penitentiary keys" to Toler. Following an extensive tour of Parchman, both journalists penned favorable reports, contending that they had investigated "all there was to be
seen."[24]

   Wiggins exploited the opening. On June 29 he announced that, effective immediately, the maximum number of lashes allowed at the
penitentiary was reduced from fifteen to ten. "Spankings," the superintendent assured the press, were never allowed to draw blood: they
were a means of discipline to which the sergeants seldom resorted, and
never were they administered without his express permission. Reports
that convicts were being abused were blown out of all proportion, he
insisted. To the contrary, Mississippi's convicts enjoyed a large number
of uncommon privileges.[25]

   All this was true, more so than free-world people could comprehend, but it no longer mattered: the old legend of Parchman Farm
was much more meaningful than fact in the intrastate skirmishing that
preceded the full-blown civil rights movement, and Bob Patterson was
experiencing increasing difficulty in holding the wolves at bay.

In early July, Tom Karsell attacked the penitentiary in a speech delivered to the Brookhaven Lion's Club. Soon he was supported by an anonymous "young convict," recently released from Parchman, who told a Memphis *Commercial Appeal* reporter that the role of vocational training and religion at the penitentiary was "greatly exaggerated," that "the main interest" was raising cotton, and that beatings were common.[26]

These things, too, were true, always had been, but now they did not sound quite right. Still, White and Wiggins remained on the offensive. After a "shakedown" of several camps produced a large assortment of grisly weapons, the *Commercial Appeal* observed that there were "two sides to the situation" at Parchman. Wiggins then invited relatives of convicts to a gala "open house." His stated motive was to "relieve some of the tension." The event attracted an estimated one thousand guests—"the largest crowd ever to visit the inmates"—and many visitors, as always, gave reporters favorable accounts of life at Parchman Farm.[27]

On July 10 Governor White traveled up to Sunflower County in the company of a host of journalists. White made no pretenses: the inspection was being conducted "to throw open the doors . . . in an effort to refute some of the charges of recent days." All of the journalists were impressed, and Gene Roper of the Jackson *Clarion-Ledger* wrote an almost idyllic account of convict life, complete with a reminder that felons were felons, after all. Governor White scolded the penitentiary's critics, remarking in the process that the state was not "running a Y.M.C.A." at Parchman. Former Superintendent Tann, interviewed in Memphis, told a reporter that those who criticized the penitentiary were ignorant. "Loving kindness and entertainment programs," he stressed, "will never replace the lash as a means of controlling the prisoners." Patterson took to the speaker's circuit during the late summer and early fall. In September he gave the McComb Lion's Club a heady account of classification, education, and recreation at Parchman.[28]

The penitentiary's detractors attempted to regain lost ground. The *Delta Democrat-Times* continued its criticism during the final six months of 1953, and Oliver Emmerich's McComb *Enterprise-Journal* joined the attack, rightly asserting that the penitentiary was "an institution of blame and punishment rather than diagnosis and therapy." Meanwhile, Parchman's legislative critics rattled their sabers, all the while laying plans for the upcoming session. In October 1953 the Jackson *Clarion-*

Ledger sized up matters very well. All the squabbling of the spring and summer, a staff writer observed, had assured that "any angle of interest that is raised in connection with the institution attracts more than usual interest."[29]

In February 1954 Alfred C. Schnur, professor of criminology at the University of Mississippi, told reporters that Parchman was a "wonderful training ground for criminals." Wiggins, the professor added, was "just a good farmer"; he and his staff were unqualified to administer a modern penal institution, and their professional shortcomings precluded the rehabilitation of convicts.[30]

Shortly one of the professor's students, Dick Anderson, was invited by Hodding Carter himself to speak before a Greenville civic group. On March 10, young Anderson lambasted the penitentiary, reportedly basing his negative comments on data drawn from the files of the FBI, the results of Schnur's research, and personal observations he had made during several visits to Parchman. Governor White was angered to the point of imprudence by the remarks of Schnur and Anderson. He stated publicly that the professor should be fired. A day later, when a journalism class from Ole Miss visited the governor's mansion, White told the students that "officials of one state institution should not publicly make derogatory remarks about another." Such talk, of course, offended the interested protectors of the First Amendment: within days the Ole Miss public relations office received copies of ten editorials from major daily newspapers defending Schnur's right to voice professional opinions.[31]

The Politics of Capital Punishment

All the controversy was shortly obscured by weightier matters. For the 1954 session of the legislature was most notable for an emotional debate on how and where Mississippi should execute those convicted of capital crimes. It was clear from the first that the state would abandon legal electrocution, universally acknowledged as a humane method of inflicting legal death only several years earlier, and adopt lethal gas, now regarded as a more humane substitute. There was a glitch, however: no legislator wanted a gas chamber in his own constituency.

The issue was nothing new. In 1940, when the state had abandoned the gallows in favor of electrocution, the only real point of dispute had been the place of execution. On that occasion political compromise had distributed the burden equally: a curious portable electric chair, hauled around in a truck, had enabled the state to execute criminals in counties of conviction.[32] Now, though, compromise was impossible. Experts advised that gas chambers could not be made portable, and county governments could not afford to purchase and maintain their own chambers. Not surprisingly, the politicians decided to foist the problem on state government.

Among the possible sites was Parchman's maximum security unit. Wiggins had begun construction in September 1953. It was a grim structure patterned after "Little Shamrock," the unit employed by the Texas penal system, and the convict-laborers, troubled by the introduction of real cages at Parchman, had dubbed the ugly building "Little Alcatraz." Wiggins hated the thing, and built it only because of his earlier agreement with Governor White; but the agreement had not stipulated the addition of a gas chamber, and the superintendent was enraged that anyone would even suggest the gassing of convicts on his plantation. He leaned on political cronies, and gained the support of an impressive array of Delta politicians led by Senator P. G. Batson and Representative Wilma Sledge of Sunflower County. "Place that thing at Parchman and you will have riots and a wholesale breakout to descend hundreds of criminals down upon our people," warned the matronly Mrs. Sledge.[33]

Wiggins and the Delta politicians scored first, shrewdly inducing the legislature to establish a "death chamber" in the newly constructed headquarters building of the Mississippi State Highway Patrol in Jackson. The capital city's mayor promptly threatened legal action, rightly claiming that the measure placed the gas chamber within a stone's throw of a heavy concentration of schools and hospitals in violation of city zoning ordinances. Soon other alternatives were being considered. Predictably enough, someone suggested placing the chamber at Oakley, the state's reformatory for black minors, but Governor White, referring to the recent interest of the federal judiciary in racial matters, squashed the idea with the comment that "we have enough Negro problems already." Thereafter the original plan of locating the chamber in Parchman's maximum security unit gained ground by default, and on September 22, 1954, during a special session of the legislature, a bill to that effect was enacted over the vehement protests of Delta politicians.[34]

Superintendent Wiggins took the news very hard. Several days after the enactment of the "gas chamber bill," he accompanied staff writer Charles M. Hills of the *Clarion-Ledger* to the site of Little Alcatraz. There, while watching his convicts work, he expressed disillusionment. "I hope we never have to use these cells," he told Hills. "They are ten times worse than the strap." Wiggins was even more concerned about the prospect of executing criminals on the grounds of the penitentiary. One member of his staff recalled that the superintendent "felt betrayed by the governor and had the look of a beaten old man." A convict-editorialist, writing in *Inside World,* stressed that capital punishment was "a legalized form of murder, contrary to the teachings of Christianity." Parchman's employees were equally disturbed, if for different reasons. "Politics, politics, politics; nobody wanted the thing [the gas chamber], so the bastards stuck it up here," remembered a staff officer. "The last thing we needed was something sensational to upset the prisoners and attract more bleeding-heart reporters."[35]

Journalists descended on the penitentiary. The Jackson *Clarion-Ledger* ran a lengthy story on the new chamber, and morbid speculation on the identity of the first victim filled the newspapers. The two likeliest candidates, murderers Minor Sorber and Gerald Gallego, granted interviews from their cells in the Hinds County jail. After both expressed relief that they would not be "fried" in an electric chair, a newsman performed the curious, heart-rending journalistic ritual so customary in the reporting of death-row interviews: a before-the-fact eulogy. Both Sorber and Gallego had served their country as soldiers; both of them wanted to atone for their crimes by donating their eyes to the blind; both of them, but especially "family man" Sorber, were good chaps gone wrong.[36]

On February 25, 1955, as Gallego's date of execution neared, Wiggins expressed grave reservations, telling a reporter that the condemned man had been a "model prisoner," that he had been converted to Christianity, and that he now saw "the error of his ways." These were strange words—the words of a farmer and not those of a professional prison man—and on the morning of March 3, as Gallego took his last meal and was read the last rites, Wiggins was visibly upset.[37]

Journalists crowded into the death cell's antechamber, positioning themselves so as to see the "death seat" through the heavy glass. Meanwhile, many of their colleagues, denied entry due to overcrowding, chattered nervously outside, glancing occasionally at the ominous guard towers above them. The victim disappointed nobody. As four condemned black convicts sobbed, and as the strains of "Up Above There's a Heaven Bright" "sounded through the grim corridors," Gerald Gallego walked the "last mile." He stood erect and smiled as he passed the distraught convicts. He encouraged them to keep singing. He seated himself in the ugly chair and cooperated as leather straps were fastened around his wrists and ankles. As the lethal gas rose, he chanted the Lord's Prayer, jerked violently, lingered for fully twenty minutes owing to miscalculations by the executioner, and at last died. Convict Allen Donaldson followed Gallego a day later; and in April, when only one journalist showed up for the third execution, an editorialist quipped that the gas chamber "wore out its popularity in a hurry."[38]

The Last Years of the Wiggins Era

Parchman Farm was never quite the same after the spate of executions: somehow the spirit of the place changed dramatically. The work chants in the fields were not as playful, the responses of the long line less animated, and one old-timer remembers sadly that "the gassins killed the soul of the farm." They almost killed Wiggins as well, but the super could at least find satisfaction in the fact that his critics broke off their attack after the execution of Gallego. The explanation, according to one former politician, was the threatening attitude of the Warren Court on the "Negro question," which "tended to make all [white] Mississippians . . . pull together."[39]

So it would appear. The landmark decision of the United States Supreme Court in the case of *Brown v. the Board of Education of Topeka, Kansas,* which knocked the legal props from under the state's segregated public schools, struck Mississippi like a bomb. Virtually every decision made by Governor White during his last two years in office was conditioned by the "Negro question," and everything suggests that White and the state's legislative leadership came to appreciate Senator Alexander's opinion that the penitentiary was no less vulnerable than the state's segregated public school system. "Scalawag" tactics, therefore, conditioned Marvin Wiggins's last years as superintendent.

The public relations of the penitentiary, still in the capable hands of Patterson, focused on the successes of convicts participating in the education program. The publicist/educational director added a sixth-grade class to his program, organized a gala graduation ceremony labeled "End of School Follies," and heaped lavish praise on his successes. Wiggins, recalling that the penitentiary had housed some 700 illiterate convicts when education was first introduced in 1944, claimed that there were now "very few prisoners who can't write their own letters."[40]

The penitentiary's official reports also advertised an expanded program of vocational education, which included formal instruction in the maintenance and operation of farm machinery. The farm manager observed that the program went "a long way towards preparing [convicts] for better jobs when they leave here." Official word also held that prisoners learned marketable skills by working in the various shops and plants of the penitentiary. The new laundry, for instance, employed 25 men, operated in "free world" fashion, and was said to qualify a convict for "a skilled position in an outside laundry upon his release."[41]

A shortening of the long line was noted as well. Official records indicated that of some 1,900 convicts on hand in September 1953, 789 were no longer in the fields. Afterward, increasing mechanization and a "steadily improving" classification system reportedly withdrew even more, and the gunmen were given a three-hour lunch break. By 1955 Patterson was championing the "moral" betterment and "rehabilitation" of convicts. He called on the legislature to finance a modern vocational training facility of adequate size and design "to provide working space for students who are studying radio repair, electricity, carpentry and other technical subjects."[42]

An expansion of the penitentiary's recreational activities was also hyped. By 1955 Parchman's music program had begun to establish a reputation in the Delta. The black prisoners still wanted nothing to do with organized music, instead carrying on as always in or near their cages, but a band composed of seven white convicts performed regularly, often for large numbers of visitors at Front Camp. The music program was advertised as a rehabilitative tool, as was the penitentiary's livestock field day, which would evolve over the years into the celebrated Parchman rodeo. Begun on a small scale in 1951, the field day was staged every October. The animal husbandman presided over the event, camp was pitted against camp, and exhibits featuring beef cattle, work stock, and horses were grouped and judged at the dairy. By 1955 competition was lively.[43]

Another widely publicized event was Pauline Wiggins's hobby contest. The event grew from a very modest beginning in 1950, but on April 8, 1956, it featured 600 contestants and drew "wide interest in the Delta area." Entries included leather goods, cabinet works, pottery, paintings, and embroidery. Exhibits were displayed in a newly constructed community house at Front Camp and judged by local civic leaders and clergymen. The contest gave convicts an opportunity to earn money through prizes and sales to visitors, and the cage economy got a considerable boost. Business was so brisk that the superintendent opened a prison bank for the convict-entrepreneurs.[44]

The publicity campaign was enhanced by the success of Wiggins's Christmas furlough program. In December 1954 the superintendent furloughed his 3,000th prisoner. Of that number, only a reported 14 had failed to return to the penitentiary since the program's inception in 1944, and but 2 of the delinquents remained at large. If those statistics are accurate, the furlough program stands as a huge tribute to the judgment of Wiggins's sergeants, perhaps as the most successful program of its type in history. In late 1954 an editorialist contended that it had "contributed to the rehabilitation of many discharged convicts."[45]

Official records also indicated improved medical services. For biennium 1953–55 the penitentiary reported not one case of heat exhaustion, not one death attributable to tuberculosis, and only 16 deaths among its entire convict population. "The health of the inmates," wrote physician Thomas A. Robinson in the summer of 1955, "has been well above the average of the outside person."[46]

In April 1955 the warden of the Illinois penitentiary, who had visited Parchman in 1944, came again with three of his subordinates. He reportedly found convict morale to be "the finest we have seen in a state prison" and "expressed himself as amazed at the tremendous improvements in the Mississippi prison." Governor White, whose opinion was perhaps less objective, claimed in June, following an inspection of Parchman, that the morale of prisoners was "higher than I have ever seen it."[47]

Of all the penitentiary's reported triumphs, however, nothing was more stunning than Superintendent Wiggins's successes in agriculture. He did it with blood in his eye, ever remembering the embarrassing deficit of 1952–53, and he did it despite unfavorable market and climatic conditions that crippled neighboring plantations. During 1953 he planted 5,895 acres in cotton, produced 6,238 bales, and brought home a profit of $268,080. In the following spring he fell prey to another debilitating drought but surprised everyone by recording a deficit of only $11,601. A year later he planted his cash crop on 5,365 acres and had the satisfaction of seeing the penitentiary record an astonishing profit of over $525,000.[48]

In February 1956, however, when the house penitentiary committee concluded a meeting with a standing ovation honoring the veteran superintendent, Wiggins knew that his days at Parchman were numbered. The new governor, J. P. Coleman, was a staunch advocate of an adult probation system, and Wiggins realized that it was only a matter of time before the legislature gave the chief executive his way. Coleman also wanted Wiggins to deemphasize agricultural operations, to implement more vocational programs, to spruce up the penitentiary's image even more. The governor was, moreover, a stickler for propriety, a man who had little patience with the petty graft that fed Parchman's engines. In early 1956 Coleman had discovered financial irregularities, had sent his "snooping henchmen" up to Parchman, and Wiggins knew full well that he could not continue to function under such conditions.[49]

The superintendent stood by silently as Coleman's probation bill progressed through the legislature, all the while wondering why nobody seemed to understand the devastating effect that a probation board would have on the composition of an already difficult convict population. The passage of the bill in the spring distressed Wiggins, and about the same time Coleman demanded the dismissal of the penitentiary's chaplain. The superintendent protested vehemently, a period of cool relations followed, and Wiggins resigned in early May 1956.[50]

"WE OWE WIGGINS OUR THANKS," pronounced a leader in the *Clarion-Ledger*. The old farmer, a journalist observed, had "undoubtedly compiled one of the best records of any penal official in the entire South, or even the nation for that matter."[51]

Perhaps the journalist went overboard, although the confused goals that characterized the administration of legal punishment in the United States during Wiggins's tenure render comparative analysis virtually impossible. Clearly, however, Wiggins had presided over an impressive transformation at the penitentiary, and between 1944 and 1956 his penitentiary had recorded net profits amounting to some $2,709,000.[52]

On July 1, 1956, when the old man bid adieu at Front Camp and drove out the gate with Pauline, he left behind him a fine stand of cotton, one that would deliver Mississippi's labor-intensive penitentiary its last fiscal-year profit.

8

The Short Reign
of the Scalawags

Generally regarded as one of the shrewdest, most competent chief executives in state history, J. P. Coleman came to office in the midst of the rapidly evolving civil rights movement, which by 1956 was targeting Mississippi's racial caste system for destruction. The governor saw that his state could not hope to combat the judicial activism of the Warren Court, that substantive reform was the only way to mitigate the approaching convulsion, and that appearances would be no less important than realities in the years ahead. Coleman was the greatest of Mississippi's latter-day "scalawags." He heard a clock ticking, and, like Bill Alexander, saw trouble in Sunflower County.[1]

A Changing of the Guard

Great pressure was placed on the governor to appoint Wiggins's understudy, Aubrey Reed, to the superintendency. Instead, Coleman chose Bill Harpole, a relatively obscure identification officer employed by the state highway patrol. Harpole was the penitentiary's first superintendent lacking experience in agriculture. That fact was exploited to the fullest by those who "hated to see the team . . . operating Parchman broken up," but even Harpole's numerous critics could not impeach his credentials as an enforcer of the law.

Until his most recent five-month stint with the highway patrol, Harpole had worked for some four years as a patrolman and had served Oktibbeha County as both sheriff and deputy. In the latter capacity he had been employed by his wife, Mary, a gifted administrator who had been elected sheriff in a county included in Coleman's old judicial district. She and her husband had impressed the future governor: Mary had followed Coleman to Jackson in a highly visible position on his personal staff. Now the governor sent the young couple up to Parchman with orders to render the penitentiary's image more compatible with modern political reality. So as to facilitate a smooth transition, the Harpoles took up residence in May, nearly two months before Wiggins's departure. With them came the Reverend Roscoe Hicks of Calhoun County and E. E. Lacey of Weir, who replaced the disappointed Reed.[2]

Harpole began his superintendency with vigor, almost immediately granting the convicts permission to install television sets in their cages, and Bob Patterson, who wisely had been allowed to stay on after Wiggins's departure, called on the media to encourage public contributions. Several sets were donated immediately, public officials spearheaded drives to obtain more, and merchants in nearby Drew allowed convicts to purchase sets through special time-payment schemes. By December antennas towered over most of the cages.[3]

Harpole and his staff made a great production of the advent of television. Patterson announced that television viewing strengthened the penitentiary's "Rehabilitation Program" by serving as a "pre-release orientation project." The grand jury of Sunflower County praised the television sets as "a morale builder for prisoners." Journalists were also impressed. Even Oliver Emmerich's McComb *Enterprise-Journal* conceded that television viewing enhanced convict rehabilitation.[4]

Coinciding with the introduction of this "pre-release orientation project" was enormously increased emphasis on religious activities. Harpole believed, or at least said he believed, that "a consciously religious person, one who is active in the church, is incapable of criminal acts."[5] He certainly acted on that hypothesis as superintendent. Upon arriving at Parchman he let the convicts know that he smiled on the religiously inclined and worked with Chaplain Hicks to organize activities through which felons might display devotion to their Maker.

On July 20, 1956, Hicks and two inmate-preachers presided over Parchman's second mass baptism. Five white men, 36 black men, and 8 black women waded into one of the penitentiary's irrigation ponds. The blacks "broke into religious songs, halting only to listen to the prayers of the chaplain as he performed his duties." The event, wrote an observer, "was carried out in a religious atmosphere, despite the presence of armed guards and trusties who discreetly, yet nevertheless watchfully, encircled the area with readied rifles and revolvers, but well to the background." By October 3, 1956, when 54 convicts were baptized "while other prisoners in choral groups sang softly," Chaplain Hicks had presided over four mass baptisms involving a total of 244 convicts. In the meantime Harpole had converted a watering trough into a more commodious baptismal site. The trough was enclosed by "white-painted brick and surrounded by carefully-tended lawn."[6]

The religious crusade was enhanced by literary contributions from the Mississippi Baptist Convention, the Salvation Army, the Gideons, the Volunteers of America, and a number of independent philanthropists. A virtual revival was staged on Christmas Day, 1956, and the convicts were showered with yuletide cheer. Harpole continued his predecessor's Christmas furlough program, every inmate received a present on Christmas morning, and the convicts were dazzled by a holiday feast. Enraptured by these events, an editorialist writing for *Inside World* unsuccessfully called on the governor to bestow suspensions and pardons as Christmas gifts.[7]

Harpole also advocated other politically correct innovations during his first six months on the job. In July 1956, amid all the hoopla surrounding his first mass baptism, the superintendent told reporters that he favored the establishment of a first offenders' ward in which young, reclaimable convicts could be removed from the baneful influence of hardened criminals. Notwithstanding the fact that probation was diverting young, reclaimable offenders from the penitentiary already, the proposal earned Harpole much praise. The Sunflower County grand jury endorsed the idea in September, and later the *Clarion-Ledger* contended that the "creation of such a camp for young prisoners . . . would help salvage and reform an increasing number of them."[8] Thereafter the superintendent raised the question on numerous occasions, and even made preliminary moves to establish such a camp, but he somehow never got around to making it a reality.

No less newsworthy was Harpole's promotion of Parchman's recreational and vocational programs. White musicians enjoyed new visibility. In July 1956 "The Insiders" made their debut, its members boasting all the markings of the "beat generation." One of them had the Lord's Prayer tattooed on his stomach. Another displayed a string of beads and had the words "cut on the dotted line" tattooed on his neck, and all but one member of the band had the word "love" tattooed on their fingers—one letter per finger. Dressed in their convict stripes, The Insiders were quite a spectacle. Only days after taking office, Harpole arranged for five local radio stations to broadcast the band's performances. Soon the musicians were drawing much attention.[9]

Another of Harpole's tactics that earned the penitentiary favorable publicity was his promotion of the convict-printed newspaper. *Inside World* had initially operated on a shoestring budget out of a small room in the old hospital, and later the editor's office had been moved to a trusty's room at Camp Five. Under the publicity-conscious Harpole, however, the newspaper was given higher priority, and its content broadened considerably.

By August 1956 *Inside World* was a thirty-page mimeographed magazine being distributed on a regular basis to sixty-eight prisons in the United States and Canada. It was, moreover, no longer a hand-to-mouth operation. Editor Donald F. Morgan, who once had worked on the newspaper staff of Michigan's penitentiary at Jackson, operated out of a newly constructed brick cubicle at Camp Five and received copy from convict-correspondents in all of Parchman's eighteen camps. Morgan's paper carried penitentiary news, general news, sports, religion, cartoons, comment on movies, and editorials described by *Clarion-Ledger* staff writer Phil Stroupe as "punchy . . . [and] mostly aimed at matters pertaining to prison politics and laws, but keenly aware of the 'free world.'"[10]

Cognizant of the newspaper's potential as a bridge between the penitentiary and the Fourth Estate, Harpole allowed his convict-editor remarkable latitude. Newsman Stroupe, who personified the success of the superintendent's tactics, concluded that *Inside World* got "a healthy peep through the physical bars of confinement to tell its story to the free world." During the second half of 1956 the convict newspaper emerged as an advocate of many penal reforms, and a number of its articles were either reprinted or paraphrased in newspapers across the state.[11]

Harpole's relatively liberal policy on the printing of *Inside World* was but a component of his broader public relations effort. He actively encouraged tours by students and teachers of state government, journalists, legislators, law enforcement officials, church and civic groups, penologists from other states, and anyone else who could be lured to remote Sunflower County. So as to lure them, the superintendent staged interesting events. In the autumn of 1956 he organized a cotton-picking contest that attracted many spectators, and in December he promoted Pauline Wiggins's old hobby contest to such an extent that the event set records for convict entries and visitors. His wife Mary, whose charm remains a subject of Delta conversation even today, dazzled visitors with her hospitality and devotion to the convicts. Meanwhile Patterson, his vitality undiminished, took to the road, speaking to civic, educational, and religious groups throughout the state, desperately trying to counter the mounting liability of the legend of Parchman Farm.[12]

In September 1956 the Sunflower County grand jury complimented Harpole for his "devotion to duty and his eagerness to do a good job." Such praise was richly deserved, commented the *Clarion-Ledger:* recent reports from the penitentiary indicated "that most of the prisoners would applaud and endorse the grand jury's compliment to the . . . superintendent." This was the reaction J. P. Coleman had wanted. On December 7 the governor pointed to "remarkable progress . . . being made at the penitentiary under Supt. Bill Harpole" and announced that soon he would visit the institution. Following Hugh White's happy precedent, Coleman invited journalists to accompany him.[13]

A week later, the governor led a number of newsmen to Parchman. Waiting on the entourage was a delegation of Sunflower County politicians: they were there to tell everyone how much they appreciated Harpole. Their plaudits were echoed by numerous prisoners, who were "loud in their praise of improvements in physical facilities and in treatment since Harpole [had] taken over." In the presence of the journalists, Coleman questioned Harpole on the status of Black Annie. There was now little need for the strap, the superintendent replied. The new maximum security unit had proved to be "a great deterrent to prison troubles": no more than four or five convicts were being disciplined by the strap each month.

Then the governor turned to the philosophy that was to guide the penitentiary in the years ahead. Money, he said, was not "the prime purpose of the operation." Rather, his administration was committed "to the rehabilitation of prisoners, the protection of society, and the welfare of prisoners who are returned to society." The executive branch of government, however, could not realize those objectives without the support of the legislature, stressed the governor. Agriculture had to be balanced with industry, and a much more extensive state-use system distributing convict-manufactured goods among state institutions had to be implemented. Furthermore, the superintendent, who was "having great difficulty keeping qualified employees," had to be given more latitude in hiring and setting the salaries of needed technicians.[14]

All this was a carefully staged performance, of course; but the plan laid out by the governor was a good one, a reasoned compromise addressing economic realities at home and political developments outside the state. As Coleman spoke, however, those around him saw little more than vestiges of the old plantation system and realized that change would not come easily. A faltering agricultural economy was, as always, causing state legislators to contract, to look suspiciously on money-bills promising to change any feature of the status quo, and that conservatism was being compounded daily by an uneasiness bred by the emerging civil rights movement. White Mississippians had been on the defensive since the days of secession. They were inclined to build barricades, to reject even a tactical offensive when threatened by outsiders, and thus a great deal of inertia confronted Coleman's criminal policy.

Toward "Progressive" Ways

The governor's visit to Parchman in December 1956 was quite successful. Among the impressed was Charles Hills of the *Clarion-Ledger*, who afterward emerged as a stout defender of Harpole and the penitentiary. Upon returning to Jackson, the journalist reported that the superintendent, "tall, quietspoken and determined, is today racking up a record . . . as a humanitarian as well as a firm administrator." A week later Hills again praised the improvements at Parchman and hailed the governor's plans for the future, not only at the penitentiary but also in the other components of the state's criminal process.[15] Even Hills, however, could not comprehend the magnitude of the changes projected by Coleman and Harpole. Their plan was to proceed with reform within the parameters of executive discretion, all the while pushing for the legislative support without which comprehensive change was impossible.

The superintendent moved forward in the spring of 1957. In March he collaborated with the state employment security commission to establish a program designed to help convicts secure gainful employment upon release. Beginning on April 1, dossiers were sent to the commission thirty days before a convict was to be released, and an active campaign to overcome the fears of prospective employers was initiated. Harpole claimed that the federally inspired innovation was "an outgrowth of the prison's accelerated rehabilitation program." Ninety-six convicts reportedly secured jobs during the next two years, and in April 1958 Senator Alexander advocated the creation of a job placement bureau at the penitentiary.[16]

Simultaneously, Harpole made the boldest stroke of his entire administration, the *official* establishment of Parchman's famous conjugal visitation program. It was risky business. Sexual relations at the penitentiary, of course, were nothing new. However, as reflected by the state's hypocritical policy on the sale and consumption of alcoholic beverages, which were illegal but subject to taxation, it was one thing to be naughty in Mississippi's Bible Belt, quite another to openly admit it. The central thrust of J. P. Coleman's public policy, though, was the introduction of measures that, while being politically dangerous in Mississippi, were calculated to impress outsiders, to protect Mississippians from themselves. The official introduction of conjugal visitation at Parchman portrayed that shaky tactic to the letter.

In early 1957 Harpole ordered the construction of a number of modest, one-room buildings, allowed spouses to visit the penitentiary for "family day" on Sundays, and made the so-called red houses available to couples of all races for designated periods. That gutsy innovation was accompanied by another, initiated in June 1956, which extended annual vacations to deserving convicts who wished to visit their families. In April 1957 the superintendent traveled to Oklahoma City for the purpose of attending the joint meeting of the Southern States Prison Association and the Southern States Probation and Parole Association. He told the delegates of his innovative annual vacations, noting proudly that only one convict had failed to return to the penitentiary since the inception of the program. He said less about the conjugal visits, perhaps because they were only then getting under way, perhaps because he feared the reaction back home; but his language reflected the new image he and Coleman sought for Parchman and the state of Mississippi. "If you place a little confidence in prisoners, they hate to betray it," he told the delegates. "After all, they are folks just like the rest of us."[17]

There is little reliable information about the formative period of Harpole's conjugal visitation program. The press had little comment, and neither the superintendent nor his department heads mentioned it in the biennial report submitted in 1957. But in the spring of 1959, when the program was established and functioning smoothly, Harpole displayed no timidity in describing his "family day" activities before the Southern Conference on Corrections in Tallahassee, Florida.[18] Shortly thereafter, Ernest A. Mitler, a New York attorney who recently had concluded a celebrated study of the nation's juvenile institutions, gave Parchman's conjugal visitation program national exposure with an article featured by *Parade* magazine.

"Family day" began at 11:30 A.M. on Sundays, when wives and children were allowed to pass through Parchman's front gate. After being searched and having their identities verified, the visitors proceeded to the administration building, where they met their convict-husbands and fathers. The families strolled and talked at Front Camp, fathers played with their children, and many attended religious services. Couples were free to go to "specially designed cottages for complete privacy as husband and wife." Unmarried prisoners often helped their married colleagues by baby-sitting: one convict worked in a commissary and frequently made children his "store assistants."

Mitler was astonished by the lack of an "air of derision or ridicule . . . [among] unmarried prisoners," and also by the absence of the "undercurrent of tension and frustration" so characteristic of prisons elsewhere. It was difficult, he observed, "to see dozens of families coming together in warm affection without some of the warmth permeating the entire feeling of the place." That warmth, he added, was partly owing to "the sympathetic administration and understanding of Harpole."[19]

The author failed to point out that family days, with virtually identical activities, had existed at the penitentiary for decades. He was correct, though, in observing that no other American penal institution had a program quite like this one, and his article was distributed to a nation of incredulous readers, many of whom otherwise believed the worst about Mississippi.

Soon the nation heard more. Newspapers everywhere carried stories describing the "Mississippi experiment." *Cosmopolitan* published Charles Knight's positive article entitled "Family Prison: Parchman Penitentiary" in March 1960. Columbus Hopper, the Ole Miss sociologist, initiated research that soon would earn him a considerable professional reputation and focus the attention of the academic world on Parchman's conjugal visits.[20]

The publicity, it seems, caught most Mississippians by surprise. At all events, there was little or no talk of coddling criminals with sexual privileges, and indeed the conjugal visits became a source of state pride. On June 19, 1959, after a St. Louis newspaper had encouraged the governor of Missouri to consider implementing the "Mississippi experiment," the *Clarion-Ledger* noted that "our Mississippi experiment may well become a national mode in this key area of prison reform." Coleman and Harpole had followed a risky course, if a well-plotted one; Harpole had managed the thing brilliantly; and by late 1959, when the state needed a victory very badly, it had one.

Although nothing could outstrip the public relations coup of family day, Harpole promoted other reforms that bolstered the image of his penitentiary. For years black convicts had competed for what they regarded as favorable work assignments in Parchman's dairy, and a degree of elitism had come to characterize the dairymen. Harpole built on that foundation, representing the dairy as an honor camp for exemplary black convicts, and created, with great ceremony, an honor camp for white males at Camp Nine.[21]

The superintendent's emphasis on religious activities never diminished. In September 1958 the *Mississippi Baptist Record* proclaimed that "Spiritual Emphasis Prevails at Parchman," and during 1959 and early 1960 Harpole butted heads with the legislature in attempting to secure funds for the construction of chapels at the penitentiary. Senator Alexander's penitentiary committee reported favorably on a bill to that effect in February 1958; but the legislature refused to enact it, and the best Alexander could do was to secure the passage of legislation allowing private donations to a chapel-building fund. In October 1959 a Jackson-based citizens' group was formed for the purpose of soliciting donations. Harpole spoke at their first meeting, where he harangued legislators for their shortsightedness. Such criticism won him few friends in the statehouse, but by February 20, 1960, private pledges totaled $10,000, plans for the construction of the first chapel were advanced, and the superintendent was calling on legislators for matching funds.[22]

Nor did Harpole neglect the penitentiary's educational program, which he regarded as "second in importance only to religious activities." In the summer of 1958 Patterson added four levels to his adult education program, thus enabling convicts to complete a junior high school education at the penitentiary. In addition, the educational director made arrangements enabling convicts to take correspondence courses through local high schools, the University of Mississippi, and Mississippi Southern College. By the summer of 1959 Patterson was bragging of "a remarkable degree of advancement" and "an increasing amount of success." In February 1960 Harpole unsuccessfully called on the legislature to establish an accredited high school at Parchman.[23]

The Failure of the Scalawags

Harpole's triumphs were impressive indeed, but none of them accomplished the first priority of the Coleman administration's criminal policy: the balancing of agriculture with industry at the penitentiary and the establishment of an expanded state-use system of convict labor. That priority was born of two crucial facts. First, Mississippi could not continue to operate a plantation system employing mostly black field hands in the face of a pervasive national movement for African American equality. Secondly, a severe glut in the cotton market, accompanied by a sharp decline in prices, coincided roughly with Coleman's inauguration.

Upon coming to office in early 1956, Coleman found allies among legislators who were concerned about the penitentiary's competition with private planters in a tightening marketplace. That concern led the legislature, on March 31, 1956, to enact a measure authorizing the penitentiary to establish a metal-working plant, to contract for the sale of metal signs to municipalities, counties, and other departments of state government, and to distribute unsalable goods among public institutions. But the statute was heavily compromised. It contained no provision granting the penitentiary a monopoly over the supply of any commodity to a public institution, it made no special appropriation, and it therefore fell far short of what Coleman desired. Late in the year the governor unsuccessfully called for appropriations to establish shops at Parchman capable of supplying state institutions with paint, disinfectants, and soap.[24]

The governor's plan was opposed by four identifiable groups. There was a sizeable body of hard-liners in the legislature who thought Coleman timid, even traitorous, in his reaction to the civil rights movement; they could be counted on to oppose almost anything emanating from the governor's mansion. There were legal retributivists who frowned on any attempt to mitigate "hard labor" at the penitentiary.

There were those representing private interests who stood to lose valuable state contracts if a state-use system triumphed. But above all else, the cotton glut had given rise to a crusade, supported strongly by Coleman himself, to balance agriculture with industry throughout Mississippi, and many of those favoring industrial development in the private sector questioned the wisdom of establishing state-supported industries at Parchman.[25]

All this added up to a standoff in the legislature, one that left the penitentiary in a most unbecoming position. Harpole, facing imminent financial collapse, could ill afford to wait on feuding politicians. In 1956 he reduced cotton acreage by 425 acres and began beating the drum of prison industry and vocational training.

Superintendent Wiggins had stressed to his critics that the old plantation system provided training in numerous vocations other than agriculture due to the presence of the many shops that made the penitentiary self-sufficient. Harpole made the same point in March 1957, emphasizing that over half the convicts worked in the penitentiary's numerous shops. Such assignments, he noted, were a valuable part of an "accelerated rehabilitation program in which prisoners learn useful trades, hobbies, occupations and skills."[26]

That was true—convicts *were* learning trades under the old plantation system, always had, and critics needed to know it. But the shops at the penitentiary generated precious little revenue, and that fact was a political liability within Mississippi. As for the cash crop, Harpole was helpless owing to the demise of the cotton market. In 1957 the penitentiary participated in the federal soil bank program, planting only 3,834.6 acres in return for a federal allowance of $71,000. That income, however, did not arrest the steady erosion of the penitentiary's financial structure. Wiggins's last crop had produced 7,487 bales and generated a net profit of well over half a million dollars. Harpole's first crop, that of 1956–57, yielded 4,527 bales and an operating deficit of $109,016. The balance sheet for the 1957–58 fiscal year was much worse, depicting an institutional deficit of $355,252.[27]

Harpole, Coleman, and their political allies broke for daylight in early 1958. The biennial penitentiary report submitted in late 1957 pleaded for legislative assistance in convict "rehabilitation," which was essentially defined as vocational training via prison industry. Then, in February 1958, Alexander's senate penitentiary committee reported favorably on a bill calling for the establishment of a soap-making plant, a mattress factory, and a metal plant capable of producing furniture, highway signs, and other equipment for use by state institutions. The bill met with strong opposition on the floor of the senate. Debate raged for two hours about the form of prison labor that would be least ruinous to the private sector. At last, after a worthwhile compromise was rejected, the opponents of the bill had their way by a narrow, two-vote margin.[28]

Afterward, as the penitentiary's financial crisis worsened, Harpole concerned himself more and more with occupying the time of his increasingly idle convicts. This he did well, taking care in the process to promote the image of the penitentiary. He created a radio, television, and electronics shop. He expanded Pauline Wiggins's old hobby contest, prudently renaming it a "hobby craft program." He established an Alcoholics Anonymous program through which many free members attended meetings at the penitentiary.[29] All the while, the hopelessly trapped superintendent, ever bemoaning the intransigence of the legislature, watched the penal farm system collapse around him.

In 1958 the penitentiary planted some 4,619 acres in cotton, increased yield per acre to such an extent that 6,144 bales were produced, but fell prey to the lean market and reported a deficit of $307,792.20 for the 1959 fiscal year. On balance, then, Harpole planted four crops and recorded an operating deficit of over $1,104,787 during his superintendency.[30]

In 1959 the superintendent actively supported Lieutenant Governor Carroll Gartin in the Democratic gubernatorial primary election against winner Ross Barnett, and on January 10, 1960, the *Clarion-Ledger* observed, "The head of one of Mississippi's ablest state officials is on the political chopping block." The ax fell shortly thereafter when Barnett announced that his campaign manager, none other than former state senator Fred Jones, would replace Harpole in March. In February, amid mounting attacks on his financial record at the penitentiary, the lame-duck superintendent told several visiting members of the house penitentiary committee that he had "no apologies to make for what we've tried to do here." And later in the month, shortly before leaving Parchman, he again emphasized that at some point Mississippi would be forced to "balance agriculture with industry" at the penitentiary.[31]

Harpole thus ended his superintendency uttering the same language with which he had begun it, a testimony to his failure to achieve his primary goal. He had achieved a great deal, but the penitentiary was adrift and entering stormy seas when he and Mary departed. The Greenville *Delta Democrat-Times,* which had tempered its traditional critical view of Parchman during the Coleman years, expressed astonishment at the dismissal of Harpole. It was, an editorialist concluded, "another example of the stupidity of the spoils system in Mississippi."[32] The journalist failed to note that the spoils system had brought Harpole to Parchman in the first place.

9

Rollin' with Ross

During the early months of 1960, the national civil rights movement gained ground rapidly, Mississippi's racially segregated institutions came under ever more determined attack, and groups of bus-riding zealots styling themselves "freedom riders" prepared to descend on Jackson from the North. Within the state, the reforming scalawags virtually disappeared, moderates changed colors, and right-wing reactionaries built barricades. The spirit of the times resembled that which had swept Mississippi a century earlier, when fire-eaters had led the state toward ruin on related grounds.

Ross Barnett was ill equipped to cope with the crisis; he, in fact, was more responsible than any Mississippian for creating it. At a time when moderation and compromise were demanded, Barnett had drummed up votes among the white electorate by scorning federal authority, by championing the sagging doctrine of states' rights, and by rattling the bones of the Confederate dead. He had asked the white electorate to "Roll with Ross," and it had responded. Now, as promised, Barnett came to office as a defender of the faith. There was pugnacity in his rhetoric: like his antebellum ancestors before him, he was fully prepared to fight the federal host.

Barnett was an accomplished lawyer and a skilled campaigner; but he did not always surround himself with competent lieutenants, and he had never learned that in politics, as in war, frontal assaults against superior force are rarely successful. The traumatic events of Barnett's administration would shake Parchman's foundations, and eight subsequent years of failed statesmanship would bring the old penal farm down.

The "Noble Experiment"

Governor Barnett's decision to entrust the state penal system to Fred
Jones seemed to be a good one. As a state senator between 1943 and
1953, Jones had played an active role in the formulation of criminal
policy, and as chairman of the senate penitentiary committee he had
been largely responsible for the sweeping reform package of 1948. But
the sixty-five-year-old Jones contrasted strikingly with Harpole, just as
Barnett contrasted strikingly with Coleman; for his background, his
appearance, his language, and his priorities smacked of the old days.

Jones was a gray-haired, cigar-chewing Delta planter who, at the
time of his appointment, was president of the Sunflower County Board
of Supervisors. He was a powerful man up Parchman way, a political
power broker who combined the best and worst features of the class
of men who ruled the Mississippi Delta. His stint in the senate had
proved him to be a cunning political in-fighter, but he had left many
enemies behind him in the theater of state politics, and his association
with Barnett had created new ones.

Jones had opposed Harpole's policies vociferously; now, he wanted
to turn back the clock. In one of his first public statements after becoming superintendent, Jones posed as a prison man of the Wiggins
school, announcing that he would restore the penitentiary as a "moneymaking proposition." He saw "plenty of land and labor"; with "proper
utilization of what we have," he asserted, "we can make money."[1]

The superintendent was extremely critical of his predecessor. "This
is a big plantation and the man in charge should know about farming,"
he proclaimed in June. "The penitentiary lost more than a million dollars during the last four years. Properly managed, it should show a financial profit." To make his point, he ridiculed the condition of farm
machinery, contending that he had farmed "30 years ago like they have
been farming here." He also announced that the production of food
crops had been abysmal, that the dairy and the meat-processing plant
had been improperly managed, and that the hospital had been operating without trained or experienced personnel.[2]

In November the superintendent displayed incredible disregard for
the legal and political currents of the day, telling journalists he had
found "bad conditions" caused by "too much whipping" when he arrived at the penitentiary. The strap, he alleged, "may have been used
. . . last year more than the public realized, especially in August of

1959, when inmates staged two sit down strikes." According to Jones, Harpole's staff "took matters into their own hands," shooters "fired into the cages," and convicts were whipped "for refusing to come out of the cages, for talking loudly in the dining hall and for other reasons." Later, the superintendent reported in an official document that "by and large the inmates are housed in buildings over 50 years old with inadequate heating, toilet or bathing facilities [with] the appearance of not having been painted in years."[3]

Jones's campaign to restore the Parchman of "the good old days" began well enough. He fired fifty employees, including some of the penitentiary's most seasoned sergeants and drivers, and replaced them with Barnett folk. Then, after planting a huge cotton crop on 6,423 acres, he lobbied the legislature for more financial latitude, advocated incentive pay for his convicts, relaxed discipline, and asked the inmates to join him in working hard for a better future. In time, Jones promised his work force in the June 1960 issue of *Inside World,* there would be "trades to learn, progressive farming, better and more schooling and [an] all-around rehabilitation program."[4]

Jones continued the conjugal visits and allowed Patterson, who somehow survived the political turnover, to introduce the Laubach literacy system, a new technique of teaching illiterates to read and write. While the director of education reported "seemingly fantastic results," the superintendent helped convince the legislature to formalize the penitentiary's chapel-building fund and successfully solicited public donations. Jones even promoted a short "hypnosis rehabilitation experiment"; it failed miserably but constituted the penitentiary's first stab at psychiatric treatment.[5]

In April 1960 Wendell Cannon, who had toured the state with his band as part of Barnett's gubernatorial campaign, was appointed the penitentiary's first director of music. The appointment portrayed the spoils system at its worst, but Cannon had his virtues, and the governor equipped him with the extraordinary power to exempt his choice of convict-musicians from field work. This plum, complemented by promises of gigs around the state, lured several of the formerly reluctant black musicians away from their cages, and by November Cannon presided over professional and amateur bands for both races as well as a quartet composed of black women. The white professional band, The Insiders, and its black counterpart, The Stardusters, were allowed to go on the road in a bus beginning in June 1960. Between August and November, The Insiders logged a reported three thousand miles, appeared on television frequently, and recorded one of Cannon's compositions. By November both bands were scheduled to perform somewhere every weekend.[6]

While Cannon and his bands traveled, Jones followed Marvin Wiggins's old and revered blueprint. In the autumn of 1960 he concluded a deal with his Delta crony, Robert Crook, the state director of civil defense, through which the penitentiary made a token payment and initiated the manufacture of mattresses for use at times of natural disaster in return for surplus farm machinery valued at over $100,000. The transaction, Jones announced optimistically, gave him "sufficient heavy equipment to throw up drainage works that make available for plantings hitherto untenable bottom lands."[7]

Impressed by the drift of events at the penitentiary, staff writer Bob Pittman of the Jackson *Clarion-Ledger* reported in November 1960 that Jones's "noble experiment" was "reversing the situation" at Parchman. In early January 1961, the popularity of the noble experiment reached a crescendo when the superintendent reported a "record crop."[8] It appeared, for a fleeting moment, that Jones would realize his boastful predictions.

Cracks in the Armor

The superintendent's experiment began to seem less noble when Austin MacCormick, the former assistant director of the federal penal system, visited Parchman for a third time in early 1961 and issued a report criticizing virtually every facet of the penitentiary's operations. The central problem, MacCormick noted, was the political spoils system. Mississippi needed a politically independent penitentiary board. The challenge for the state was "to get the prison out of politics."[9]

MacCormick's observations were ignored by state officials, who preferred talk of money. In February the governor announced proudly that already the penitentiary's transfers to the state treasury were over $250,000 more than had been projected by the state budget commission. What Barnett failed to announce was the fact that disbursements were running well ahead of receipts, that the penitentiary was in route to a fiscal-year deficit of over $336,000, and that Jones and the commissioners were fighting like cats and dogs.[10]

The conflict between the superintendent and the board revolved around the very thing Austin MacCormick had observed during his recent visit—the political spoils system. The commissioners were concluding a number of dubious contracts with the private sector. As always, graft was diminishing productivity, but now there was apparently more of it. Meanwhile, Jones's furious attempt to revive plantation agriculture was an expensive proposition. All these factors combined to carry disbursements to an appalling level.

A standoff between politics and penal farming was also discernible in staff appointments. Unlike his predecessors, Governor Barnett did not seem to understand that remunerative operations at Parchman required a degree of competency among staff members. Responding to the wishes of his cronies, he foisted an unprecedented number of political appointees on the penitentiary, thereby destroying long-standing relationships between staff and convicts, and heightening conflict about leftover patronage among the penitentiary's administrators. All this elevated tensions in the cages and undermined the delicate balance of power between the commissioners and the superintendent. The commissioners blamed Jones; Jones blamed the commissioners; matters heated up daily.

In late March a trusty sent on an out-of-state mission for the penitentiary drove a truck to Texas, turned right, and went home to Montana. There was not much anybody could do about it, and great embarrassment ensued. The *Delta Democrat-Times* called for a "new attitude" at Parchman, and the political opponents of the governor seized the opportunity to heap ridicule on his administration. According to Cliff Sessions of United Press International, a rumor circulated in Jackson that hundreds of persons had applied for admission to the penitentiary because "convicts are treated so nicely."[11]

Barnett, who had a wonderful sense of humor, brushed off the incident with a glib question—"If you can't trust a trusty, who can you trust?"—but the escape brought the conflict between Jones and the commissioners to a head. The commissioners demanded a curtailment of Jones's liberal policy on leaves from the penitentiary. The superintendent recoiled like a rattler, things went from bad to worse, and on April 18, 1961, apparently without first conferring with the governor, the commissioners fired Jones.

Barnett issued a vague statement promising to "straighten things out." A joint legislative committee departed for Parchman. Letters from the Delta supporting the ousted Jones swamped legislators. The

Delta Democrat-Times, somewhat confused by it all, called for the re-instatement of a superintendent with "a long background in penal re-form." With the integration melee heating up daily, many powerful state politicians thought it unwise to change horses in midstream, so great pressure was placed on the commissioners to reconsider. After much wrangling, the board reluctantly agreed to reinstate the super-intendent.[12]

Jones came back with a flourish, expanding Harpole's old job-placement program and renewing his plea for incentive pay for convicts. His attitude impressed the *Delta Democrat-Times,* which featured a story hailing the superintendent's many accomplishments, but Jones's honeymoon was short-lived.[13]

On May 31, 1961, lethal gas at Little Alcatraz martyred the much-litigated Robert Lee Goldsby, a black murderer whose case had been exploited by civil rights advocates to challenge policies that excluded blacks from state voter registration lists, and thus from trial juries.[14] Only days later, freedom riders appeared at Jackson's bus stations, resulting in mass arrests and yet another unsettling collision between the emerging principle of African American equality and Mississippi's constitutional and statutory law.

Under the provisions of the state code, the freedom riders were guilty of misdemeanors, so they were dispatched to the Hinds County penal farm. Problems developed very quickly. By June 12, 1961, the county penal farm had admitted eighty-four of them and overcrowd-ing was acute.[15] Furthermore, the young activists had come to Missis-sippi seeking to challenge the authority of a racist regime, had suc-ceeded in provoking a reaction, and now the question for state officials was what to do with them. The passions of most white Mississippians had been aroused: there was reason to fear that the incarcerated zealots would be abused, even murdered, and thus martyred, like Goldsby, in the eyes of the nation.

The attitude of the civilian guards at the county penal farm was bad enough, but it was nothing when compared to the hostility of the convicts. Trusties grumbled about favored treatment afforded the "riders." Other prisoners refused to associate with them. Tensions mounted daily. It was a sticky issue, perhaps one without solution, but the solution adopted only made matters worse. In mid-June the Hinds County Board of Supervisors succeeded in foisting their problem on the state penitentiary. Buses began to transport the unmanageable freedom riders to Sunflower County. By June 24, sixty-six of them, including twenty-three women, were at the penitentiary; by August 5 Parchman housed one hundred, with more on the way.[16]

The transfer of these misdemeanants to a statutorily defined institution for felons placed Superintendent Jones and his sergeants in an unbecoming position. There were, of course, legal problems. While increasing numbers of FBI agents descended on the penitentiary, the American Civil Liberties Union filed a petition for a writ of habeas corpus on behalf of the freedom riders. Justice Hugo Black denied the petition to the delight of state officials, but in the aftermath of Black's holding it was clear to everyone that the state's case would fall apart if the misdemeanants were abused.[17]

That possibility was very real. James Hendricks, editor of *Inside World,* attacked the freedom riders as fools "suckered into coming down here to disturb the peace." They were hypocrites who did not care about black Mississippians, wrote Hendricks, and their time would be more wisely spent if they directed their efforts toward Northerners who labeled black people "spooks, smokes, boogies, greaseballs," and the like instead of toward those who labeled them "niggers." The editor evidently spoke for a large number of Parchman's inmates. A former white convict recalls that "we wanted to kick their asses," and a black one remembers that "we [the black convicts] were really pretty ignorant about things back then and weren't especially fond of them [the freedom riders]." Governor Barnett, comprehending that the riders were seeking to provoke a damaging reaction by state officials, cautioned Superintendent Jones to avoid incidents at all costs, and the commissioners ordered a tightening of managerial procedure.[18] The scenario that had haunted Governor Coleman was unfolding: the eyes of the nation were fixed on Parchman Farm.

Jones placed the unwanted intruders in the maximum security unit and in the yet-unoccupied first offenders camp, thus shielding them from the wrath of his other convicts. The superintendent was, however, in a no-win situation. The stark, sweltering cells of Little Alcatraz did not please the freedom riders. One of them launched a hunger strike, reportedly losing forty pounds in twenty-three days, and another, James Farmer, a founder of the Congress of Racial Equality, claimed that Jones's policy was "the dehumanization of the riders to make us as animals." Jones refuted the charges and did everything imaginable to keep the lid on, but shortly he and the Barnett administration were sent reeling by a scandal of major proportions.[19]

The Kimble Berry Scandal

In December 1961 Kimble Berry of Greenville, a furloughed convict who had fled to Lynn, Massachusetts, told a *Boston Globe* reporter an incredible story. He had been given leave and supplied with a car, a pistol, and power of attorney to open a safe deposit box in an Arkansas bank. His instructions had been to go to the bank, to retrieve stolen currency and negotiable securities, and to deliver the loot to several friends of the governor, who had promised to reward him with a pardon.

Later reports, among which were a number of unsubstantiated rumors, painted an even darker picture. Berry, it was said, had secured a furlough not on merit but instead at the request of Lieutenant Governor Paul B. Johnson Jr., son of the former governor and a native of Hattiesburg. The money and the securities in question had been stolen in a recent robbery in Hattiesburg. Five men had been convicted and sentenced to Parchman for the robbery. Parties close to the governor had conferred with one of the convicted men only days before Berry's release, had provided Berry with the car, had left the penitentiary with Berry, and had been seen with him in Greenville.[20]

The reports were given credence by the behavior of the implicated parties, who made public remarks casting odium on the Barnett administration. The governor sought to deflate the mushrooming scandal through an in-house investigation, afterward announcing that everything was exaggerated, but the *Delta Democrat-Times* ridiculed Barnett's effort as a "maneuver . . . to keep the press off his back." Legislative leaders agreed, in late January appointing a special investigating committee composed of members from both chambers. The committee elected Senator W. B. Lucas of Macon chairman. Lucas, the dean of the senate who was said to be "as mean as a yard dog," led his committee to Parchman on January 29 and began to review personnel records as well as documents relating to paroles, suspensions, and furloughs. Next day word broke that Superintendent Jones had fired his music director, Wendell Cannon, for stirring up trouble among the prisoners and the staff.[21]

After the state of Massachusetts granted Berry asylum, Barnett ordered Jones to tighten his leave policies and asked the legislative committee to include the organization and management of the penitentiary in its investigation. Heeding the earlier advice of Austin Mac-Cormick, the governor suggested the creation of "a constitutional, staggered board, with authority to select the Superintendent and other specified administrative personnel."[22]

On April 3, 1962, the Lucas committee released the first of three separate reports. It addressed the bizarre events surrounding Berry's release, explained that a "veil of mystery hung over the entire investigation," noted the impropriety of pursuing a criminal prosecution based on inmate testimony, and cleared Lieutenant Governor Johnson. The next day the committee released its second report, this one addressing the issue of leaves, suspensions, and furloughs. The problem, found the committee, was attributable neither to the governor nor to his appointees at Parchman, but instead to a "faulty system." That interpretation was supported by a lengthy account of how the system had failed, concluding with a harmless proposal for the creation of a five-man board, much like the old board of pardons, to assist the governor in the granting of leaves and suspensions.[23]

So far, so good: actors in state government, it seems, were giving and taking with a spirit of compromise. However, between April 4, when the second report was made public, and April 19, when the committee's third and final report was released, something transpired that dramatically altered the attitudes of the yard dog and his colleagues on the committee.

The third report contended that the penitentiary was a "mess because of politics, illegalities and conflicts." Everything was "conducted in an air of uncertainty and confusion due to conflicts over the exercise of authority between the Governor, the penitentiary commissioners and the superintendent." Indeed, "Every phase of the operation . . . [was] controversial, including the hiring and firing of personnel, the granting of leaves and suspensions, the operation of the various departments of the penitentiary, including purchases of supplies, and the supervision and control of the prisoners." Purchases had been made "in an irregular, unusual, and oft-times illegal manner." Owing to the conflict of authority, "cross-currents of dissension, discordance and disagreement [filled] the atmosphere."[24]

Before the release of the committee's third report, the governor, the commissioners, and the superintendent—all with daggers drawn but in it together—had managed with difficulty to present a united front. Now Lucas's committee produced correspondence and testimony revealing the hostile currents beneath the surface, and the actors aired their dirty laundry with a vengeance produced by long-repressed frustrations.

"If I had a governor like White or Wright or Bailey, it would be all right," said Jones. But it was impossible for a superintendent to administer the penitentiary properly when a governor constantly foisted incompetent political cronies on him. On a "good many" occasions, claimed Jones, he had fired employees on grounds of incompetence, only to have Barnett force him to rehire them, and on one occasion the governor had sent a private investigator to Parchman because he "wanted some records swiped . . . at the hospital."

The superintendent was even more adamant in his attack on the commissioners. Supplies for the penitentiary, he charged, were bought from a supply company partly owned by a son of Commissioner Tom Ross. Most of Parchman's groceries were bought from a firm in which Commissioner Walter Scruggs was a principal stockholder. Over 50 percent of the cotton produced at the penitentiary in 1961 had been delivered to a company Scruggs directed. Furthermore, all the commissioners, but especially Ross, said Jones, had "agitated among convicts and other people and I am certain that they have been promised better jobs if I leave here."

The commissioners met fire with fire, denying Jones's allegations and attacking him for lax discipline, a dangerous leave policy, failure to follow rules, incompetent farm management, and gross financial mismanagement. They charged further that the Berry scandal never would have occurred had not Barnett, house speaker Walter Sillers, and other politicians forced them to rehire Jones. That, however, had been nothing new. Politicians constantly exerted pressure for the hiring of favored parties; indeed, the influence of the governor and various legislators accounted for the presence of every employee at the penitentiary.[25]

Barnett delayed his formal reply until the afternoon of April 23. Then, characteristically peering over his eyeglasses at anxious reporters, he unblushingly defended his exploitation of the penitentiary's patronage and dismissed the report of Senator Lucas's committee contemptuously. The governor fired Superintendent Jones a day later.[26]

Parchman Adrift

Barnett replaced Jones with Marvin Wiggins's old farm manager, C. E. Breazeale, fended off the deposed superintendent's continuing attacks, and set out to block several distasteful bills sponsored by his enemies in the legislature. In Breazeale, Barnett chose a superintendent who could follow orders and keep his mouth shut. Jones's mouth, however, was seldom shut, and it was especially active in the weeks following his ouster. "I placed my head on Ross Barnett's chopping block," he cried to reporters. The people and the legislature, he predicted, would "rise up with righteous indignation and demand that this institution be set up on a plan such as most other southern prisons are operated."

Jones did his best to rouse the people. His dismissal, he asserted publicly, had come because of his long-standing opposition to brutality and because of his objections to a system that kept "the worst employees for political reasons." Later, he wrote to a member of the probation and parole board, claimed he had a number of affidavits proving that "good friends of the governor" had offered to arrange paroles for payoffs, and sent a copy of the letter to the press.

Mississippians did not rise up with righteous indignation. Jones, however, was not without his supporters, the reports of the Lucas committee left many questions unanswered, and the governor still faced an uphill battle. If Jones was regarded as a villain within the Barnett camp, he was seen as a martyr by many of the convicts. They grew extremely restless, even volatile, after the governor fired "the old reformer." The trusty-shooters were disarmed. Deputies and highway patrolmen reinforced the penitentiary's hopelessly outnumbered civilian guards. Barnett alerted the national guard. Order was maintained, but the convicts remained sullenly defiant, and an unidentified employee saw trouble ahead. "Let me tell you something, those prisoners aren't so dumb," he told a reporter. "They'll wait a couple of days 'til the officers quit patrolling so heavily . . . [and] then they'll do something."[27]

More threatening to the governor were the thrusts of his detractors in the legislature and the lingering possibility of criminal proceedings against members of his administration. Barnett moved quickly to squelch both threats, reportedly leaning on legislative allies and demanding that the Lucas committee turn over its records to the grand jury of Sunflower County. On May 2, 1962, the senate constitution

committee killed a bill advocating a constitutional board of penitentiary commissioners. A week later the Lucas committee delivered its
findings to the grand jury. Not surprisingly, that body found no basis
for indictments.[28]

Meanwhile, everything was done to promote the myth that all was
well at Parchman. An Associated Press reporter interviewed a number
of prisoners and heard not one complaint. *Inside World* dutifully praised
virtually every facet of convict life. Assistant Superintendent Minga
Lawrence claimed that most convicts enjoyed a lifestyle "better than it
was in the free world." Breazeale remarked that Black Annie had not
been used since Jones's departure.[29]

Similar tactics had proved quite successful in fending off the penitentiary's critics on earlier occasions. But this time all the smiles and all
the assurances failed to deceive even the dullest of Mississippians, and
there were powerful men in the legislature who thought it unwise to
let Barnett and his cronies off so easily. One such man was W. H. Jolly
of Columbus, now chairman of the senate penitentiary committee.
Concluding that Superintendent Jones had done his best "under the
most trying circumstances," Jolly introduced legislation calling for the
creation of a powerful board of commissioners composed of five pro-
fessionally qualified members serving staggered terms. Unlike the earlier bill, which had been squelched by the senate constitution committee, this one was assigned to Jolly's own committee, which was beyond
Barnett's reach. Amendments in committee transformed the original
measure into a sweeping penal reform package. In the end, four separate bills came to the floor of the senate with powerful backing.[30]

In late May, Parchman's once vaunted security system collapsed. A
flurry of escapes threw folks in the Delta into a "tizzy," wrecking Superintendent Breazeale's public relations campaign and indeed carrying the affairs of the penitentiary to the point of absurdity. One journalist satirized the escapes. Less amused, both houses of the legislature
passed Jolly's reform package while convicts were yet "running around
like rabbits in the fields and woods."[31]

After having recommended most of the proposed reforms himself
in February, Governor Barnett now astonished everyone by vetoing
the two bills that sought to alter the political structure of the penal
system. The vetoes sent legislative leaders into a rage. Jolly and Bob
Anderson, the chairman of the house penitentiary committee, lambasted Barnett and his "henchmen" at the penitentiary while the *Delta*

Democrat-Times burst forth with lethal invective. At last Barnett had shown "his true political colors," an angry editorial proclaimed. The governor had displayed all too clearly "that he prefers to use the penal farm as a political pork barrel, with employees hired and fired according to his dictates, and with prisoners given lengthy furloughs on the basis of their political connections."[32]

Legislature leaders, incapable of overriding the unpopular vetoes, exacted a degree of revenge by reducing the penitentiary's appropriation by some $150,000 during the last days of the session, but all the turmoil subsided when the legislators left Jackson. The governor then traveled up to Parchman and announced that he had "never seen greater unity" at the penitentiary. Two weeks later, Commissioner Scruggs toured the penitentiary and spoke of a wonderful transformation. He was followed in late July by Barnett's chum, Senator R. D. Everett. The governor, Everett told the press after a tour, had been "wise and courageous" in vetoing the penitentiary reform bills. Since 1934, the senator added, the state of Mississippi had had "about as nearly perfect laws governing the penitentiary as it is possible to make."[33]

The comments of Barnett and his friends were nonsense, political rhetoric calculated to disguise the fact that Superintendent Breazeale was in deep trouble. The reduction in the penitentiary's appropriation came at the worst possible time. Superintendent Jones's first cotton crop had been a good one, but still the penitentiary had recorded a substantial deficit. The 1961 crop was worse. Now operating with insufficient capital and headed toward a fiscal year deficit of nearly $308,000, Breazeale was forced to cut overhead expenses.[34]

Although Superintendent Jones had spoken of the sorry condition of the physical plant in 1961, Breazeale reported no major physical improvements during the 1962 fiscal year and recommended none for the 1963–65 biennium. Typhoid and influenza immunizations were discontinued. The hospital operated with only one qualified nurse. The state hospital commission voiced grave concern about conditions in the operating room. The penitentiary's director of dentistry admitted that it was "almost impossible to do all the dental work that is necessary." Obsolete and worn equipment allowed the canning plant to operate only "at about fifty percent efficiency." The chaplain complained that his department was not meeting the needs of the convicts. Both the education program and the public relations of the penitentiary suffered an irretrievable loss when Patterson resigned.[35]

In October 1962 Senator Hayden Campbell of Jackson warned of disaster. Twenty-five staff positions were unfilled, and soon insufficient appropriations would force the abandonment "of at least 2,000 acres of cotton-producing land," he told journalists. On a recent visit to Parchman, Campbell added, he had observed a "pressing need" for shoes, boots, and winter underwear. In one cage, most of the 116 convicts were "almost barefooted."[36]

The penitentiary was sliding backward at a most inopportune time, a fact that was perhaps reflected by a significant increase in reported escapes and deaths among convicts. Surely the cutbacks in staffing, food services, medical services, and the other essentials of life figured prominently in both developments, and no doubt the rising escape rate was partly attributable to a substantial reduction in leaves and suspensions. But one must also consider the continuing shift in the profile of the convict population.

Of the prisoners admitted between July 1, 1962, and June 30, 1963, over 40 percent were white, nearly 86 percent were literate, and less than 43 percent were farmers and farm laborers. By comparison, of the convicts admitted during the 1933 fiscal year, less than 24 percent had been white, some 70 percent had claimed literacy, and almost 75 percent had been farmers and farm laborers.[37]

These changes were of great significance. White men always had constituted the penitentiary's most unmanageable inmates; they remained so, and now there were many more of them. Literate convicts had proved to be less willing than illiterates to buckle under to Parchman's labor-intensive regimen. The shift from farmers and farm workers to artisans and skilled laborers, most of them from urban areas, allowed Breazeale to place fewer effective hands in the fields, and many of the black inmates, inspired by the civil rights movement, were less manageable than in the past. Compounding the dilemma was the continuing effect of probation, which diverted the best of the state's felons from the penitentiary, and of parole, which gave early releases to the best of the rest. The hard fact is that Breazeale faced challenges that were unknown to Superintendent Williamson in 1933, and now the stakes were considerably higher.

Yet the governor and the legislature continued their suicidal standoff on penitentiary affairs throughout 1963, Barnett's last year in office. The result was predictable. A large increase in cotton sales was reported, and the chief executive promised a financial recovery in July;

but a continuation of the downward spiral of farm operations was obvious by January 1964, and several months later a fiscal-year deficit of nearly $300,000 was reported. The governor was no less emphatic in proclaiming Parchman a "model prison" during the summer of 1963. That boast, however, seemed ridiculous later in the year when three shotgun-brandishing trusties escaped, a furloughed murderer passed bad checks in Greenville, and two men broke into the administration building, making off with $2,500. "That's a hell of a way to run a prison," quipped the *Delta Democrat-Times*.[38]

When Barnett left office, Parchman was largely undone. Marvin Wiggins would not have recognized the old plantation. The "vulchers" were in control. They had carried graft to alarming levels, compromising what could not be compromised, bringing the penitentiary to its knees. Their appointments had gutted management, penetrating even the ranks of the veteran sergeants. Most of the old men in the cages, the loyal cagebosses, were gone, replaced by truculent younger men, and all of the white camps were time bombs waiting to explode. The shooter system was also showing signs of collapse. Clearly, all of it was resulting in an unprecedented degree of human abuse.

Furthermore, sixteen long years of revolutionary improvements had gone for naught, as had the public relations triumphs of Patterson and Harpole. Scandal was now the rule, not the exception, and the gap between fact and fiction in the old legend of Parchman Farm was narrowing daily. The cat, in fact, was out of the bag, and the clock J. P. Coleman had heard in 1956 continued to tick, louder and more ominously than before, for the iniquities of state penitentiaries were beginning to attract the attention of the federal judiciary.

10

Caught Betwixt and Between

In January 1964, shortly after Lieutenant Governor Paul B. Johnson Jr. succeeded Barnett as chief executive, the legislature took up the problems of the penitentiary. Fred Jones was back in the statehouse, now as a member of the lower chamber, and his rough treatment at the hands of Barnett had convinced him that no improvement was possible unless the penal system could be ruled by a nonpartisan board with members serving staggered terms. Others, observing the faltering cotton market, stressed the absurdity of state competition with the private sector and the advantages of instituting vocational training under a state-use scheme of convict labor.

Still others argued that Parchman's system could never withstand the civil rights movement. The penitentiary remained racially segregated. The staff included no one but Caucasians. Black men continued to shuffle along as members of the long line. Winchester-brandishing shooters continued to stalk them. The strap continued to hang from the belts of the sergeants. In January Senator McDonnell put "the fear of God" in the commissioners by threatening to go into federal court "to stop violation of the civil rights of prisoners." Later he joined Jones, a powerful group in the senate, and the *Delta Democrat-Times* in advocating the statutory abolition of Black Annie.[1]

The debates were unusually hot, and along the way much dirty laundry was hung out for the world to see. Superintendent Breazeale admitted frankly that nothing resembling a rehabilitation program existed. McDonnell accused the Sunflower County legislative delegation of caring nothing about Parchman "as long as they got the [superintendent's] job for their man." Another senator produced written evidence that convicts were buying their way out of the penitentiary. McDonnell, alleging that convicts had been whipped unmercifully in the past, threatened to report all future abuses to the United States Attorney and to act as "assistant prosecutor" in civil rights litigation.[2]

Through it all, there was a profound absence of leadership, a failure to go to the root of the problem. In June 1964 a greatly amended bill claiming to reorganize the penitentiary was at last enacted.[3]

The Penitentiary Act of 1964

The penitentiary act of 1964 replaced the three gubernatorial appointees on the old board of commissioners with a board consisting of five gubernatorial appointees. The duties of the new commissioners were left somewhat vague. The idea, one must suppose, was to make them inspectors. At any rate, the statute specified that they were to oversee the business affairs of the penitentiary. But there the purview of the commissioners ended and, serving concurrent rather than staggered terms, they remained the servants of the governor who appointed them. So did the superintendent: he was to be appointed by the governor, to hold office at the pleasure of the chief executive, and to have "exclusive management and control of the penal system." Neither the superintendent nor the commissioners were required to have anything resembling professional qualifications.

The statute did not outlaw Black Annie. It left a faltering trusty-shooter system untouched. It did not remedy a well-documented degeneration of living conditions at the penitentiary. It evaded the question of racial inequity altogether. It authorized the penitentiary to establish vocational training programs, but no money was appropriated to establish them, and nothing was done to effect a viable state-use scheme of convict labor. In the face of eight consecutive years of deficits, a glutted agricultural marketplace, and a pervasive national crusade for African American equality, the politicians clung to the old ideal of remunerative plantation agriculture.

The only substantive provisions of the statute were those that established token qualifications for sergeants, drivers, and guards, and those specifying that released prisoners would receive a little more money and a bus ticket to either the state line or their county of conviction. "Yep," a perceptive journalist had observed amid the debates, "what's wrong with Parchman may well be us . . . [because] we refuse to yield enough money to keep up a good farm and rehabilitation, expect the best from nothing and cuss loud and long when we don't get what we think we deserve."[4]

Little Paul's Folly

Meanwhile, Governor Johnson's close ties with the former administration led him to retain Superintendent Breazeale and most of Barnett's other appointees at the penitentiary. Johnson knew better, one must suspect, because in early February 1964 he went up to Parchman, called all the employees together, and admonished them for their numerous sins. He would not permit "peanut politics to interfere with the job that must be done"; he would fire any employee who sent him a gift; anyone depending on politics for continued employment was a "dead pigeon." If deficits continued, Johnson added, a council of Delta planters would be formed to advise the chief executive.[5]

Then the governor and the commissioners, taking stock of the fact that a great deal of federal money was available, began to talk of convict rehabilitation. In July 1965 board chairman Harvey West announced plans to open formal classes in diesel mechanics, automotive mechanics, sheet-metal working, welding, building trades, air conditioning maintenance, and bookbinding. The plan called for the probation and parole board to screen convicts who desired vocational training and for classes to be offered to those whose graduation coincided with their anticipated date of release. The state department of education, in collaboration with federal agencies, would provide aptitude tests for "prospective convict-students" so as "to ascertain to what employment a prisoner is best suited." Initially the program would operate in temporary facilities, but soon construction would begin on a large educational complex.[6]

In October 1965 Superintendent Breazeale got the program under way on a small scale. By January 1966 "quite a lot of personnel" had been transferred into the training program, and by April sixty-two inmates were at work in a "real life laboratory" consisting of classes in building trades, sheet metal, welding, automobile mechanics, and diesel mechanics. The book-bindery opened on May 18, 1966, under the supervision of an "expert" from Pennsylvania. Soon the facility was restoring, renewing, and rebinding an average of 1,400 textbooks daily at a cost of roughly one dollar per book. By August 1966 the bindery had restored a reported forty thousand books, and the entire vocational training program was employing 190 "students."[7]

In October 1967 the *Clarion-Ledger* hailed the dedication of Parchman's new vocational training facility as a "major breakthrough in the history of inmate rehabilitation in Mississippi." Governor Johnson, a host of journalists, and a number of elected state officials went up for the ceremony and toured the huge building. It consisted of 75,000 square feet of floor space capable of accommodating three hundred convict-students.[8]

After the opening of the facility, the curriculum was expanded. By the summer of 1969 fifteen courses were being offered, and the vocational training program was operating on a $375,000 annual budget. Paul Mellenger, the new director of the school, reported that only 6 percent of his graduates were committing crimes that brought them back to Parchman.[9]

The Johnson administration complemented the vocational training program with other newsworthy innovations. The board adopted a policy banning the use of Black Annie. On May 25, 1965, formal dedication ceremonies marked the opening of what was advertised as the penitentiary's first comprehensive library system. On Christmas eve 1966 the convicts were at last taken out of their striped uniforms and issued new outfits consisting of trousers with white drill stripes and blue denim shirts. In 1968 a grant from the new Law Enforcement Assistance Administration facilitated the creation of a reception center and a diagnostic clinic. Next year a similar grant led to the opening of a pre-release center that was said to be racially integrated, and about the same time Camp Seven was converted into an "inpatient clinic."[10]

All the reforms made for good press and tended to obscure the fact that the first priority of the Johnson administration was the restoration of remunerative agricultural operations at the penitentiary. In July 1964 the board of commissioners reduced cotton acreage by 1,600 acres, ordered the expansion of soybean and truck crop production, and announced that the penitentiary would no longer ship surplus canned fruits and vegetables to other state institutions. Then the governor and the board lobbied vigorously for special appropriations to purchase modern machinery and for the technical assistance of the Cooperative Extension Service of Mississippi State University.[11]

Their efforts were enhanced by the perception of prosperity spawned by President Lyndon B. Johnson's domestic and foreign policies. Beginning in 1965, the legislature heaped lavish appropriations earmarked for machinery and other agricultural improvements on the penitentiary. As the machinery arrived, Superintendent Breazeale removed increasing numbers of gunmen from the fields, and in 1967 "Progress Through Cooperation" came when the Mississippi Cooperative Extension Service lent the penitentiary its considerable expertise in agriculture and animal husbandry. Improvements in farm operations were noted in 1966, and in late 1967 the mechanized penitentiary reported a very misleading "profit."[12]

All this resulted in disaster. Johnson had begun his term of office by giving the employees of the penitentiary a tongue-lashing for their ruinous backbiting. Then, amid much publicity, he had supported legislation that addressed neither the source of the backbiting nor what was clearly a dysfunctional structure of penal administration. And then, with the penitentiary operating under the same superintendent, the same staff officers, the same sergeants, the same underlings, and the same managerial principles, the governor and the board of commissioners had mandated sweeping changes in Parchman's means of production. They had altered the cash crop, replaced convict labor with machines, exploited the expertise of the Cooperative Extension Service, sold large amounts of cotton, soybeans, vegetables, and fruit on the open market, and reported a profit. But it was a mere "paper" profit, the stuff of politicians, and the tactics that fashioned an improved balance sheet spawned a wide range of other problems.

In 1956 the penitentiary's sale of cotton in a glutted marketplace had excited great criticism. Now the cotton glut was much worse, and as private planters were investing heavily in alternative crops, the state matched them dollar for dollar, all the while exploiting public lands, publicly paid technicians, unpaid laborers, and tax exemptions in the name of penal farming. Understandably, the private sector howled plenty, and the joint legislative penitentiary committee recommended in early 1968 that the state should "avoid unfair competition" with private enterprise.[13]

Johnson's decision to retain Superintendent Breazeale and the bulk of Barnett's employees at the penitentiary also fostered problems. According to several former staff members and convicts, the major weakness of the governor's policy came with the fact that "he left a timid farmer" in charge of a staff that was "a pack of back-biting, corrupt scoundrels." In August 1965 a prison official told a reporter that there were thirty members of one family on the payroll. Several months later the house penitentiary committee, noting that dissension was rife among staff members, recommended a reduction in the number of employees who were related to others employed by the state. In early 1966 yet another scandal involving the penitentiary's leave policy confirmed either graft or woeful incompetence among Parchman's staff. While local and state politicians protested vehemently, Senator McDonnell remarked that Superintendent Breazeale was a "good farmer, but we can't legislate him into a warden."[14]

Yet nobody of importance was replaced at the penitentiary, and later the innovations of the Johnson administration exacerbated an already serious problem. Quite simply, old dogs refused to learn new tricks. Increased mechanization, the introduction of scientific farming, and the "meddling of those educated fools from the cow college" (the Cooperative Extension Service of Mississippi State University) did not go down well with many employees.[15]

From the first there was dissension between those who administered farm operations and those who presided over the vocational training program and the other innovations that diverted gunmen from the fields. A reporter found Superintendent Breazeale grumbling only weeks after the board announced that the vocational training program would be instituted. He was "much worried about use of a storage house near the administration center for a vocational school." The building afforded great public visibility, and the commissioners liked that, but it could not be guarded properly.[16]

Later, a journalist reported that the penitentiary's employees were divided on the issue of vocational training. One group regarded the program as an important tool in convict rehabilitation; others believed "a crook is a crook and if you teach him to handle a welding torch he will use it to cut the face off a safe." Apparently the latter opinion held the upper hand. "The whole vo-tec thing was bull shit," recalled an employee. "It excited everyone who was ignorant, pissed off everyone who wasn't, and divided the ass-kissers in the administration building from the sergeants."[17]

In early 1968 legislators found unqualified, insecure employees, great bickering among staff members, serious problems in the chain of command, and evidence that visiting politicians were fomenting discontentment. Two years later the house penitentiary committee recommended a study to determine the veracity of recurring reports that the vocational training program was interfering with farm operations.[18]

Many of the problems resulted from a fundamental contradiction in the policies of the Johnson administration, a contradiction that revolved around the traditional mission of the penitentiary. Parchman was a *penal* farm, and the idea was to operate it with *convict* labor. But in their haste to make a good financial showing, state officials divorced the farm from the prison.

At the base of Johnson's policy was increased mechanization and the removal of progressively larger numbers of convict laborers from the fields. In February 1968 a legislative committee noted that most of the penitentiary's crops were being harvested by machines and, pointing to the greater productivity of mechanized agriculture, predicted that more work would be done by machines in the future. That prediction was sound. In early 1970 Representative Malcolm Mabry was stunned to learn that only some 500 of the penitentiary's 1,700 inmates were available for farm labor. Mabry and his colleagues on the house penitentiary committee were appalled. To them it seemed that penal authorities had lost sight of the primary function of the penitentiary; they strongly recommended that, farm profits or no farm profits, more of the convicts should be engaged in hard labor.[19]

Old principles of convict management supported the views of the committee. In 1943 Superintendent Love had stressed that intensive farm labor was the key to the maintenance of order at the penitentiary. That opinion was not original: it went to the philosophical foundations of the old penal farm system. In 1965 a group of Parchman's older employees told a reporter that cotton was picked by hand because "a tired cotton-picking inmate [was] less likely to promote mischief than one who [stood] around watching a machine do the job."[20] But now machines were doing the job, or at least the better part of it, and increasingly idle inmates posed a problem of no small proportion.

Governor Johnson and the commissioners theorized that the new vocational training program and the maze of other innovations would fill the void. They were wrong. As late as February 1970, merely 165 convicts were involved in vocational training, and at all events the program served only well-behaved inmates who were about to be released. Somewhere in the shuffle, too, the penitentiary's religious and educational programs fell on hard times. The 1968 joint legislative report

on the penitentiary stressed the need to strengthen religious programming and noted critically that an educational director was not on the
payroll.[21]

Then there was the dark side of inmate classification. Many nice
things could be said about the new classification system. There was the
reception center, where all sorts of testing went on, and dating from
1968 two psychologists from nearby Delta State College helped assure
that convicts were properly assigned.[22] The first offenders were sent to
the new first offenders' camp, the physically disabled to the disability
camps, the psychologically unbalanced to the in-patient clinic, those
with clerical skills to Front Camp, those with medical training to the
hospital, and skilled artisans to wherever they could most fruitfully ply
their trades. After behaving themselves for a designated period, convicts could apply for the vocational training program. And some three
weeks before their scheduled date of release, "short-timers" went to
the pre-release center where they ate good food, watched television,
enjoyed conjugal pleasures with visiting spouses, and reflected on what
awaited them in the free world.

This state-of-the-art scheme had one notable weakness: it concentrated the worst of the convicts in the farm units, now dubbed "hog
camps." There, antisocial tendencies were reinforced by association,
and bitterness was engendered by harsh discipline; by the late sixties
the farm camps were festering sores. But all things being relative, the
commitment of greater numbers of confirmed social deviants, combined with the steady introduction of farm mechanization, dispersed
more and more unmanageable convicts among all the camps and sub-
verted the classification process. By the late sixties, recidivists were being
assigned to the first offenders' camp.[23]

The Crumbling Penal Farm System

As early as August 1965 a journalist noted a new tension at Parchman.
You could "feel in your bones" that all was not "happiness and sunshine." There were many convicts "who would as soon cut your throat
as look at you," and a visitor would be well-advised "not [to] let
your pocketbook hang out." The newsman observed, moreover, that
greater numbers of convicts were attempting to escape. A recent break
had resulted in three deaths; and a prison official led the journalist to
Camp Five, pointed to the spot where the corpses had lain, and told

of his great relief when he saw "armed guards in charge instead of prisoners." Even the female inmates were becoming unruly. Only recently, several white women working at the canning plant had staged a revolt.

Confronted with these conditions, Superintendent Breazeale was tense, distrustful, and mindful of a need to enclose the cages with fences, while the penitentiary's guards were "pleasant, but never friendly." No longer were visitors simply waved in and out of the front gate. Automobile trunks were opened and searched, and guards maintained that even the governor did not escape their security checks.[24]

The security system of the penitentiary was no better than its trusty-shooters, who continued to hold sway despite the introduction of a number of civilian guards. In October 1965 a reporter found them extraordinarily vigilant at one farm camp. There, four full-blooded Choctaw Indians served as shooters, and the gunmen toiling under their scrutiny showed "genuine respect" for the gun line. "You just can't step an inch over the line around here," said a gunman. "Everyone knows if you do those Indians would pure love to scalp you with that 30–30."

But shooters like these Choctaws were few and far between by the autumn of 1965. Old-timers reiterated the time-honored maxim that long-term convicts made the best trusty-shooters, lamented that parole had stripped the penitentiary of the best long-term men, and expressed grave reservations about the existing convict constabulary, especially the new probationary half-trusties, who so often went "over the hill."[25]

A certain tension existed even among the trusty-servants who worked at the guest house. In former times these grinning, shuffling blacks had charmed most visitors, and nobody had complained about the open violation of the 1934 statute denying trusty status to "conspicuous or notorious criminals." By 1966, however, this crème de la crème of the convict population neither grinned nor shuffled quite as much as they had several years earlier. Indeed, they seemed to be somewhat truculent, scheming, and derisive. In March 1966 a reporter observed murderers serving food in the guest house and expressed alarm. Somehow the face of Parchman Farm had changed utterly: the old plantation was no longer like it had been in the "good old days."[26]

The superintendent had little choice in the matter. He employed conspicuous and notorious criminals as trusties because the operation of probation and parole assured that the penitentiary housed little else; because the legislature would not allow him to employ a sufficient number of civilian guards; because low pay, terrible working conditions, and the penitentiary's isolated location normally rendered the few civilian guards he employed inefficient, corrupt, or both; and because those same factors usually caused the better civilian guards to depart after a short time. Security, then, was a serious and worsening problem, and Parchman's employees, "almost without exception," stressed that order could not be maintained without Black Annie, which was now employed in violation of a toothless board policy. The house penitentiary committee noted the degeneration of the trusty system, decided that it was "financially impossible" to replace trusty-shooters with civilian guards, and concluded in the face of disaster that the old system was generally satisfactory.[27]

On January 25, 1968, while Superintendent Breazeale was away, thirty-nine gunmen at Camp Five, a white hog camp, bucked the line, ignored the threats of their keepers, and "severely assaulted" three of their colleagues who attempted to go to work. Trusty-shooters and drivers stormed the cage, overcame the striking gunmen, and bodily carried them to the maximum security unit. Six days later the penitentiary committees of the house and senate arrived and got an earful of testimony.

The chaplain told of being offered "as much as $1,000 to get somebody paroled." Kenneth Bagwell, the veteran sergeant at Camp Five, assured the politicians that he had seen problems brewing for a long time. There was a severe shortage of manpower in the fields due to other assignments, the new machinery was not compensating, and convicts in the hog camps resented what they rightly regarded as unequal treatment. J. B. Mabus, sergeant at Camp Eight, agreed with Bagwell, adding that fully 40 percent of his gunmen were gal-boys. Both sergeants criticized the new regime for its declining emphasis on religious training and for its restrictions on the use of the strap. Too many compromises had been made: none of these problems had existed in Mr. Marvin's day.

Those opinions, which attributed all the problems to the recent departure from tried and true principles, were contested by Superintendent Breazeale, who blamed everything on his inability to implement new principles. The sergeants did not need the strap to maintain order, he claimed; they needed more machinery. A nice start had been made, but it had not been followed through, and difficulties were only natural due to a conflict between the old Parchman and the new.

The convicts did not like anything, old or new. They complained that they were mistreated, overworked, fed terrible food, and forced to endure hordes of pushy homosexuals. They alleged that drivers, shooters, and civilian guards administered "merciless whippings" with a wide belt, that hair was plucked from the faces of convicts as a means of torture, and that drugs were forced down the throats of gunmen. One convict testified that he had turned blue after being denied heating in the maximum security unit. Lifer Lawrence Hessian warned, "Another riot could easily happen anytime." One Bumgardner, a former editor of *Inside World,* summed up all the complaints with an articulate harangue against the Parchman "system."[28]

An investigative reporter visited the penitentiary after the departure of the legislators and discovered further damaging information. Only days before the riot at Camp Five, a convicted murderer serving a life term had snatched a pistol from a guard and terrorized the inmates of the first offenders' camp. A convict who had been given a Christmas furlough was in police custody in Jefferson Parish, Louisiana, under multiple charges, including the attempted murder of a law enforcement officer. Four other felons granted furloughs had not returned to the penitentiary.[29]

The joint report of the house and senate penitentiary committees did not address the causes of the riot at Camp Five; that matter, legislative leaders decided, would be broached in a later document. Still, the report was hardly an endorsement of the policies pursued by the outgoing Johnson administration. Politicians continued to involve themselves with staff arrangements and day-to-day operations. Management was poor. There were many unqualified employees. Staff dissension was rampant. Trusties were guilty of abuses. Support services were weak.[30]

The legislative committee's later report on the riot omitted a great deal of evidence that the press had revealed earlier; and shortly after it was released, Theodore Smith of Corinth, a member of the senate penitentiary committee, told journalists that the report was "misleading, incomplete, and did not reflect the consensus of the joint committee." A day later the house indirectly refuted Smith by giving Representative Bob Anderson and his investigating team an extraordinary vote of confidence. Then, however, Senator Corbett Lee Patridge entered the fray. Patridge, who had been stripped of the chairmanship of the senate penitentiary committee in January at the insistence of Lieutenant Gov-

ernor Charles Sullivan, was not in a cooperative mood. He threatened
to "name names" in a penitentiary report of his own. "I can tell you
today that there is brutality, insufficient clothes, homosexuality and insufficient food at the penitentiary," he stressed defiantly.[31]

Meanwhile, Governor John Bell Williams succeeded Johnson and
replaced Superintendent Breazeale with Tom Cook—a farmer, a college graduate, and a former sheriff of Oktibbeha County. Shortly after
Cook arrived at Parchman, the Sunflower County grand jury attacked
the trusty system, labeled the meat-processing plant a health hazard,
complained about the presence of hardened felons in the first offenders'
camp, and criticized state officials for pursuing financial profit instead
of convict rehabilitation.[32]

Cook sought to make amends, but within days Parchman was criticized along with the penitentiaries of Louisiana and Arkansas in a report released by the Atlanta-based Southern Regional Council (SRC).
A biracial, nonprofit research group actively involved in the disclosure
of civil rights violations, the SRC found that prison administrators in
the three Southern states were "without funds," a shortcoming that
left their convicts "without hope." In all three states, the report added,
"archaic and brutal instruments" were used to exact labor and maintain discipline amid alarming racial discrimination. Following on the
heels of the SRC report was yet another scandal, this one involving
the discovery of a counterfeiting ring at Parchman by federal agents.
While that investigation continued, a female convict working in the
governor's mansion murdered one of the other trusties.[33]

As these events rocked the penitentiary, Rex Jones of Hattiesburg,
the archconservative chairman of the House Subcommittee on Paroles
and Probation, proceeded with another investigation of leaves, furloughs, paroles, and pardons. Jones produced a galling report, and in
April 1968 the house passed a measure restricting the terms upon
which repeat offenders could be granted parole. Two months later the
House Constitution Committee reported favorably on a resolution to
vest the pardoning power of the governor in a three-member panel of
state judges. Both pieces of legislation failed; but the debates on them
exposed the state's criminal policy to a bitter tug-of-war, and in November the parole system became even more suspect when criminal
proceedings were initiated against Martin Fraley, the former chairman
of the probation and parole board, for allegedly selling a parole.[34]

In early 1970 Senator Patridge, now restored to the chairmanship of the senate penitentiary committee, introduced legislation calling for the termination of farm operations at Parchman and Lambert.[35] Patridge's colleagues rejected his proposal, but soon the death of Danny Calhoun Bennett further undermined the protectors of the status quo.

At Parchman, as at other penal institutions, inmates sometimes disappeared or died under suspicious circumstances without exciting any great interest by the public. Not so with the death of Bennett. He was young, he had received a light sentence, he had predicted that he would be murdered only days before his death, and there was, to say the very least, confusion surrounding the cause of his death.

Preliminary official reports attributed death to heatstroke, but an undertaker from Ripley, Mississippi, noticing that the body was badly bruised, suspected foul play and alerted authorities outside the penitentiary. A subsequent investigation revealed that Bennett had been beaten savagely with an ax handle and a rubber hose by trusties, that he had been tossed in a bus to die, that several hours had passed before the corpse had been taken to the hospital, and that there was reason to suspect a cover-up by penal authorities. In the end, two trusties were convicted of murder, a civilian guard was dismissed, and citizens far and wide began to suspect that the homicide was but the tip of an iceberg at the penitentiary. A composer from Tupelo actually wrote and recorded a song about the death of Bennett.[36]

The 1970 report of the house penitentiary committee reflected unprecedented disillusionment. Inspecting Parchman in February, the legislators found that supervision was lax, that too few of the convicts were involved in manual labor, that conflicts between supervisors continued, and that dire financial irregularities recommended the institution of a daily audit. So serious were the problems that the committee actually endorsed Senator Patridge's earlier recommendation, suggesting a feasibility study to determine whether the penitentiary's lands should be leased to private planters. One veteran legislator saw no hope for Parchman. "I've concluded after years of service . . . that we will never straighten Parchman out until it is taken out of politics," he wrote. "I don't intend to worry myself about it any more because there isn't anything we can do."[37]

Toward the Abyss

Nobody in Jackson, it seems, worried themselves about the mounting woes of Parchman Farm as the decade of the seventies dawned. At any rate, the October 1970 presentment of the Sunflower County grand jury contained an uncommonly critical section on the penitentiary. Then, in early 1971, the vulnerability of the penitentiary was underscored when the United States Fifth Circuit Court of Appeals, reviewing the case of 250 civil rights demonstrators who had been arrested and shipped from Natchez to Parchman in 1965, held in *Anderson v. Nosser* that state and local officials had acted in violation of state and federal law. Indeed, the court stated in the opinion that the treatment of the demonstrators was so horrendous that state officials should be mindful that "we deal with human beings, not dumb driven cattle."[38]

That devastating indictment, as well as the implications of a recent federal court holding against Arkansas's Cummins penal farm,[39] convinced Mississippi's legislative leadership that perhaps a little reform was necessary after all. But the politicians who gathered in Mississippi's pretentious statehouse, well above the foundations of the old antebellum penitentiary, were certain of neither diagnosis nor cure.

What to do? J. P. Coleman had been right: the time to get cracking had come and gone years ago. Yet even now, as the seventh decade of the twentieth century dawned, Mississippi's political establishment remained moribund, incapable of breaking out of the defensive mindset and suicidal inertia that had throttled all public policy for some twenty years.

A goodly number of state politicians, reflecting on the awesome power of their colleagues from the Delta, threw their hands in the air, convinced that discretion was the better part of valor. Whistling in the dark was also quite popular; and there were, to be sure, more than a few ostriches in the statehouse. One also discerned a great deal of romanticism among the legislators: everything would be all right, the romantic observed with numbing earnestness, if only the state could carry Parchman back to the tried and true principles of better days.

Others thought a little tinkering, a face-lift of sorts, would set things right: a few black employees, perhaps some new paint, and a better public relations campaign might work wonders. And of course many politicos, among them the interests who were doing quite well under existing arrangements, damned the federal menace and insisted that a bit of political jockeying, a stroke here, a rub there, would ward off the threat.[40]

This latter point of view carried the day. The penitentiary act of 1971 stipulated that, beginning in January 1972, the five members of the penitentiary's board of commissioners, still appointed by the governor, would serve staggered six-year terms. The statute also mandated that a board-appointed superintendent would "possess qualifications and training which suit him to manage the affairs of a modern penal system," and that the board could choose a superintendent who was not a native Mississippian. That provision was vague, purposely so one must suspect, but at least it raised the possibility that someone other than a political hack might superintend the penitentiary.

The legislature bit the bullet on the trusty-shooters as well: the much-maligned "headhunters" were to be disbanded by July 1, 1974. But the statute neither created nor financed staff positions to replace the convict constabulary, it did not ban the lash, and it altogether ignored the threatening question of racial inequity.[41] The penitentiary act of 1971, therefore, was modest work, the stuff of reluctant, backpedaling politicians, and it displayed appalling shortsightedness.

Shortly after the close of the legislative session, a young man who had formerly served as a correctional officer in the state of Massachusetts was employed as a driver at Parchman. "The sight of more than a hundred inmates quietly marching down the gravel road with hoes slung over their shoulders" impressed him: "It was a far cry from Massachusetts, where prisoners belonged to a union and 'citizen-observers' were permitted in the cellblocks to spy on correctional officers," he recalled.[42] Yet here was the rub: Parchman's system of convict discipline was indeed a "far cry" from that practiced in states thought to be progressive. Furthermore, the fact that the overwhelming majority of the inmates "quietly marching down the gravel road with hoes slung over their shoulders" were African Americans was altogether at odds with the pervasive civil rights movement.

The young driver was also struck by the extent to which Mississippi's penitentiary suffered from political neglect.[43] By all appearances, the place once had been a remarkably commodious prison. Now, though, the buildings were rat-infested and badly dilapidated. His sergeant, Tom Bennett, escorted him to his new home near the cage:

> As we approached the steps leading to the front door, I marvelled at the sight that stood before me. Actually, the first thing that caught my attention was the smell—after all, there were a hundred turkeys living twenty-five feet from my front door. . . .
>
> Although walking, I was still turned to look at the turkeys when the sergeant grabbed my shoulder, shouting for me to watch out. The first of

the three wooden steps leading to the front porch of the house was rotted out. Reaching for the screen door, he had to pull on it several times before it finally opened with a flourish, only to hang cock-eyed on the bottom hinge. . . .

I caught a glimpse of the first one out of the corner of my eye. Be calm, I thought, it was merely imagination, not a rapidly moving shadow silently disappearing into a gaping hole in the plaster wall. But then my worst suspicions were confirmed; I froze in my tracks, feet paralyzed in the doorway. . . . As Tom Bennett suddenly hollered and stomped his foot on the hardware floor, a dozen mice squealed and scurried in every direction, including one who, in an apparent state of confusion or wanton bravery, ran toward me. . . .

How could I expect my wife and son to live in such a mess, I wondered. She was terrified of mice; the place had no air conditioning; there was no telephone (only those holding the rank of sergeant or above had phones); the dust and dirt were everywhere. I kept thinking about the comfortable apartment we had left behind in Massachusetts.[44]

If Parchman's physical plant was largely unfit for human habitation, and if the old labor system was a legally threatening anomaly, the degree of brutality in the inmate-run cages was galling. Upon entering his cage, the young driver found a wailing inmate and asked for an explanation. "The cageboss and some of his buddies have been threatening all night to fuck him," he was told. Then there was "Pappy," an old shackshooter, who was well known "for his intemperate behavior and volatile outbursts," even for his penchant "to fire his rifle into the cages on occasion, just because the inmates were 'talking too loud.'"[45]

The smoothly run prison of Wiggins's day was on the rocks, but shortly matters worsened. In January 1972, when William Waller succeeded John Bell Williams as governor, the board of commissioners demonstrated the weaknesses of the 1971 statute by appointing an untrained, inexperienced kinsman of Waller's wife, John Allen Collier, to the superintendency. That ill-advised appointment was followed roughly a month later by a warning from the state board of health that Parchman might have to be closed because of an obsolete water system, an inadequate sewage system, an improper system of waste disposal, dubious fire protection, and violations of state milk-processing regulations. Almost simultaneously, several convicts overpowered and killed a trusty-shooter, commandeered a bus filled with other convicts, and headed for the nearby town of Drew, brandishing firearms.[46]

With no meaningful reforms forthcoming, Parchman drifted toward the federal litigation that Bill Alexander, J. P. Coleman, and their "scalawag" supporters had foreseen years earlier. And the old penal farm drifted most unbecomingly, directionless, scandal-ridden, the victim of failed statesmanship. "Parchman has always been an embarrassing subject to discuss with an official," a *Clarion-Ledger* editorialist had written on February 6, 1966. "Usually the response to a Parchman question is a sad shake of the head and a vague statement to the effect that things are bad at Parchman but that it is an impossible situation." That was a fair assessment. By 1972 the penitentiary stood as a monument to confused thinking, poor planning, and inept public administration. It was the victim of a ruinous political stalemate, an institution caught squarely between the past and the future.

Epilogue

Judge William C. Keady's initial finding of fact in *Gates v. Collier* was handed down on October 20, 1972. It held the state of Mississippi in violation of the First, Eighth, and Fourteenth Amendments and, not incidentally, of several provisions of its own code mandating minimal standards at Parchman Farm. Those findings prefaced orders for both immediate and long-term relief.

Among the court's subsequent orders were those that led to the destruction of the first cages at Parchman. Yet the troubled souls who witnessed that symbolic spectacle during the mid-seventies had no conception of what was to come. *Gates* was a class action, and the classes recognized by the district court (all convicts generally, and all African American convicts in particular) assured that the case would never die for want of a plaintiff. After 1972, and extending well into the 1990s, Judge Keady and his successor conducted an ongoing judicial inquisition, a virtual daily audit of the Mississippi penal system that produced well over 150 orders providing relief for state convicts.

Collectively, the orders of the district court have afforded Mississippi's felons those protections of the Bill of Rights deemed compatible with a judicial definition of the essential interests of prison discipline and security. Such a definition, of course, differs widely from that which existed in Mississippi before federal intervention. During the 1980s and 1990s, Parchman Farm and its legendary system of convict discipline were dismantled piece by piece, and a cellblock prison conforming to the now homogenized national model of criminal corrections slowly rose from the flatlands of the Yazoo Delta.

Was the intervention of the federal judiciary necessary? Yes. There was no way to defend the Parchman of 1972. There was no reason to think that state actors could get the job done. There was no alternative to an inquisition by the federal bench.

Has federal intervention brought improvement? Again, yes, provided one subscribes to the so-called justice model of criminal corrections, which essentially defines the inmates of American penal institutions as the unwilling wards of a parental state and places primary emphasis on the constitutional parameters of their confinement.

The racial inequity that so profoundly influenced Judge Keady's early orders has been redressed. The old Parchman practiced racial segregation; the contemporary prison is fully integrated. The old had no black employees; the current staff reflects a considerable triumph for affirmative action employment.

The justice model also affords inmates much more protection from their keepers. Before federal intervention, legal resources were generally not available to convicts; today, inmates have access to law libraries, to writ writers, and to legal counsel at all times. Before federal intervention, prisoners had no right to due process in disciplinary proceedings: the superintendent and his sergeants served as judge and jury whenever their charges violated rules, and they imposed sanctions, including corporal punishment and solitary confinement, without notice, a hearing, or a mechanism for external review. Today, an exacting definition of due process governs all disciplinary proceedings, corporal punishment is disallowed, and solitary confinement is limited in duration and governed by rules specifying minimal standards of treatment.

The new penitentiary also maintains strict culinary and medical standards. It offers a wide array of educational, vocational, recreational, and religious opportunities. And it houses its inmates in modern structures conforming to guidelines mandated by the district court.

All this, no doubt, adds up to a greatly improved standard of living for Mississippi's incarcerated felons. Quite another question, though, is whether the justice model of criminal corrections has led to improvement within the broader realm of penal jurisprudence. Has it strengthened the essential punitive foundations of public law? Has it deterred crime more effectively? Has it more successfully incapacitated dangerous felons? Has it enhanced convict rehabilitation? In real terms, are convicts better off?

In June 1991 I conducted a telephone interview with one of Judge Keady's old legislative colleagues and heard an interesting opinion:

> Bill was right to lower the boom. But he went too far. He forgot the good things that existed at Parchman under Wiggins and Harpole. He

forgot the terrible impact of the civil rights movement on Mississippi politics; hell, things weren't normal back then; it was obviously a period of chaotic transition that would pass. He forgot what criminal process was all about too, and he damn sure forgot what a state penitentiary is in business for. Anyhow, in writing your book, don't assume, like everybody else seems to, that things are necessarily better at Parchman now than they were in Wiggins's last years. They're better than they were when Bill got involved—God, anything would be—but racism or no racism, I'll put Wiggins's Parchman, and maybe Harpole's too, up against anything in the country, then or now.

There is much truth in this assessment. Available evidence suggests that the Parchman of the mid-fifties realized the traditional goals of corrective justice, including the health and general welfare of its convicts, to a much greater extent than the Parchman of the late 1990s. Furthermore, even the "shabby, trusty-run plantation" Judge Keady found so lacking in 1972 stacks up pretty well with the prison of today.

There has been a phenomenal rise in the number of commitments since the initial holding in *Gates,* notwithstanding a dramatic increase in the number of probatory sentences handed down by the courts of criminal jurisdiction and a considerable diminution in the length of time served by those felons sentenced to confinement. Inmate involvement in educational programs, religious programs—indeed, in anything that might be considered rehabilitative in nature—has dropped off appreciably. A divisive, gang-oriented inmate subculture has evolved. There has been a substantial increase in convict-on-convict brutality. The rate of recidivism has risen a great deal. In short, on penological grounds the prison is certainly no better, and arguably much worse, than the one that existed in 1972, although costs have risen prodigiously.

How is this possible? Old Parchman Farm, after all, resembled a slave plantation. The bulk of its inmates were black. They were forced to work in cotton fields. Overseers, all of them white men, literally rode herd over them. The place was racially segregated as well, and it had well-documented abuses, some of them galling. The answer lies in perspective.

There is nothing remarkable about a penal institution that housed a predominantly black convict population: the lowest socioeconomic classes have always filled the prisons of the United States, the progeny of former slaves have always been well represented within them, and today African Americans constitute a grossly disproportionate percentage of the nation's convicts.

There is nothing remarkable about a penal institution that employed an all-white staff and segregated its convicts by race prior to the
civil rights movement: that was the rule, not the exception, across the
nation.

There is nothing remarkable about a penal institution that forced its
convicts to endure disgusting labor: the prisons of every state have done
so more or less, and the material difference between chain gangs, penal
factories, penal mines, and penal farms escapes the convict.

There is nothing remarkable about a penal institution in which abuses
occurred: convicts are, after all, convicts; they are confined against their
wills; and anyone who studies the resulting tactics of brute force employed in American prisons discovers a chronicle of what most free-
world folk regard as abusive treatment.

Nor is there anything remarkable about a penal institution with features that recall the days of domestic slavery. Legal incarceration is, by
definition, an abridgment of liberty that reduces free human beings
to a condition of servility. Indeed, "penal servitude" lies at the heart
of the penitentiary concept, and the notion that convicts were "slaves
of the state" prevailed among American jurists until only recent times.

None of these doleful features, therefore, distinguish Mississippi's
old penal farm among the prisons of its era. Parchman Farm, however,
was a remarkable place for other reasons, and its history is perhaps instructive for a nation that currently incarcerates such a huge percentage
of its citizens with so few discernible benefits.

Mississippi's convict lease system was erected by the Republican
emancipators of the African American immediately after the Civil War
and later extended to numbing limits by the state's "redeeming" Democrats. Convict leasing was, as one contemporary noted, a scheme of
penology "worse than slavery": arguably, nothing in American history
offers a more galling chronicle of public corruption and human abuse.

Penal farming on public lands replaced the convict lease system in
Mississippi. Parchman Farm was the state's principal instrument in that
endeavor, and the establishment of the isolated prison constituted a
revolution in criminal policy, a penal reform that remains unsurpassed
to this day. Indeed, the reform enhanced the realization of every ideal
of corrective justice, if not the yet unrealized ideal of racial justice, and
it absolutely accrued to the advantage of convicts.

James Kimble Vardaman, the political strongman most responsible
for the consummation of this far-reaching shift in policy, believed that

Mississippi's former slaves and their progeny were both genetically and morally unprepared for a status of social equality, that they were predisposed to criminality, and that their demonstrable behavior justified the worst fears of civilized white society. Vardaman's racial bigotry and steadfast defense of white rule shock a modernity so far removed from the horrors of civil war and postwar reconstruction. His fears, however, were hardly ill founded.

Given the ugly fact of slavery, and considering also the terms on which the slave was freed, rampant criminality among the black freedmen was inevitable. It occurred. It occurred on a monumental scale, threatening the persons and property of black and white Mississippians alike, and it increased with the steady migration of rural blacks to the state's cities as the twentieth century progressed. Moreover, rampant criminality by Mississippi's African Americans continues today, decades after the death of Jim Crow and in a state that has more black elected officials than any other.

Since the Civil War, therefore, coping with the felonious members of a large African American underclass has been a necessary focus of public policy in Mississippi. Racial prejudice, to be sure, has figured in the equation: the inequities and iniquities of the state's former racial caste system are hardly fictitious. Preconceived notions about criminality have no doubt undone more than one black citizen: labeling is a pervasive factor in criminal process everywhere. But crime by African Americans, very real crime, has been, and is, a cold fact of life in Mississippi. Even today, as the new millennium approaches, public officials, black and white, grapple with the ugly criminological legacy of slavery. The state's convict population remains well over 70 percent black, and the number of incarcerated African Americans has increased dramatically since the triumph of the civil rights movement.

Vardaman was the first public official in Mississippi to grapple with this phenomenon proactively. Despite his racial bigotry, he accepted the black man as a permanent fixture, knowing full well that the white man was dependent on his labor, and he empathized with the plight of the state's Africans. But Vardaman found the criminality of blacks ruinous, at odds with the foundations of Western civilization, and a major factor in the racial strife that so thwarted Mississippi's development.

Vardaman assigned a hefty measure of blame to the policies of his political predecessors. Among those policies, none was more counterproductive, he thought, than the exploitation of convict labor by private parties. The practice fell heaviest on the black man; it was morally indefensible; but above all else it was impolitic, destructive of the harmonious if unequal relationship that had to exist between the black man and the white man. The penal philosophy Vardaman willed to posterity confronted that shortcoming: it sought to check long-standing human abuse, to instill a work ethic, to teach marketable skills, and to release contented, productive convicts back into society.

Vardaman's motives are despicable by today's lofty egalitarian standards: they were clearly rooted in principles of social control, not those of social justice. Social justice, however, has little to do with penology anywhere, yesterday or today; and, ironically enough, the emphasis of Mississippi's "White Chief" on humane treatment and "correction" made him a flaming penological liberal in early twentieth-century America.

The penal farm Vardaman willed to posterity was therefore quite progressive for its time. Today, of course, the notion of putting African Americans to work in cotton fields is obnoxious. In early twentieth-century Mississippi, though, that was hardly the case. Given the alternatives of convict leasing, a public works system employing chain gangs, and confinement in a cellblock prison, it seemed perfectly rational and indeed humane to subject black felons to the same regimen of life and labor that characterized the law-abiding members of their race. The regimen established at Parchman Farm did precisely that.

Vardaman's scheme afforded convicts an uncommon degree of protection: no state penal system of the early twentieth century operated under a more exacting system of checks and balances. A popularly elected board of penitentiary inspectors is rare indeed in the history of American penology. So is a maze of informants representing so many diverse political interests—a "snitch system" extending from the statehouse to the prison trenches. And the segregation of the races at Parchman Farm, with each cage supervised by a black or white cageboss in cahoots with a responsible prison administrator, precluded many of the iniquities that abounded in other American prisons.

Vardaman's emphasis on remunerative convict labor also had merit. Throughout the history of Parchman Farm, profits always delivered hefty legislative appropriations while red ink normally reduced the penitentiary to the financially starved status of prisons in other states. Healthy legislative appropriations, in turn, enhanced convict life. Convicts have no meaningful political constituency, and thus little leverage in public-sector finance. Parchman's history suggests that a revenue-generating penal institution, even in a relatively poor state like Mississippi, can mitigate the effects of this unfortunate glitch in republican political economy.

Operating upon Vardaman's principles, Parchman Farm began with a flourish, profiting from the dominance of its political architect, then sputtered in the wake of his fall, at last floundering during the years of the Great Depression. Between 1936 and 1944, however, the penal farm experienced steady improvement under the leadership of superintendents Jim Thames and Lowery Love, and between 1944 and 1952 Superintendent Marvin Wiggins carried Parchman to its zenith.

The ever-rising market value of cotton was the common denominator in the rise of the Mississippi penal farm: even those white politicians who frowned on appropriations for black felons were willing, indeed eager, to support a goose laying golden eggs. Yet the thing required management, political as well agricultural, and here Wiggins closed the deal.

Mr. Marvin, in fact, stands among the most accomplished penologists in American history, and the penitentiary over which he presided in the late 1940s and early 1950s was among the most effective in the nation. Security was relatively tight. Abuses were relatively rare. Culinary and medical arrangements were relatively good. Inmates were healthier than the great majority of free Mississippians, and certainly more so than those who languished in most of the nation's other prisons.

A full-blown philosophy of operant learning also flowered at Wiggins's Parchman, holding out uncommon incentives to convicts and effectively inspiring hard work and good behavior. A relatively successful adult education program was in place, complementing an equally successful program of vocational education through which convicts managed the support services of a huge, largely self-sufficient plantation.

Among Wiggins's innovations was the nation's first furlough program, which evidently achieved more success than any of its type in history. Parchman's rodeo, its hobby crafts program, its award-winning inmate newspaper, and its celebrated music program were also the legacy of Wiggins, and the foundations of the penitentiary's famous conjugal visitation program were laid by the venerable super. At the same time, Wiggins's penal farm boasted an incredibly low recidivism rate and was the only revenue-generating prison in the United States.

What went wrong? The seed of Parchman's problems was planted early on, long before Wiggins's time, with the demise of Vardaman's old watchdogs, the elected board of trustees, via the penitentiary act of 1934. After January 1, 1936, when the strong-governor scheme of prison administration went into effect, the penal farm's fiscal integrity was threatened, the welfare of its inmates at risk, owing to the heavy demands of politics.

The resulting scandals, however, produced an extraordinary penal reform movement within Mississippi during the late forties and early fifties, one that championed the most enlightened principles of the new "corrections." Few states can boast of the likes of Howard McDonnell. No state can claim editors more devoted to the cause of penal reform than Hodding Carter and Oliver Emmerich. Nowhere does one discover a body of correctional lobbyists more active than those who represented the Mississippi Association of Crime and Delinquency.

Ironically, though, the successful initiatives of these Mississippians contributed to the demise of Parchman Farm. The old "Mississippi System" was hardly designed to accommodate the economic and demographic changes that visited the state after the surrender of Japan in 1945, but the piecemeal adoption of policies rooted in failed Northern prisons assured disaster.

Wiggins's arrival at Parchman was preceded by the adoption of such a policy: the enactment of the state's parole statute in 1944. Most of Wiggins's long tenure was devoted to programs designed to counter the debilitating effects of parole, and along the way he made his mark on the history of American corrections. Yet the effect of parole was far from fortunate. After 1946, the most manageable of Parchman's convicts—its veteran trusties and, above all, the best of its cagebosses and shooters—departed.

Demographic changes thickened the plot considerably during the 1950s. The most far-reaching of these was a dramatic increase in the number of Caucasian commitments. Parchman's system was designed to accommodate Mississippi's rural black farmhands, and white men, who regarded the prison's regimen of labor as socially degrading "nigger work," had always been problematic. The arrival of greater numbers of white convicts, the bulk of them from the state's emerging cities, altered relationships within the inmate subculture, bred mounting tension, and reduced productivity. So did the arrival of more African American convicts from urban areas: people, black or white, who have never put in a day in the cotton rows find it galling.

Mississippi's federally inspired solutions to the problems bred by these unsettling changes only compounded the woes of the penitentiary. Anyone who knows old Parchman Farm recalls an astonishing degree of camaraderie, an us-against-the-world attitude, among both the keepers and the kept: the now-yellowed pages of *Inside World* reveal it very clearly, as do the compositions of the institution's blues artists and the recollections of many old-timers. There was, in fact, a curious warmth about the place, even in the cotton rows, much of it attributable to the distinctly paternalistic leadership of its superintendents, especially Wiggins.

But Mr. Marvin was incapable of explaining it to state legislators, or perhaps they did not listen to him. At any rate, the construction of the maximum security unit, Little Alcatraz, and more especially the placement of the gas chamber within it, had a devastating effect on Parchman Farm. Confinement in the dark cells undermined the social chemistry of the prison, and something about the spirit of the place died with Gerald Gallego on March 3, 1955.

Shortly thereafter, Mississippi enacted its much-debated probation statute, thereby assuring that the penitentiary housed an even less manageable convict population. Then the cotton market went belly up, Wiggins retired, and the political foundations of the penitentiary eroded down in Jackson. Old Parchman Farm was dead in the water, its means of production and system of convict management long gone, well before the civil rights movement visited Mississippi.

After the advent of civil rights agitation, moreover, Governor J. P. Coleman's attempt to bring the old penal farm abreast of a rapidly changing world fell prey to political reaction. That phenomenon, too, is easily explained. Save only Virginia, no Southern state suffered more than Mississippi during the Civil War and its tragic aftermath, and the generation of white Mississippians who beheld the beginning of the crusade for African American equality during the late 1950s had grown to maturity on the knees of Confederate veterans. Not surprisingly, they responded much like their ancestors of a century earlier, who had been confronted by a strikingly similar initiative by the federal power.

The decision of the electorate to "Roll with Ross" in the gubernatorial election of 1959 sealed the fate of Parchman Farm. Governor Barnett's policies deprived the institution of veteran leadership, bred scandal on an unprecedented scale, and alienated the legislature, thus assuring a diminution in state appropriations and a resulting degeneration of living conditions at the worst possible moment.

Barnett also chose to ignore the sound advice of his predecessor, Coleman, and recommitted Parchman to a policy that was frankly stupid—a suicidal attempt to restore plantation agriculture in direct competition with the state's planters and despite one of the greatest social movements of modern history. Meanwhile, the governor, seemingly oblivious to the strength of the forces arrayed against him, approved the commitment of large numbers of civil rights activists to Parchman, thereby identifying the institution with his much-publicized defense of institutionalized racism and focusing the attention of a critical nation on Sunflower County.

The crippling effects of Barnett's penal policy were compounded during the gubernatorial term of the younger Paul Johnson. Everything suggests that Johnson meant well, but he was hamstrung by the legacy of his predecessor, the legislature was truculent, and the policies of his administration left the penitentiary in no-man's-land, caught squarely between the traditional demands of penology and those of the new civil rights. Parchman Farm never recovered. William Keady did not bring Mississippi's old penal farm down. Far from it: he presided over an autopsy of the institution and attempted to chart a course for a future that even now remains uncertain.

The old gravel road running south from Clarksdale to the state penitentiary in Sunflower County is now paved, but it still winds its way through the flatlands of the Yazoo Delta, invading the rich buckshot soil that once made cotton king. Along the way, though, one finds few of the old shotgun shacks. Mechanization has long since driven the sharecropper off the land, and the smell, the feel, of the depopulated Delta is different.

So, too, is what awaits at journey's end, for only a shadow of old Parchman Farm remains. Thousands of the acres Marvin Wiggins developed are leased to local planters, and the remaining lands of the penitentiary hold but faint resemblance to earlier days. The depot, once the site of humming gins, bulging cotton houses, and busy industry, is gone. Upon entering Front Camp, formerly the heart of the great plantation, one feels the bland presence of bureaucracy, so characteristic of prisons everywhere. Driving west, toward the great river, the visitor observes a scarred, eroded landscape, rotting cottages, and at last the chilling monuments to Bill Keady's notion of a "modern operation": gray, foreboding structures rising ominously from the flatlands. These are real cages, cellblocks of cold steel surrounded by electronically guarded chain-link fences topped by coiled razor wire.

Black Annie is now a relic of history, a dinosaur spoken of sheepishly by the new generation of employees and displayed naughtily by a handful of old-timers who pay lip service to old ways. Gone, too, is the fabled long line, where the dreaded shooters held sway with hard eyes and shining Winchesters. Shadowy memories of Mr. Marvin linger. The old-timers speak longingly of his greatness, of the "golden age" of Parchman Farm when the land flowered with cotton, but all that is a distant memory.

The prison has gone the way of the nation, for better or for worse. Mississippians are being dragged along slowly, all the while wondering naively why a plantation of over fifteen thousand acres with legions of captive laborers cannot feed, clothe, and otherwise support itself. Meanwhile, more and more of the grim cellblocks go up, with private contractors growing wealthy at public expense, and penal authorities—ever reminding legislators of the mighty federal judiciary—lobby for still more of them. At present, only a handful of Mississippi's municipalities have populations greater than that of the state penal system; and with more convicts arriving daily, the nexus of state correctional policy is a search for a means of passing felons through a prison treadmill more rapidly.

All this, to be sure, is a sorry state of affairs, but none of it is unique to Mississippi. Throughout the nation, the justice model of criminal corrections is collapsing under its own weight, and public officials are desperately searching for answers. Perhaps it is time for them to abandon the reign of reaction that has so dramatically affected legal punishment since the advent of the civil rights movement.

There is nothing pretty about imprisonment: at best it is a lesser of evils, and the similarity between slavery and legal incarceration is manifest. That fact, one must suspect, has been the driving force behind the nation's abandonment of time-honored maxims of corrective justice: conscience-stricken Americans understandably chafe at the presence of so many African Americans—the descendants of former slaves—in their prisons and seek to make amends. Social justice, however, is one thing, criminal justice quite another, and long experience suggests that the two cannot be combined in a single scheme of public policy.

With that fact clearly before them, policymakers might do well to contemplate the nation's easily demonstrable shortcomings in the social sphere, the probity of an expansive and mushrooming body of legal commands and penal threats, and the woefully conventional cast of a failed concept of legal incarceration. And in the course of such deliberation, perhaps they might revisit the old penal farm in Mississippi's Yazoo Delta. There, the ironic similarities between Governor Vardaman's penal philosophy and the loftiest correctional ideals of modernity might well come clear, along with the paradox offered up by Parchman Farm at high tide.

Parchman's Camp 8 (Negro), ca. 1950. MDAH.

Parchman's Camp 6 in flush times, ca. 1950. MDAH.

A camp dining hall, ca. 1940. MDAH.

Parchman's brickyard, ca. 1950. MDAH.

Farm buildings at Parchman, ca. 1950. LLH.

Negro cattlemen at Parchman, ca. 1940. MDAH.

Mail call, ca. 1940. MDAH.

Female convicts at the slaughterhouse, ca. 1940. MDAH.

Governor Hugh White and entourage inspecting a hog unit, ca. 1953. MDAH.

"Little Alcatraz," the maximum security unit at Parchman, ca. 1960. LLH.

Death Row at Little Alcatraz, ca. 1976. Courtesy of Tyler H. Fletcher (hereafter cited as THF).

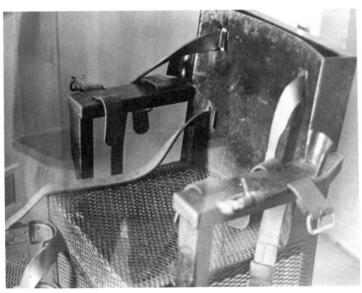

The death seat within the gas chamber, 1975. THF.

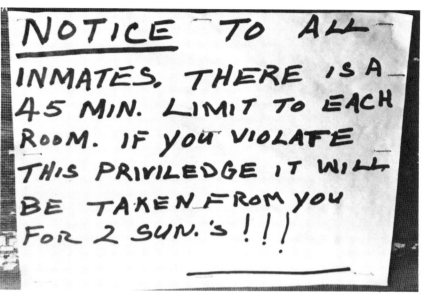

Sign posted on a "red house," ca. 1974. THF.

The Parchman prison band, ca. 1980. MDOC.

Old Camp 10, abandoned and awaiting demolition, ca. 1974. MDOC.

Flames engulf an old cage in the wake of *Gates v. Collier*, ca. 1976. MDOC.

The fruits of federal intervention: the new face of Parchman, ca. 1980. MDOH.

Notes

Introduction

1. I first heard this chant at Parchman Farm in 1975. All of the quotations in this introduction were either heard or recorded in the course of my visits to Parchman in 1975 and 1976.

2. Donald Cabana, *Death at Midnight: The Confession of an Executioner* (Boston: Northeastern University Press, 1996).

Chapter 1: Born of Politics

1. F. A. Johnston, "Suffrage and Reconstruction in Mississippi," *Publications of the Mississippi Historical Society* [hereafter *MHS*] 6 (1902): 237; A. D. Kirwan, *Revolt of the Rednecks: Mississippi Politics, 1876–1925* (Gloucester, Mass., 1964), pp. 78–79.

2. For accounts of the antebellum penitentiary and the postbellum convict lease system, see W. B. Taylor, *Brokered Justice: Race, Politics, and Mississippi Prisons, 1798–1992* (Columbus, Ohio, 1993), pp. 15–66.

3. Ibid., pp. 66–69.

4. Jackson *Clarion-Ledger*, Jan. 26, 1899.

5. *Laws of the State of Mississippi* [hereafter cited as *Miss. Laws*], 1900, pp. 63–65, 67–69, 245–46. See also *Mississippi Legislature, Senate Journal* [hereafter cited as *Senate Journal*], 1900, p. 63; and *Mississippi Legislature, House Journal* [hereafter cited as *House Journal*], 1900, pp. 106, 178.

6. Penal farming on state-owned properties outside the Jackson area was first advocated in August 1886 by Senator George C. Dillard in a letter to the editor of the *Vicksburg Post*. Afterward the scheme was embraced by the leadership of the Farmer's Alliance as an alternative to the convict lease system and advocated by a number of newspapers affiliated with the agrarian faction of the state Democratic Party. In the late 1880s Ethelbert Barksdale, editor of the powerful Jackson *Clarion-Ledger*, championed the idea, as did Governor John

M. Stone in his address to the Mississippi legislature in January 1896. For further information on the Dillard scheme and its continuing role in state politics, see Taylor, *Brokered Justice,* pp. 58–82.

7. Ibid., pp. 63–65, for accounts of the legislative committee reports of 1888 revealing the extent of graft and human abuse within the convict camps of the lessee, the Gulf and Ship Island Railroad Company. See also Enoch Wines, *The State of Prisons and of Child-Saving Institutions in the Civilized World* (1880; reprint, Montclair, N.J., 1968), pp. 111–12, 196.

8. Taylor, *Brokered Justice,* p. 71.

9. *Senate Journal,* 1902, p. 8; "Works Project Administration: Historical Records Survey," RG 60, vol. 6, p. 403, Mississippi Department of Archives and History, Jackson, Miss. [hereafter cited as MDAH]; "Lands of the Mississippi State Penitentiary," comp. P. J. Townsend Jr. and E. McBride (Office of the Governor, Sept. 3, 1980), pp. 7–28 [hereafter cited as "Penitentiary Lands"]; *Biennial Report of the Board of Control of the Mississippi State Penitentiary,* 1899–1901, pp. 3–4 [hereafter cited as *PR,* followed by the years constituting the biennium, as are the biennial reports of the penitentiary's board of trustees (1906 through 1935) and board of commissioners (1936 through 1975)].

10. *The Constitution of the State of Mississippi, Adopted . . . November 1, 1890,* comp. G. L. Rice (Jackson, Miss., 1936), pp. 94–95; *Journal of the Proceedings of the Constitutional Convention . . .* (Jackson, Miss., 1890), pp. 123–24; Jackson *Clarion-Ledger,* Sept. 2, 1890; S. Curtis, "Penitentiary Reform in Mississippi, 1875–1906" (master's thesis, Mississippi College, 1974), p. 53.

11. Taylor, *Brokered Justice,* pp. 67–70.

12. Jackson *Daily Clarion-Ledger,* Nov. 2, 1947. See also "Penitentiary Lands," pp. 71–73, for an analysis of land potential at Parchman.

13. These charges were advanced in the reports of two subsequent legislative committees. See *House Journal,* 1902, pp. 58–67; 1906, pp. 615–28, 916–18, 1328–29. See also W. F. Holmes, *The White Chief: James Kimble Vardaman* (Baton Rouge, 1970), p. 152, and Kirwan, *Revolt of the Rednecks,* pp. 170–71. For accounts of the distribution of the convict population during the two years following the purchase of Parchman Farm, see *PR,* 1901–3, p. 4, and the Warden's Papers for 1901 and 1902, MDAH, RG 49, vols. 6 and 7.

14. Holmes, *The White Chief,* pp. 151–52. See the share contract between the state and planter H. C. Watson for the year 1897, MDAH, RG 49, vol. 3. For a vivid picture of Bourbon tactics regarding the award of share contracts, see H. J. McLaurin to A. J. McLaurin, Nov. 4, 1895, MDAH, Governor's Papers, Series E, p. 99. For a galling report by a medical examiner of the condition of convicts on one privately owned Delta plantation, see R. D. Farish, M.D., to Penitentiary Board of Control, May 23, 1896, ibid., p. 110.

15. *PR,* 1895–97, p. 92; *Senate Journal,* 1900, p. 33; Kirwan, *Revolt of the Rednecks,* p. 170; Holmes, *The White Chief,* p. 154.

16. Kirwan, *Revolt of the Rednecks,* pp. 171, 174, 308, 312. See Macon *Beacon,* Feb. 15, 1896, for arguments by the African American editor supporting share agreements on fiscal grounds.

17. Holmes, *The White Chief,* pp. 93–96.

18. *Miss. Laws,* 1900, pp. 245–46; Jackson *Clarion-Ledger,* Sept. 5, 1901.

19. *House Journal,* 1902, pp. 58–67; Vicksburg *Herald,* Jan. 9, 15, 22, 1902; Jackson *Clarion-Ledger,* Jan. 16, Feb. 6, 20, 1902; Kirwan, *Revolt of the Rednecks,* pp. 170–71.

20. Jackson *Clarion-Ledger,* Jan. 16, Mar. 6, 1902; *House Journal,* 1902, pp. 146–47, 451–61; *Senate Journal,* 1902, p. 62.

21. *Miss. Laws,* 1902, p. 54; Kirwan, *Revolt of the Rednecks,* pp. 173–74.

22. Kirwan, *Revolt of the Rednecks,* pp. 122–35; Holmes, *The White Chief,* pp. 96–97; E. F. Noel, "Mississippi's Primary Election Law," *MHS* 8 (1904): 239–45.

23. Holmes, *The White Chief,* pp. 101–15. For details of the state's first primary election, see Kirwan, *Revolt of the Rednecks,* pp. 144–61.

24. Holmes, *The White Chief,* xii; N. P. McLemore, "James K. Vardaman, A Mississippi Progressive," *Journal of Mississippi History* [hereafter cited as *JMH*] 29 (Feb. 1967): 2; H. Ladner, "James Kimble Vardaman, Governor of Mississippi, 1904–1908," *JMH* 2 (Oct. 1940): 175; Curtis, "Penitentiary Reform in Mississippi," p. 83. See generally C. Lopez, "James K. Vardaman and the Negro: The Foundation of Mississippi's Racial Policy," *Southern Quarterly* 3 (Jan. 1965): 155–78; and G. Osborn, "A Country Editor Finds Himself: James K. Vardaman Champions Reform," *JMH* 8 (April 1946): 81–93.

25. Holmes, *The White Chief,* pp. 31–32.

26. Greenwood *Commonwealth,* Oct. 17, Nov. 7, 14, 1902.

27. *House Journal,* 1906, pp. 19–20. See M. E. Wolfgang's chapter on Lombroso, F. A. Allen's chapter on Garofalo, and T. Sellin's chapter on Ferri in H. Mannheim, ed., *Pioneers in Criminology,* 2d ed. (Montclair, N.J., 1973), pp. 232–91, 318–40, 361–84.

28. Greenwood *Enterprise,* June 19, Oct. 31, 1890; Mar. 21, July 4, 1891; July 21, 1893; June 29, 1894; and Holmes, *The White Chief,* pp. 30–33, 160. Holmes suggests (pp. 32–33n) that Vardaman "may well have been influenced" by the published views of J. P. Altgeld, governor of Illinois. Altgeld's *Our Penal Machinery and Its Victims* (1884) advanced a deterministic view of criminality and a reformative concept of penology. See R. Ginger, *Altgeld's America: The Lincoln Ideal Versus Changing Realities* (New York, 1958), pp. 65–66.

29. *House Journal,* 1906, pp. 20–22.

30. Ibid., p. 19; Greenwood *Commonwealth,* April 15, May 6, 20, Aug. 12, 1897; Sept. 29, 1899; Jan. 19, 1900; Feb. 22, 1901.

31. *House Journal,* 1906, pp. 19–22. For brief summaries of Vardaman's views on criminality and penology, see Kirwan, *Revolt of the Rednecks,* pp. 172–73, and Holmes, *The White Chief,* pp. 30–33, 159–60.

32. For elaboration, see H. Carter, *Lower Mississippi* (New York, 1942), pp. 289–91; W. C. Harris, *Presidential Reconstruction in Mississippi* (Baton Rouge, 1967), pp. 18–36; and F. E. Smith, *The Yazoo River* (New York, 1954), 169–86.

33. Holmes, *The White Chief,* pp. 4–5.

34. For analysis of the political legacy of Reconstruction, see C. V. Woodward, *The Burden of Southern History,* enl. ed. (Baton Rouge, 1970), pp. 89–107. For Vardaman's support of lynching, see Holmes, *The White Chief,* pp. 36–38, 88–89, 109. See ibid., pp. 132–34, for evidence that, once inaugurated as governor, Vardaman attempted to halt lynching.

35. Holmes, *The White Chief,* pp. 81–90.

36. Ibid., pp 34–39, 88–90, 102–3, 132–33, 187–88, 193–94, 198–99, 285–91, 326–27, 269–70, 384–86. D. M. Oshinsky, *"Worse Than Slavery":* *Parchman Farm and the Ordeal of Jim Crow Justice* (New York, 1996), pp. 23–29, 32–34, 127–33, relates the extraordinary amount of heinous crime in Mississippi during the decades following the Civil War.

37. Jackson *Clarion-Ledger,* Mar. 16, 1905; Kirwan, *Revolt of the Rednecks,* p. 163.

38. See, for example, G. Harris, "A Defense of Governor Vardaman," *Harper's Weekly* 49 (1905): 238.

39. For an account of state educational policy for African Americans in the age of Jim Crow, including comment on Vardaman's views, see N. R. McMillen, *Dark Journey: Black Mississippians in the Age of Jim Crow* (Urbana and Chicago, 1989), pp. 72–108. See generally J. D. Anderson, *The Education of Blacks in the South* (Chapel Hill, N.C., and London, 1988).

40. McMillen, *Dark Journey,* pp. 197–223, constituting the chapter entitled "Jim Crow's Courts."

41. Vardaman advanced this philosophy most succinctly in his address to the legislature of January 1906 (*House Journal,* 1906, pp. 17–23). See also his editorials in the Greenwood *Enterprise,* April 13, 20, 27, 1894.

42. Holmes, *The White Chief,* pp. 54–56, 182.

Chapter 2: Dust in the Delta

1. Holmes, *The White Chief,* p. 150, summarizing articles in the Jackson *Clarion-Ledger,* Nov. 2, 1904, and the Brookhaven *Leader,* Dec. 16, 1905, and also drawing on an interview of May 1, 1968, with J. K. Vardaman Jr.

2. Kirwan, *Revolt of the Rednecks,* pp. 171–72; Holmes, *The White Chief,* pp. 152–54, 158–59; Curtis, "Penitentiary Reform in Mississippi," p. 106. For elaboration, see *PR,* 1903–5, v-viii; "State Penitentiary, 1901-6," MDAH, RG 49, vol. 30, pp. 242–43; Jackson *Clarion-Ledger,* Dec. 7, 9, 14, 20, 21, 1905; Jan. 25, Mar. 8, 1906; and Jackson *Evening News,* Dec. 7, 1905.

3. H. B. Lacey, "The Mississippi Penitentiary System," in *The Official and Statistical Register of the State of Mississippi 1904,* ed. D. Rowland (Nashville, 1904), p. 302.

4. *PR,* 1903–5, v–viii.

5. *House Journal,* 1906, pp. 17–22. See also Kirwan, *Revolt of the Rednecks,* pp. 172–73, and Holmes, *The White Chief,* pp. 159–60.

6. *House Journal,* 1906, pp. 615–28, 916–18, 1328–29. For the minority report, see ibid., pp. 638–44. See also Kirwan, *Revolt of the Rednecks,* pp. 173–74, and Holmes, *The White Chief,* pp. 161–63.

7. *Miss. Laws,* 1906, pp. 142–43; *The Mississippi Code of 1906 . . .* (Nashville, 1906), pp. 1012–13 [hereafter cited as *Code of 1906*]. See also Holmes, *The White Chief,* pp. 165–76, recounting the concessions in educational policy made by Vardaman in return for the package of penitentiary legislation.

8. Interview by author with a former employee of the Mississippi penal system, Parchman, Miss., Oct. 1978 [hereafter cited as Interview 1].

9. *Code of 1906,* p. 1012.

10. Governor Stone had advocated a similar scheme in 1896 (*Senate Journal,* 1896, p. 46).

11. *PR,* 1905–7, pp. 5–6; Board of Trustees Minute Book, 1906–1916, entries of 1906 and 1907, MDAH, RG 49, vol. 31 [hereafter cited as TMB 1906–16].

12. *Miss. Laws,* 1910, p. 160; *PR,* 1907–9, p. 15, and 1909–11, p. 4; "Penitentiary Lands," pp. 32–36.

13. TMB 1906–16, entries of 1907–12, chronicling the tactics of centralization; "Penitentiary Lands," pp. 37–41; *PR,* 1907–9, pp. 4–5.

14. For these and other pertinent statistics, see *PR:* 1905–7, pp. 5, 21, 52; 1907–9, pp. 3, 51–2, 85, 88; 1909–11, pp. 3, 21, 28–46, 49; 1911–13, pp. 3, 35, 54; 1913–15, p. 5; 1931–33, p. 18.

15. *Senate Journal,* 1912, pp. 348–49.

16. *Miss Laws,* 1914, pp. 176–77, and 1916, pp. 52–53; *House Journal,* 1918, pp. 1642–49; *PR,* 1917–19, p. 21.

17. *PR,* 1915–17, pp. 34–37.

18. M. L. Hutson, "Mississippi's State Penal Systems" (master's thesis, University of Mississippi, 1939), pp. 5–7.

19. *PR:* 1913–15, p. 116; 1915–17, pp. 17–19, 194, 207; 1917–19, pp. 120, 124; 1919–21, pp. 126, 134, 136; 1921–23, p. 144; 1923–25,

pp. 143, 146; 1925–27, pp. 139, 148, 151; 1927–29, pp. 4, 140; 1929–31, pp. 4, 129–30, 135; 1931–33, pp. 14, 26. See also L. Q. Stone, "Prison Problems in Mississippi," *Proceedings of the Annual Congress of the American Prison Association . . . 1917* (Indianapolis, n.d.), pp. 111–12 [hereafter cited as *APA 1917*]; *Proceedings of the Annual Congress of the American Prison Association . . . 1921* (New York, n.d.), p. 257 [hereafter cited as *APA 1921*]; *The Annotated Mississippi Code . . . 1917 . . .*, comp. W. Hemingway (Indianapolis, n.d.), p. 2646 [hereafter cited as *Code of 1917*]; and *Miss. Laws*, 1934, p. 359. My interview with a former employee of the Mississippi penal system (Cleveland, Miss., June 1979; hereafter cited as Interview 2) provided information amplifying that provided by the published sources listed above.

20. *PR*, 1915–17, pp. 36–39, 61–62, and 1933–35, p. 6; Hutson, "Mississippi's State Penal Systems," pp. 28–29. For further details on operations, see generally the Board of Trustees Minute Book, 1917–1934, MDAH, RG 47, vol. 28 [hereafter cited as TMB 1917–34].

21. Interviews 1 and 2; *PR:* 1905–7, p. 5; 1907–9, p. 3; 1915–17, p. 5; 1919–21, pp. 5, 8; 1921–23, p. 3; 1923–25, pp. 3, 14; 1925–27, p. 3; 1927–29, pp. 4–5; 1929–31, p. 4; 1931–33, pp. 4, 16–19; 1933–35, p. 15.

22. Interviews 1 and 2; H. J. Zimmerman, "Penal Systems and Penal Reform in the South Since the Civil War" (Ph.D. diss., University of North Carolina, 1947), p. 322; Hutson, "Mississippi's State Penal Systems," p. 38. For statutes mandating convict labor on the levees, see *Miss. Laws:* 1912, pp. 155–56; 1916, pp. 625–26; 1934, p. 569. For specific examples of such labor, see *PR:* 1901–3, p. 7; 1915–17, pp. 40–43; 1927–29, p. 4.

Chapter 3: The Mississippi System

1. Interview 1; *PR*, 1925–27, p. 24; *Proceedings of the 55th Annual Congress of the American Prison Association . . . 1925* (New York, n.d.), p. 80 [hereafter cited as *APA 1925*]; N. B. Bond, *The Treatment of the Dependent, Defective and Delinquent in Mississippi* (n.p., n.d.), pp. 27, 83. The rules and regulations governing convicts were formulated at least as early as 1890, adopted officially in 1907, and mandated by statute without revision in 1934. See *PR*, 1890–91, p. 32; TMB 1906–16, entry of Feb. 8, 1907; and *Miss. Laws*, 1934, pp. 364–65.

2. Interview 2.

3. Published works shedding light on Parchman's early years are scarce, and much of the information in them is dubious owing to an almost universal assumption by authors that what existed at a later time also existed earlier. The same is generally true of unpublished works dealing with Parchman's early years, although some of them contain valuable information. The most useful unpublished works include R. E. Cooley, "A History of the Mississippi Penal

Farm System, 1890–1935: Punishment, Politics and Profit in Penal Affairs" (master's thesis, University of Southern Mississippi, 1981); L. G. Shivers, "A History of the Mississippi Penitentiary" (master's thesis, University of Mississippi, 1930); the already-cited thesis of M. L. Hutson, "Mississippi's State Penal Systems"; a manuscript in Parchman's library by S. Sullivan entitled "Prison Without Walls: A History of Mississippi's Penal System"; a manuscript by W. L. McWhorter entitled "Inmate Society: Legs, Half-Pants and Gunmen: A Study of Inmate Guards at the Mississippi State Penitentiary" (1981); and a manuscript by C. Quarles entitled "A Study of the Mississippi State Correctional System" (1973).

4. Interviews 1 and 2.

5. Ibid.

6. Donald A. Cabana, *Death At Midnight*, pp. 55–56, relates the continuation of this ritual in 1971.

7. Interviews 1 and 2.

8. W. Ferris, *Blues From the Delta* (New York, 1978), pp. 31–33; Alan Lomax, *The Land Where the Blues Began* (New York, 1993), pp. 260, 263. Oshinsky, *"Worse Than Slavery,"* pp. 145–47, offers a representative sample of the calls and the nicknames of the callers. Further information is located in "Parchman Folder," 76–13–4, David Cohn Collection, University of Mississippi Archives, Oxford, Miss.

9. Oshinsky, *"Worse Than Slavery,"* p. 30, quoting L. W. Levine, *Black Culture and Black Consciousness* (New York, 1977), pp. 212–15, and Lomax, *Land Where the Blues Began*, p. 263.

10. Interviews 1 and 2.

11. Ibid.

12. Ibid.; *APA 1925*, p. 85; Hutson, "Mississippi's State Penal Systems," p. 20.

13. Interviews 1 and 2; *Senate Journal*, 1924, pp. 888–89.

14. Interview 2.

15. Interviews 1 and 2.

16. Ibid.; *PR*, 1888–89, pp. 11, 14; *Proceedings of the American Prison Association . . . 1910* (Indianapolis, 1910), pp. 123–24 [hereafter cited as *APA 1910*]; Bond, *The Treatment of the Dependent, Defective and Delinquent in Mississippi*, pp. 87–88; Hutson, "Mississippi's State Penal Systems," p. 6. See Cabana, *Death at Midnight*, pp. 58–61, for an account of a driver and his shooters handling a rabbit in the row in 1971.

17. Interviews 1 and 2.

18. Interview 2; *Miss. Laws*, 1922, pp. 323–24, and 1928, p. 216; Bond, *The Treatment of the Dependent, Defective and Delinquent in Mississippi*, p. 87. Between 1907 and 1922 there were 157 discharges for "meritorious service" and only 123 suspended sentences. Between 1922 and 1929, 294 suspended

sentences were granted. See *PR:* 1907–9, p. 88; 1909–11, p. 49; 1911–13, p. 54; 1913–15, p. 116; 1915–17, pp. 194, 207; 1917–19, pp. 120, 124; 1919–21, pp. 126, 133; 1921–23, pp. 143–44; 1923–25, pp. 143, 145; 1925–27, pp. 148, 150; 1927–29, p. 140; 1929–31, p. 129; 1931–33, p. 14. For data on attempted escapes, see *PR,* 1919–21, p. 143, and 1923–25, pp. 143 and 145. See also *House Journal,* 1930, p. 12, for comment by the governor.

19. Interviews 1 and 2; *PR,* 1903–5, p. 256; *House Journal,* 1910, p. 59, and 1916, p. 47; *Senate Journal,* 1912, p. 24, and 1920, pp. 349, 929, 955, 1595–97; *Miss. Laws:* 1916, pp. 138–39; 1922, p. 357; 1924, pp. 222, 589; Jackson *Weekly Clarion-Ledger,* Aug. 4, 1910; Hutson, "Mississippi's State Penal Systems," p. 42; L. T. Balsamo, "Theodore G. Bilbo and Mississippi Politics, 1877–1932" (Ph.D. diss., University of Missouri, 1967), pp. 95–96; W. D. McCain, "The Triumph of Democracy, 1916–1932," in R. A. McLemore, ed., *A History of Mississippi,* 2 vols. (Hattiesburg, Miss., 1973), 2: 59–62; P. B. Foreman and J. R. Tatum, "A Short History of Mississippi's State Penal Systems, *Mississippi Law Journal* 10 (April 1938): 271.

20. F. Wallace, "A History of the Conner Administration" (master's thesis, Mississippi College, 1959), pp. 59–60.

21. Drawing on the pardon files at MDAH, Oshinsky, *"Worse Than Slavery,"* pp. 181–86, quotes from correspondence relating to clemency for black convicts but omits any reference to that relating to white convicts.

22. Interviews 1 and 2.

23. The famous song, of course, is "The Midnight Special." This verse appears in all recorded versions known to me, although slight variations in wording appear in some of them.

24. See, for example, Jackson *Clarion-Ledger,* May 12, 1940, describing Governor Paul Johnson's "mercy court" proceedings at Parchman.

25. Jackson *Daily Clarion-Ledger,* Nov. 2, 1915, Oct. 31, 1933; W. F. Minor, "They Ate Their Way to Freedom," *The Times-Picayune New Orleans States Magazine,* Jan. 9, 1949; P. de Kruif, *Hunger Fighters: A Social History of Pellagra in the South* (Westport, Conn., 1972), pp. 92–96.

26. Jackson *Daily Clarion-Ledger,* Jan. 1, 20, 1932.

27. *PR:* 1907–9, p. 88; 1909–11, p. 49; 1911–13, p. 54; 1913–15, p. 116; 1915–17, pp. 194, 207; 1917–19, pp. 120, 124; 1919–21, pp. 126, 133; 1921–23, pp. 143–44; 1923–25, pp. 143, 145; 1925–27, pp. 148, 150; 1927–29, p. 140; 1929–31, p. 129; 1931–33, p. 14.

28. Oshinsky, *"Worse Than Slavery,"* p. 226; Jackson *Clarion-Ledger,* Jan. 15, 1936, and Mar. 14, 1939; Interviews 1 and 2; interview by author with a former convict who served time at Parchman from the late 1930s until the early 1950s, Jackson, Miss., June 1984 [hereafter cited as Interview 3].

29. Jackson *Clarion-Ledger,* Jan. 16, 1938.

30. Interview 1; Hutson, "Mississippi's State Penal Systems," p. 32.

31. Interview 2.

32. C. B. Hopper, *Sex in Prison: The Mississippi Experiment with Conjugal Visiting* (Baton Rouge, 1969), pp. 52–81.

33. Interview 1. For a similar assessment, see Hopper, *Sex in Prison,* p. 95.

34. Hopper, *Sex in Prison,* pp. 79–80.

35. Interview by author with a former employee of the Mississippi penal system, Hattiesburg, Miss., May 1995 [hereafter cited as Interview 4].

36. The passage cited here, as well as other descriptive comment about the state penitentiary, is available in the Works Progress Administration publication *Mississippi: A Guide to the Magnolia State* (1938).

37. Interview 1.

38. Interviews 1, 2, and 4.

39. Hutson, "Mississippi's State Penal Systems," pp. 22–23; Bond, *The Treatment of the Dependent, Defective and Delinquent in Mississippi,* p. 85; Hopper, *Sex in Prison,* p. 35.

40. *APA 1910,* p. 124.

41. *PR:* 1909–11, p. 51; 1911–13, pp. 54–55; 1913–15, p. 120; 1915–17, p. 196; 1917–19, p. 22; 1919–21, p. 130; 1921–23, p. 147; 1923–25, p. 137; 1925–27, p. 140; 1927–29, p. 141.

42. Oshinsky, *"Worse Than Slavery,"* p. 150, quoting Lomax, *Land Where the Blues Began,* p. 257. Both authors accept the same convict's allegation that "They'd kill um like that," notwithstanding the fact that nobody (including the convict who made the allegation to Lomax, the triumphant convict-plaintiffs in the first round of *Gates v. Collier,* or the considerable number of convicts who have subsequently filed suit in federal court) has ever provided the name of a single person killed by Black Annie. An allegation of homicide resulting from the application of a blunt strap to the "naked butt" of a human being is suspicious on biological grounds alone, and only one of the twenty-two convicts I interviewed for this book made such an allegation. When asked to name the murdered parties, however, the convict quickly recanted, explaining that he had "just heard tell of it" (interview by author with a convict serving time at Parchman, Parchman, Miss., May 1979; hereafter cited as Interview 5).

43. Interview 4.

44. Ibid., and Interviews 1, 2, and 3.

45. One "Lundy," writing in the June 1957 number of Parchman's inmate newspaper, *Inside World,* provides a good account of this phenomenon. Oshinsky, *"Worse Than Slavery,"* p. 190, goes much further, albeit without documentation, stating: "And some prisoners took matters into their own hands, quite literally, by drinking poison, slitting their wrists, severing Achilles tendons, or chopping off a limb, a process of self-mutilation known as

'knockin' a joe.'" I have found no evidence to support such a statement, although it seems reasonable to speculate that inmates at Parchman, like those of all prisons and indeed many members of free-world society, sometimes poisoned and mutilated themselves.

46. Jackson *Weekly Clarion-Ledger*, Oct. 7, 1909.

47. Interview 4; *Jackson Daily News*, Jan. 28, 1952. See also Oshinsky, *"Worse Than Slavery,"* p. 151.

48. *PR:* 1905–7, pp. 21, 52; 1907–9, pp. 51, 85; 1909–11, pp. 26, 46; 1931–33, p. 18, the latter depicting financial accounts from 1911 through 1933.

49. *House Journal*, 1910, p. 20; *PR*, 1923–25, p. 14.

50. Quoted by Jackson *Daily Clarion-Ledger*, June 23, 1914.

51. Quoted from the record jacket of Lomax's album, *Negro Prison Songs from the Mississippi State Penitentiary*, released by Tradition Records in 1947.

52. David Cohn, *Where I Was Born and Raised* (South Bend, Ind., 1967), pp. 103, 110. Oshinsky, *"Worse Than Slavery,"* p. 136, suggests that Cohn's account "may have been apocryphal" because "White Southerners liked to believe that blacks did not much mind going to prison—that there was no shame to it, no loss of status, no fear of what lay ahead." This judgment, which is offered without documentation, implies that white Mississippians did not regard their penitentiary as punitive. That is certainly not true; and oddly enough, it seems to run counter to the entire thesis of Professor Oshinsky's book: that white Mississippians hated blacks and maliciously imposed on them a prison that was "worse than slavery." At any rate, all evidence confirms that the lifestyle of black convicts incarcerated at Parchman Farm during the early decades of the century was remarkably similar to that of the great majority of *employed* African Americans in free-world Mississippi.

53. Interview 4.

54. Interviews 1 and 2.

55. Kirwan, *Revolt of the Rednecks*, pp. 174–75.

56. For Noel's efforts, see *Senate Journal*, 1910, p. 18, and 1912, p. 24; *House Journal*, 1910, p. 59; and Jackson *Weekly Clarion-Ledger*, Aug. 4, 1910. For Brewer's efforts, see *Senate Journal*, 1912, p. 124; *House Journal*, 1912, pp. 861–62; and Cooley, "A History of the Mississippi Penal Farm System," pp. 103–5. For Whitfield's efforts, see *Senate Journal*, 1924, pp. 201, 212–14, and 1926, pp. 295–98. For Bilbo's efforts, see Balsamo, "Theodore G. Bilbo and Mississippi Politics," pp. 95–96; McCain, "The Triumph of Democracy," pp. 59–62; and Cooley, "A History of the Mississippi Penal Farm System, 1890–1935," pp. 107–9. See also Bilbo's speech to the legislature in *Senate Journal*, 1917, p. 43.

57. For numerous examples of Yerger's, Thames's, and Montgomery's efforts on behalf of the convicts, see TMB 1906–16 and TMB 1917–34.

58. Jackson *Daily Clarion-Ledger,* Mar. 15, 1936.

59. For Montgomery's remarks, which were addressed to the senate penitentiary committee, see ibid., Mar. 13, 1934. For numerous examples of her efforts on behalf of the convicts, see generally the entries of 1926–34 in TMB 1917–34.

60. For examples of Williamson's efforts, see *PR,* 1929–31, p. 22, and 1931–33, p. 13. For examples of Fox's criticism of the legislature and recommendations for reform, see ibid., 1923–25, pp. 14–15, and 1925–27, p. 28.

61. For information on the embezzlement scandal, see "Pen Board President Demands Changes," *Mississippi State Penitentiary Investigation* (1914); *Senate Journal,* 1914, pp. 65–66; TMB 1906–16, pp. 498–500; Balsamo, "Theodore G. Bilbo and Mississippi Politics," pp. 80–82; Holmes, *The White Chief,* pp. 328–29; Kirwan, *Revolt of the Rednecks,* pp. 237–39; and C. M. Morgan, *Redneck Liberal: Theodore G. Bilbo and the New Deal* (Baton Rouge and London, 1985), p. 36. For information on the official negligence that resulted in the fatal fire at Oakley, see *Senate Journal,* 1914, pp. 1430–31.

62. See generally TMB 1906–16 and TMB 1917–34, for occasional notations concerning abuses by employees. See also "Pen Board President Demands Charges of Brutality Be Probed," MDAH, subject file: "Penitentiary, 1840–1938."

63. *Senate Journal,* 1908, pp. 27–28, 32–33; *PR,* 1927–29, p. 143; Bond, *The Treatment of the Dependent, Defective and Delinquent in Mississippi,* p. 9; B. McKelvey, *American Prisons: A History of Good Intentions* (Montclair, N.J., 1977), p. 85.

64. *APA 1925,* p. 84; Interview 2.

65. Interviews 1, 2, and 4.

66. J. L. Gillem, *Taming the Criminal: Adventures in Penology* (New York, 1931), p. 13; Bond, *The Treatment of the Dependent, Defective and Delinquent in Mississippi,* p. 91.

67. Holmes, *The White Chief,* pp. 328–30; Kirwan, *Revolt of the Rednecks,* pp. 237–39. The Parchman and O'Keefe land deals had two things in common: both delivered clearly inferior land with poor drainage at premium prices, and both involved very suspicious political appointments. Immediately after the purchase of Parchman Farm, J. M. Parchman was appointed warden; and Ernest J. O'Keefe, who served as superintendent from 1915 to 1921, was actually the chief executive officer of the state penal system when the floodplain his family owned, the O'Keefe Farm, was purchased by the state. Interestingly, neither land deal and neither appointment came during the years when Vardaman held sway.

68. *PR,* 1925–27, p. 28; *Senate Journal:* 1917, p. 43; 1924, p. 212; 1930, pp. 12–13; P. W. Garrett and A. H. MacCormick, *Handbook of American Prisons and Reformatories, 1929* (New York, 1929), p. 257.

69. *Proceedings of the Annual Congress of the American Prison Association. . . 1919* (Indianapolis, 1919), p. 210; *House Journal*, 1930, pp. 601–3, and 1932, p. 55; Jackson *Daily Clarion-Ledger*, May 3, Oct. 24, 1933; *PR:* 1919–21, p. 5; 1921–23, pp. 3, 12–20; 1923–25, pp. 12–22; 1925–27, pp. 20–28; 1927–29, pp. 15–18; 1931–33, pp. 3–11.

Chapter 4: The Magnolia New Deal

1. See generally *PR*, 1931–33. For Trustee Montgomery's assessment, see Jackson *Daily Clarion-Ledger*, Mar. 13, 1936.

2. *PR*, 1931–33, p. 18.

3. For evidence of the unfolding political duel between Conner and Montgomery, see Jackson *Daily Clarion-Ledger*, Nov. 8, 1933; Jan. 6, 16, 25, Feb. 4, 7, 27, Mar. 2, 4, 1934. For reports of the final deliberations of the legislature, see ibid., Mar. 2, 4, 13, 23, 1934; *House Journal*, 1934, pp. 433–35; and *Senate Journal*, 1934, pp. 662–64, 686, 693, 726.

4. *Miss. Laws,* 1934, pp. 347–70. See also Cooley, "A History of the Mississippi Penal Farm System, 1890–1935," pp. 140–43; Bond, *The Treatment of the Dependent, Defective and Delinquent in Mississippi*, p. 87; Hutson, "Mississippi's State Penal Systems," p. 6; and R. F. Saucier, "A History of the Mississippi Penal System, 1935–1970" (master's thesis, University of Southern Mississippi, 1982), pp. 1–2, 4–5.

5. Jackson *Daily Clarion-Ledger*, Mar. 23, June 7, 1934.

6. Ibid., Mar. 13, April 14, 1934; *PR*, 1933–35, p. 18.

7. Jackson *Daily Clarion-Ledger*, July 5, 6, 20, 22, 1934.

8. Ibid., Nov. 5, 1936; Nov. 5, 1937; Board of Commissioners Minute Book, 1944–1959, MDAH, RG 49, vol. 27, entry of Oct. 4, 1950 [hereafter cited as CMB 1944–59].

9. For an account of the "hands-off" doctrine that shielded state penal systems from judicial intrusion until the late 1960s, see Taylor, *Brokered Justice*, p. 194.

10. Interviews 2 and 4; interview by author with a former employee of the Mississippi penal system, Clarksdale, Miss., Dec. 1980 [hereafter cited as Interview 6]; interview by author with a former employee of the Mississippi penal system, Cleveland, Miss., Dec. 1980 [hereafter cited as Interview 7]; interview by author with a former state legislator, Jackson, Miss., Feb. 1980 [hereafter cited as Interview 8]; interview by author with a convict who worked in Parchman's guest house during the forties, Natchez, Miss., May 1980 [hereafter cited as Interview 9].

11. Interviews 2, 3, and 7.

12. Jackson *Daily Clarion-Ledger*, Feb. 4, 1934.

13. Ibid., Jan. 27, 1936; Oct. 22, 1937; Jan. 26, 1938; Jan. 16, 1940; Jackson *Clarion-Ledger,* Nov. 18, 1942; July 1, 1944; Feb. 26, Aug. 24, 1952.

14. Jackson *Daily Clarion-Ledger,* Mar. 24, 1935; Nov. 20, 21, 1940; *PR,* 1939–41, p. 3.

15. *PR,* 1933–35, pp. 3–5, 12, 18–20, 46, 51.

16. Ibid., p. 3; Jackson *Daily Clarion-Ledger,* Jan. 31, Mar. 29, 1935.

17. Ibid., Jan. 10, 23, 1936.

18. *PR,* 1937–39, pp. 3–5; 1939–41, pp. 4–6.

19. Jackson *Daily Clarion-Ledger,* April 1, 1937; Jan. 16, 1940; *PR:* 1935–37, pp. 3, 22; 1937–39, pp. 3, 20, 25–26; 1939–41, pp. 16–17.

20. Ibid., 1939–41, p. 3.

21. Jackson *Daily Clarion-Ledger,* Nov. 13, 14, 1941; *Senate Journal,* 1941, p. 84.

22. *PR,* 1941–43, pp. 4–5; Jackson *Clarion-Ledger,* Oct. 29, 1942.

23. *PR,* 1941–43, pp. 20, 34.

24. Jackson *Clarion-Ledger,* Dec. 6, 1943.

25. *PR:* 1941–43, pp. 30, 34; 1943–45, pp. 3, 21, 23; *Senate Journal,* 1944, pp. 15–16.

26. For pithy accounts of the progression of criminological thought, see F. P. Williams III and M. D. McShane, *Criminological Theory,* 2d ed (Englewood Cliffs, N.J., 1994), and W. B. Pelfrey, *The Evolution of Criminology* (Cincinnati, 1980). For an account of related developments that transformed penology into "corrections," see McKelvey, *American Prisons,* pp. 34–196, 234–67.

27. Ibid., pp. 10, 27, 49, 238, 292, 300–310.

28. Garrett and MacCormick, *Handbook of American Prisons and Reformatories,* pp. 527–29. See also Foreman and Tatum, "A Short History of Mississippi's State Penal Systems," pp. 271–72.

29. For editorials in the Jackson *Daily Clarion-Ledger* and Jackson *Clarion-Ledger* defending corporal punishment, see the editions of Nov. 8, 1934, July 20, 1935, and May 7, 1936. For defenses of the trusty system, see the editions of July 14 and 16, Aug. 1, and Oct. 19, 1934. For defenses of the suspension system and attacks on the concept of parole, see the editions of Sept. 2, 1934; Jan. 2, Mar. 28, 31, 1935; Jan. 7, Feb. 21, 1937; Sept. 3, 1938; Mar. 19, April 18, 1939; and Dec. 18, 1940. For criticism of the state-use system of prison labor, see the edition of Mar. 4, 1936. For defenses of the penitentiary's organization and physical arrangements, see the editions of Dec. 22, 1942, and Dec. 6, 1943.

30. Ibid., Mar. 5, 8, 1937.

31. Ibid., June 16, 1938. See also the editions of June 25, 1935; May 15, 1938; and Nov. 5, 9, 1940.

32. Ibid., Nov. 17, 19, 1940.

33. Ibid., Sept. 3, 1938; Jan. 9, 1941.

34. Ibid., Nov. 26, 1941. See also Howard A. McDonnell, *In the Throes of Criminal Justice* (Bryn Mawr, Penn., 1986).

35. *Miss. Laws,* 1940, pp. 73, 711–13; 1942, pp. 38, 384–86. For an account of the state's drift toward the establishment of a reformatory for black youth, see Jackson *Clarion-Ledger,* Jan. 15, 1950.

36. *Senate Journal,* 1938, pp. 891, 912, 918; *PR,* 1937–39, p. 6; Jackson *Daily Clarion-Ledger,* Nov. 13, 1936; April 12, 1939; May 4, 1940; Nov. 26, 1941.

37. Interviews 7 and 8.

38. Jackson *Daily Clarion-Ledger,* Aug. 9, Nov. 10, 1940; Dec. 8, 1941; Mar. 14, May 13, 16, Sept. 19, 1942; Jan. 6, 1944; *House Journal,* 1942, pp. 361–63; *Senate Journal,* 1942, pp. 427, 701; *Miss. Laws,* 1942, pp. 62–63.

39. Interviews 7 and 9; *PR,* 1943–45, p. 5; Jackson *Clarion-Ledger,* Feb. 19, 1942; Feb. 8, 1944.

40. Interviews 7 and 8.

41. Jackson *Clarion-Ledger,* Sept. 14, 1941; Mar. 10, 11, 20, June 20, 1943; Feb. 8, 1944; *Senate Journal,* 1944, p. 5; *PR,* 1941–43, pp. 6–7.

Chapter 5: A Little of This, a Little of That

1. *House Journal,* 1944, pp. 62–63; Jackson *Clarion-Ledger,* Jan. 19, 21, 22, Feb. 8, 17, 25, 27, 1944.

2. Ibid., Feb. 18, 19, 27, 1944.

3. For reports on the progress of the parole bill and comment by legislators, see ibid., Jan. 21, Feb. 8, 17, 22, Mar. 14, 1944. For the parole statute, see *Miss. Laws,* 1944, pp. 574–79. For the debates on the accompanying penitentiary bill, see *Senate Journal,* 1944, pp. 780–81. For the journalistic criticism, see Jackson *Clarion-Ledger,* Mar. 26, 1944.

4. *Miss. Laws,* 1944, pp. 554–71.

5. *Senate Journal,* 1944, pp. 190–91, 578–83; Jackson *Clarion-Ledger,* Feb. 22, 1944.

6. Ibid., July 1, 7, 1944.

7. For comment on Wiggins's managerial skills and assessments of the efficiency of his staff, see *PR,* 1947–49, pp. 8–9, 12; 1951–53, p. 21; and Jackson *Clarion-Ledger,* Jan. 2, 1951; Feb. 26, Aug. 24, 1952.

8. Interviews 2, 6, 7, 8, and 9.

9. Interviews 2, 6, 7, and 8.

10. Ibid.

11. Interviews 7 and 8; *PR:* 1943–45, p. 3; 1945–47, pp. 3–4; 1947–49, p. 4; 1949–51, pp. 3, 15; Jackson *Clarion-Ledger,* Jan. 16, Sept. 18, 1946; Jan. 19, 1947; July 31, Nov. 9, 1948; July 24, Oct. 14, 1949.

12. Ibid., Dec. 10, 1944; Aug. 30, 1946; Dec. 19, 1947; Nov. 9, 1948; CMB 1944–59, entry of Jan. 6, 1948; *PR:* 1945–47, pp. 3–5; 1947–49, pp. 3, 7–8.

13. See, for example, Jackson *Clarion-Ledger,* Jan. 27, Feb. 12, Mar. 2, May 6, June 29, Sept. 17, Oct 12, 30, 1943; Jan. 12, Feb. 4, Oct. 24, Nov. 4, 5, 7, 1944; Mar. 9, April 24, 30, Dec. 16, 18, 1945; Jan. 27, Feb. 5, 13, May 7, July 10, Nov 24, 1946; Jan. 26, 28, Feb. 2, 13, Mar. 1, 31, April 13, 1947; Mar. 4, Nov. 27, Dec. 30, 31, 1948.

14. Ibid., Jan. 18, Mar. 11, June 30, Nov. 29, 1946, Jan. 21, Dec. 8, 1947; *Senate Journal,* 1946, p. 640.

15. Interview 7; Jackson *Clarion-Ledger,* Jan. 19, 1947, reporting one of Wiggins's accommodating responses to the criticism of his detractors.

16. Interview 7.

17. Jackson *Clarion-Ledger,* Oct. 7, 1944.

18. Ibid., Aug. 8, Sept. 27, 1946.

19. Ibid., Jan. 19, 1947.

20. *PR,* 1945–47, p. 11; interview by author with a former convict who served time at Parchman, Natchez, Miss., Feb. 1982 [hereafter cited as Interview 10].

21. CMB 1944–59, entries of May 1, Sept. 4, 1945; Interviews 7 and 10.

22. Jackson *Clarion-Ledger,* Aug. 18, 1946.

23. Ibid., Jan. 19, 1947; *PR,* 1945–47, p. 11; Interview 10.

24. Jackson *Clarion-Ledger,* Dec. 11, 1945; June 14, 1948; April 19, 1952; CMB 1944–59, entry of Mar. 5, 1946; *PR:* 1945–47, p. 11; 1949–51, p. 25; 1951–53, p. 39.

25. For the progress of the parole board during its first five years of operation, see the agency's published biennial reports: 1944–45, p. 3; 1945–47, pp. 3–4; and 1947–49, p. 2. See also *PR:* 1943–45, p. 16; 1945–47, p. 6; CMB 1944–59, entry of Jan. 2, 1945; and Jackson *Clarion-Ledger,* Jan. 16, July 7, Dec. 15, 1946; Jan. 19, 1947; Jan. 9, 1949.

26. Interview 7; CMB 1944–59, entry of Mar. 5, 1946.

27. *Hattiesburg American,* May 3, 1947; Jackson *Clarion-Ledger,* May 4, Dec. 17, 19, 1947.

28. Interviews 7 and 8.

29. Interview 8.

30. Ibid.; Jackson *Clarion-Ledger,* Mar. 20, 23, 24, May 10, 1948.

31. *Miss. Laws,* 1948, pp. 640–65, 704–7. See *Senate Journal,* 1948, pp. 155, 191, 381, for accounts of unsuccessful attempts to abolish the strap, to employ a music teacher, and to establish a probation system and an "honor camp" for meritorious convicts.

32. Interviews 7 and 8; Jackson *Clarion-Ledger,* Mar. 23, 24, 1948.

33. Interview 7; *PR,* 1947–49, p. 7.

34. *Miss. Laws,* 1948, p. 54; Jackson *Clarion-Ledger,* Nov. 28, 1948; *PR:* 1947–49, pp. 4, 5, 11; 1949–51, pp. 3, 17–18; 1951–53, pp. 3–4, 15.

35. Jackson *Clarion-Ledger,* July 31, 1948; *PR:* 1947–49, pp. 3–4, 7–8, 10; 1949–51, p. 13.

36. Ibid, 1947–49, p. 4; Jackson *Clarion-Ledger,* Nov. 9, 1948; July 24, Oct. 14, 1949.

37. Ibid., Feb. 19, 1944.

38. Ibid., April 3, 1945; Jan. 16, Sept. 18, Nov. 27, 1946; Jan. 19, Nov. 2, 1947; July 31, 1948; *PR:* 1945–47, p. 4; 1947–49, pp. 4–5, 10; 1949–51, pp. 3, 15. See the Christmas Day menu in Jackson *Clarion-Ledger,* Dec. 25, 1945.

39. *PR:* 1943–45, p. 10; 1945–47, pp. 17, 19; 1947–49, pp. 26, 29; 1949–51, pp. 30, 33; 1951–53, pp. 7, 12; Jackson *Clarion-Ledger,* Jan. 2, 1951.

40. Interviews 7 and 10.

41. *PR:* 1947–49, p. 21; 1949–51, p. 25; Jackson *Clarion-Ledger,* June 28, 1950.

42. Interviews 1, 7, 9, and 10; *PR,* 1949–51, p. 27.

43. Ibid., 1947–49, p. 20.

44. Ibid., 1949–51, pp. 24, 26–7; 1951–53, p. 41; Jackson *Clarion-Ledger,* Dec. 1, 1949.

45. *PR:* 1947–49, pp. 23–4; 1949–51, p. 25.

46. Ibid., 1951–53, p. 6; Interview 6; interview by author with a former convict who served time at Parchman, Leland, Miss., April 1982 [hereafter cited as Interview 11].

47. *PR,* 1949–51, pp. 13, 25; CMB 1944–59, entry of April 5, 1949.

48. *PR,* 1947–49, p. 25; Jackson *Clarion-Ledger,* Dec. 3, 12, 1946; Dec. 13, 1947; May 10, 11, Dec. 2, 1948; Oct. 6, 1950; Nov. 25, 1952.

49. For reports on the penitentiary's kennel and the methods employed in the event of escapes, see Jackson *Daily Clarion-Ledger,* May 15, 1938, and Jackson *Clarion-Ledger,* Jan. 26, 1958. For official statistics on escapes, see *PR:* 1939–41, pp. 22, 27; 1941–43, pp. 9, 14; 1943–45, pp. 7, 10; 1945–47, pp. 17, 19; 1947–49, pp. 26, 29; 1949–51, pp. 30, 33; 1951–53, p. 12.

50. Jackson *Clarion-Ledger,* Jan. 31, 1947.

Chapter 6: High Tide

1. Interviews 6, 7, and 8; interview by author with a former employee of the penal system, Jackson, Miss., May 1995 [hereafter cited as Interview 12].

2. Interview 12. See Cabana, *Death at Midnight,* pp. 165–66, for brief comment on Wiggins's political clout in Jackson and the lofty opinion of his penitentiary held by professional penologists.

3. Interview 12.

4. Interviews 6, 7, 8, 9, 10, 11, and 12.

5. Interview 8; Jackson *Clarion-Ledger,* Aug. 24, 1952.

6. Interview 12.

7. Oshinsky, *"Worse Than Slavery,"* pp. 166–68, 193–94, tells of the legendary Wagner and Mullins. For an example of journalistic exploitation, see Jackson *Clarion-Ledger,* Jan. 12, 1950, relating one of the brutish Mullins's successful collars.

8. *The Mansion,* pp. 48–49; E. Newhall, "Prisons and Prisoners in the Works of William Faulkner" (Ph.D. diss., UCLA, 1975).

9. Quoted by P. Oliver, *Blues Fell This Morning* (New York, 1960), p. 200. Black Mississippians were hardly alone in fearing the "Long-Chain Man." Among those who grew up with me in the Mississippi Delta during the early fifties, the word was that Long-Chain Charlie would "gitcha if ya don't watch out."

10. The terrified victim of the troubled father and the judge was the author of this book, but I was by no means the only youngster on whom such tactics were employed. Working in the cotton rows outside Greenwood, I heard black parents raise the specter of Parchman Farm when their children got lazy or careless in the fields; and at school one day, a police officer wound down his pitch for law and order, reminded the class of Parchman Farm, pointed his finger at us, and remarked threateningly: "Them sergeants up there will make you think the principal's paddle was a lot of fun."

11. For a modern account of the legend surrounding prison graveyards, this one addressing the unmarked graves at the Louisiana State Penitentiary at Angola, see New Orleans *Times-Picayune,* Oct. 14, 1990.

12. Interview 1.

13. Ibid.

14. Interview 12.

15. Jackson *Clarion-Ledger,* Aug. 6, 1950.

16. Interview 12.

17. Interview by author with the wife of a former employee of the Mississippi penal system, Drew, Miss., May 1982 [hereafter cited as Interview 13].

18. Interview 12.

19. The lynching of blacks by white mobs was certainly widespread in the South during the last years of the nineteenth century and the early years of the twentieth, but lynchings diminished appreciably as the new century progressed. On May 12, 1940, a leader in the Jackson *Clarion-Ledger* proclaimed proudly and accurately: "Not A Lynching In South Over A Full 12–Month Period."

20. Interviews 7, 12, and 13. Subsequent quotations in the next few paragraphs are also from these interviews.

21. Interview 12.

22. Ibid. For a recent account of this phenomenon, see J. Timilty, *Prison Journal* (Boston, 1997).

23. Interview 12. See Cabana, *Death at Midnight,* pp. 41–42, for favorable comment on the role of manual labor in convict management at Parchman.

24. For a good summary of the operant learning theory propounded by Skinner and more recently given criminological application by C. Ray Jeffrey, and of the related "social learning theory" advanced by Robert Akers, see Williams and McShane, *Criminological Theory,* pp. 118–27. For a good summary of the manifestation of such theory in the evolution of progressive stages within prisons and reformatories, see Max Grunhut, *Penal Reform* (1948; reprint, Montclair, N.J., 1972), pp. 83–94. See also W. B. Taylor's chapter on Maconochie's "Mark system" and E. E. Dooley's chapter on Crofton's "Irish system" in "The Foundations of Modern Penal Practice: A Symposium," comp. W. B. Taylor, in *New England Journal of Prison Law* 7 (Winter 1981): pp. 54–96.

25. Interview 12.

26. Interview 3.

27. Interviews 3, 9, 10, and 11.

28. Jackson *Clarion-Ledger,* Oct. 9, 1953.

29. Interview 3. See Cabana, *Death at Midnight,* p. 42, for a favorable assessment of the effectiveness of Parchman's shooters. Oshinsky, *"Worse Than Slavery,"* pp. 141–42, lists the several known disasters involving trusties at Parchman.

30. Interview 12. McWhorter, "Inmate Society," pp. 10–26, gives a good general account of the shooter system.

31. Interview 12. See Jackson *Clarion-Ledger,* May 22, 1987, for Alan Lomax's remarks on the high profile of dogs at Parchman.

32. Ibid.; Jackson *Clarion-Ledger,* May 16, 1952.

33. Interview 7. Oshinsky, *"Worse Than Slavery,"* p. 150, states: "Escape attempts carried an unspeakable penalty: a whipping without limits." The only documentation offered to support this statement is Superintendent Oliver Tann's account of the measures he took in 1935 when a mass breakout in a white cage resulted in the murder of a shooter: "I had whippings given to the eight we caught who weren't wounded. Before the young ringleader confessed, I had him lashed on the buttocks, calves, and palms, then gave him fifteen lashes on the soles of his feet. This cleared his mind" (Memphis *Commercial Appeal,* July 29, 1953). In no way does Tann's account of the manner in which he dealt with the murder of a trusty by convicts in 1935 confirm the existence of a uniform policy mandating "a whipping without limits" whenever convicts attempted to escape. Indeed, all parties whom I interviewed for this book found such a suggestion puerile. After the construction of Parchman's maximum security unit in the mid-fifties, captured rabbits were uniformly sent

to the hole. See Cabana, *Death at Midnight,* pp. 63, 139, confirming that both rabbits and convicts who bucked the line were sent to the maximum security unit when he arrived at Parchman in 1971.

34. Interview 7. See also Oshinsky, *"Worse Than Slavery,"* p. 144, confirming the later existence of this policy via an interview with convict Robert Phillips.

35. Interviews 6, 7, and 12. Cabana, *Death at Midnight,* pp. 139–41, relates his reinstatement of this policy during the 1980s.

36. Interview 12.

37. Jackson *Clarion-Ledger,* July 12, 1953.

38. Ibid., Oct. 9, 1953.

39. Ibid., July 12, 1953.

40. Ibid., Feb. 3, 1955; May 9, 1956.

41. Interview 12.

42. Ibid.

43. Ibid. ; Oshinsky, *"Worse Than Slavery,"* pp. 139–41.

44. Interviews 3, 4, 5, 6, 7, 9, and 12.

45. See Cabana, *Death at Midnight,* pp. 63–64, 69–71, for interesting comment on the relationships that existed among sergeants, drivers, shooters, and cagebosses in 1971.

46. Interview 11.

47. Interview 10; interview by author with a female who served time at Parchman during the 1950s, Natchez, Miss., Jan. 1983 [hereafter cited as Interview 14]. See also Cabana, *Death at Midnight,* p. 50, for comment on the cage economy that existed in the early 1970s.

48. All parties interviewed gave this account of Parchman's "snitch system," and former driver, warden, and acting commissioner of corrections Donald A. Cabana confirms that it was alive and well in the early 1970s. Hereafter my interviews with Cabana, which were conducted intermittently for almost a decade, are cited as "Cabana Interviews."

49. Interview by author with a former employee of the Mississippi penal system, Jackson, Miss., May 1984 [hereafter cited as Interview 15].

50. Oshinsky, *"Worse Than Slavery,"* p. 227, drawing on interviews with convicts Horace Carter and Matthew Winter, the latter being one of the original plaintiffs in *Gates v. Collier.*

51. Jackson *Clarion-Ledger,* Feb. 26, Aug. 24, 1952.

52. Interview 7; Jackson *Clarion-Ledger,* Sept. 24, 1958, quoting Superintendent Bill Harpole.

Chapter 7: Parchman Under Siege

1. Jackson *Clarion-Ledger,* Jan. 17, 1952, reporting Alexander's critical speech.

2. Interview by author with a former state legislator, Jackson, Miss., Mar. 1986 [hereafter cited as Interview 16].

3. Jackson *Clarion-Ledger,* May 23, Aug. 6, Dec. 23, 1950; Jan. 2, 20, 1951; *True Detective* 54 (Dec. 1950): 40–43, 69–71.

4. Interview 16.

5. Jackson *Clarion-Ledger,* Jan. 17, 1952. The proposal to establish a state department of corrections was rooted in Northern penal reform and in the emphasis on bureaucratic reorganization that swept the country after World War II. Governor Wright's address to the legislature of Jan. 3, 1950, proposed governmental reorganization, and later in the year a legislative committee endorsed the amalgamation of all "correctional agencies" under a single department of state government. See *House Journal,* 1950, pp. 30–31, and Jackson *Clarion-Ledger,* Nov. 8, 1950.

6. *Senate Journal,* 1952, p. 217.

7. Jackson *Clarion-Ledger,* Feb. 26, 1952.

8. Ibid., Mar. 15, May 14, 16, Aug. 5, 1952.

9. Ibid., Feb. 3, 22, 1952. See ibid., Feb. 23, 1958, for retrospective comment on Alexander's pamphlet *The Lash,* a copy of which is on file at MDAH.

10. Jackson *Clarion-Ledger,* Jan. 17, 29, 1952.

11. *Senate Journal,* 1952, pp. 433, 438, 481, 900; *House Journal,* 1952, pp. 352, 354, 407, 652; Jackson *Clarion-Ledger,* Feb. 3, 22, Mar. 2, 15, April 19, June 16, 1952.

12. Interviews 7 and 16.

13. Jackson *Clarion-Ledger,* Feb. 3, 1952.

14. *House Journal,* 1952, pp. 204, 244, 274; Jackson *Clarion-Ledger,* Jan. 29, Feb. 2, 3, 1952; Interview 16.

15. Interview 7; Cabana Interviews. For comment on these problems, see Jackson *Clarion-Ledger,* Apr. 15, July 9, 12, Sept. 22, 1953. For comment on the problems posed by white convicts, see Jackson *Clarion-Ledger,* May 6, 1936; A. R. Beasley, "More Information about Mississippi Prison Conditions," *Mississippi Baptist Record,* Sept. 24, 1947; and Oshinsky, *"Worse Than Slavery,"* pp. 164–65.

16. *PR:* 1941–43, p. 20; 1951–53, p. 5.

17. Jackson *Clarion-Ledger,* Aug. 24, 1952; Interview 7.

18. Interviews 6 and 7.

19. Jackson *Clarion-Ledger,* April 18, 1953.

20. Greenville *Delta Democrat-Times,* April 24, June 23, 1953; Jackson *Clarion-Ledger,* April 15, 26, June 25, 26, 1953; New Orleans *Times Picayune,* June 26, July 12, 1953; Memphis *Commercial Appeal,* July 11, 1953.

21. *PR,* 1951–53, pp. 4–5.

22. Jackson *Clarion-Ledger,* June 23, 1953.

23. Ibid., June 30, July 11, 1953; New Orleans *Times Picayune,* July 5, 1953; Interview 10.

24. Memphis *Commercial Appeal,* June 30, 1953; Jackson *Clarion-Ledger,* June 26, 30, 1953.

25. Ibid., June 30, 1953; New Orleans *Times Picayune,* July 5, 1953.

26. Memphis *Commercial Appeal,* July 11, 1953; Jackson *Clarion-Ledger,* July 9, 1953.

27. Memphis *Commercial Appeal,* July 5, 1953.

28. Jackson *Clarion-Ledger,* June 26, July 9, 11, 12, 29, Oct. 1, 1953.

29. McComb *Enterprise-Journal,* Sept. 30, 1953; Jackson *Clarion-Ledger,* July 21, Oct. 9, 1953; Feb. 24, 1954.

30. Ibid., Feb. 24, 1954.

31. Ibid., Mar. 11, 12, 1954.

32. For reports of the earlier debates, see Jackson *Daily Clarion-Ledger,* Mar. 12, 1936; Mar. 7, April 5, 1940. For an account of the portable electric chair, see Craddock Goins, "The Traveling Executioner," *American Mercury* (January 1942): 93–97.

33. Interview 16; Jackson *Clarion-Ledger,* Sept. 13, 1954. See ibid., July 25, Aug. 2, 1953, reporting on-site inspections by state officials of the maximum security units at Atmore, Alabama, and Huntsville, Texas, and the resulting decision to adopt the Texas model. For a description of Little Shamrock, see R. C. Copeland, "The Evolution of the Texas Department of Corrections" (master's thesis, Sam Houston State University, 1980), pp. 129–32. For a description of Little Alcatraz, see Jackson *Clarion-Ledger,* Sept. 26, 1954, and Cabana, *Death at Midnight,* pp. 36–37. For brief comment on Wiggins's opposition to placing a gas chamber at Parchman, see ibid., p. 166.

34. Jackson *Clarion-Ledger,* Jan. 20, May 8, 13, Sept. 12, 13, 14, 15, 17, 20, 23, 26, 29, 1954; *Senate Journal,* 1954, pp. 27, 141, 145, 167; 1954–55 (Extra Session), pp. 27, 94; *Miss. Laws,* 1954, pp. 44–46.

35. Jackson *Clarion-Ledger,* Sept. 26, 1954; *Inside World,* Oct. 1954; Interview 7.

36. Jackson *Clarion-Ledger,* Dec. 9, 12, 1954.

37. Ibid., Feb. 26, 1955; Interviews 7 and 16; Cabana, *Death at Midnight,* p. 167.

38. Jackson *Clarion-Ledger,* Mar. 4, May 1, 1954; McDonnell, *In the Throes of Criminal Justice,* pp. 256–59; Interviews 7 and 16.

39. Interviews 12 and 16.

40. Jackson *Clarion-Ledger,* April 3, 1955; *PR,* 1953–55, p. 34.

41. Ibid., pp. 20, 34–35.

42. Ibid., pp. 7, 20, 34.

43. Jackson *Clarion-Ledger,* Oct. 23, 1953; April 3, 1955; Interview 7.

44. McComb *Enterprise-Journal,* Sept. 30, 1953; Jackson *Clarion-Ledger,*

Mar. 11, April 1, 1956. For a description of the handiwork produced by convicts participating in the hobby contest, see D. Evans, "Afro-American Folk Sculpture from Parchman Penitentiary," *Mississippi Folklore Register* 6, no. 4 (Winter 1972): 141–52.

45. *PR*, 1953–55, p. 13; Jackson *Clarion-Ledger*, Dec. 16, 1954.

46. *PR*, 1953–55, pp. 24–30.

47. Jackson *Clarion-Ledger*, May 1, June 25, 1955.

48. *PR:* 1953–55, pp. 5, 17–18, 33; 1955–57, p. 6.

49. *House Journal*, 1956, p. 417; Interview 7; interview by author with a state official, Hattiesburg, Miss., Oct. 1986 [hereafter cited as Interview 17].

50. For reports of the key debates on the probation bill, see *Senate Journal*, 1956, p. 22, and Jackson *Clarion-Ledger*, Jan. 18, Feb. 23, Mar. 21, 1956. For the statute, see *Miss. Laws*, 1956, pp. 312–18. For Wiggins's letter of resignation, see CMB 1944–59, entry of June 5, 1956.

51. Jackson *Clarion-Ledger*, May 9, 1956.

52. *PR:* 1943–45, pp. 10, 23, 27; 1945–47, pp. 17–18, 21–2; 1947–49, pp. 6, 26, 29; 1949–51, pp. 4, 30, 33; 1951–53, pp. 5, 7; 1953–55, pp. 5, 17–18, 33; 1955–57, p. 6.

Chapter 8: The Short Reign of the Scalawags

1. For assessment of Coleman's racial strategy and tactics, see N. R. McMillen, "Development of Civil Rights 1956–1970," in McLemore, *A History of Mississippi*, 2: 158–59; E. Terry Jack, "Racial Policy and Judge J. P. Coleman: A Study in Political-Judicial Linkage" (Ph.D. diss., University of Southern Mississippi, 1979), pp. 61–94; Greenwood *Commonwealth*, May 10, 1984; and *Life*, April 15, 1957, pp. 93–98.

2. Jackson *Clarion-Ledger*, Mar. 9, June 6, Aug. 17, 1956; CMB 1944–59, entry of Aug. 7, 1956; Interviews 7 and 16; interview by author with a former state official, Jackson, Miss., Jan. 1982 [hereafter cited as Interview 18].

3. Jackson *Clarion-Ledger*, July 15, Dec. 2, 1956.

4. Ibid., Aug. 2, Sept. 12, 1956; McComb *Enterprise-Journal*, Aug. 1, 1956; *PR*, 1955–57, p. 37.

5. Jackson *Clarion-Ledger*, Sept. 24, 1958.

6. Ibid., July 22, Oct. 4, 1956.

7. Ibid., Dec. 20, 1956; *PR*, 1955–57, pp. 38–9; *Inside World*, Dec. 1956.

8. Jackson *Clarion-Ledger*, July 21, Sept. 12, Dec. 8, 1956.

9. Ibid., Aug. 5, 1956.

10. Ibid.

11. Ibid. ; *Inside World*, Sept. and Dec. 1956; *PR*, 1955–57, p. 36.

12. Ibid., pp. 36–8; Jackson *Clarion-Ledger,* Dec. 16, 1956.

13. Ibid., Sept. 12, Dec. 8, 1956.

14. Ibid., Dec. 16, 1956.

15. Ibid., Dec. 16, 23, 1956.

16. *PR,* 1957–59, pp. 6–7; *Inside World,* Mar. 1957; Jackson *Clarion-Ledger,* April 8, 1958; June 28, 1959.

17. Ibid., April 18, 1957.

18. Ibid., May 17, 1959.

19. *Parade,* May 17, 1959. See also Jackson *Clarion-Ledger,* June 19, 1959.

20. Professor Hopper's first article was "The Conjugal Visit at the Mississippi State Penitentiary," published by *The Journal of Criminal Law, Criminology and Police Science* 53, no. 3 (Sept. 1962): 340–43. It was followed in 1969 by Hopper's celebrated book, *Sex in Prison.*

21. *Inside World,* Sept. 1957; Jackson *Clarion-Ledger,* Oct 6, 1957. See also ibid., June 28, 1959, reporting the favorable opinion of nineteen state circuit judges who inspected the white honor camp.

22. Interview 15; *Mississippi Baptist Record,* Sept. 4, 1958; *Senate Journal,* 1958, p. 287; *Miss. Laws,* 1958, p. 246; Jackson *Clarion-Ledger,* Feb. 23, 1958; Oct. 9, Nov. 13, 1959; Feb. 21, 1960.

23. Interview 15; Jackson *Clarion-Ledger,* June 18, 1958; Feb. 21, 1960; *PR,* 1957–59, p. 35.

24. *House Journal,* 1956, pp. 369, 430, 575, 812, 845, 977, 1045; *Miss. Laws,* 1956, pp. 325–26; Jackson *Clarion-Ledger,* Feb. 2, Dec. 16, 1956.

25. Interview 17.

26. Jackson *Clarion-Ledger,* Mar. 10, 1957.

27. *PR:* 1955–57, pp. 6, 19–21; 1957–59, pp. 3, 5, 7–8, 18.

28. *PR,* 1955–57, pp. 3, 7–8, 21, 36; *Senate Journal,* 1958, pp. 287, 549, 578; Jackson *Clarion-Ledger,* Mar. 21, 1958.

29. *PR,* 1957–59, pp. 31, 36–37; Jackson *Clarion-Ledger,* June 28, 1959.

30. *PR:* 1957–59, p. 21; 1959–61, pp. 6, 23.

31. Jackson *Clarion-Ledger,* Feb. 21, Mar. 6, 1960; Greenville *Delta Democrat-Times,* Feb. 25, 1960.

32. Ibid., Mar. 28, 1960. I am indebted to Mr. Harpole, a state senator until his death in the autumn of 1990, for reviewing and confirming the accuracy of the portions of this chapter relating to his superintendency.

Chapter 9: Rollin' With Ross

1. Jackson *Clarion-Ledger,* Mar. 24, 1960.

2. Ibid., June 6, 1960.

3. Ibid., Nov. 20, 1960; *PR,* 1959–61, p. 4.

4. Ibid., p. 24; Jackson *Clarion-Ledger,* June 5, 1960.

5. *Miss. Laws,* 1960, pp. 595–96; Greenville *Delta Democrat-Times,* June 19, 1960; Jackson *Clarion-Ledger,* June 10, 1960; Feb. 21, 1961; *PR,* 1959–61, p. 44.

6. Interview by author with a former inmate who served time at Parchman, Vicksburg, Miss., April 1982 (hereafter cited as Interview 19); Jackson *Clarion-Ledger,* Nov. 20, 1960.

7. *PR,* 1959–61, pp. 5, 45.

8. Jackson *Clarion-Ledger,* Nov. 20, 1960; Jan. 10, Feb. 5, 1961.

9. Ibid., Jan. 25, 1961; Greenville *Delta Democrat-Times,* Jan. 25, 1961.

10. Jackson *Clarion-Ledger,* Feb. 7, 1961; *PR,* 1959–61, p. 6.

11. Greenville *Delta Democrat-Times,* Mar. 28, 1961; Jackson *Clarion-Ledger,* Mar. 26, 1961.

12. Ibid., April 19, 20, 21, 1961; Greenville *Delta Democrat-Times,* April 21, 1961; Board of Commissioners Minute Book, 1960–1964, MDAH, RG 49, vol. 40, entry of April 24, 1961 [hereafter cited as CMB 1960–64]. See also Saucier, "A History of the Mississippi Penal Farm System, 1935–1970," p. 40.

13. Greenville *Delta Democrat-Times,* May 7, 17, 1961.

14. For accounts of the unfolding case, which featured Ross Barnett as one of the attorneys representing the husband of Goldsby's victim and charges by state officials and journalists that the federal judiciary was thwarting criminal process, see Jackson *Clarion-Ledger,* Feb. 27, June 16, Oct. 13, 18, 28, Nov. 3, 8, 25, 1959, and June 1, 1961.

15. Ibid., June 13, 1961.

16. Ibid., Aug. 6, 1961; CMB 1960–64, entry of June 14, 1961.

17. Jackson *Clarion-Ledger,* July 27, Aug. 6, 1961; Interview 17.

18. *Inside World,* Sept. 1961; CMB 1960–64, entry of Nov. 7, 1961; Jackson *Clarion-Ledger,* Aug. 6, 1961; Interview 19; interview by author with a former inmate who served time at Parchman, Jackson, Miss., Mar. 1986 [hereafter cited as Interview 20]. For general comment, see A. Moody, *Coming of Age in Mississippi* (New York, 1968), particularly p. 275; and Saucier, "A History of the Mississippi Penal Farm System, 1935–1970," pp. 41–42.

19. Jackson *Clarion-Ledger,* July 5, 6, 8, 30, Sept. 30, 1961; interview by author with a former employee of the Mississippi penal system, Greenwood, Miss., Mar. 1982 [hereafter cited as Interview 21].

20. Jackson *Clarion-Ledger,* Jan. 1, 3, 6, 10, 1962; Greenville *Delta Democrat-Times,* Jan. 4, 8, 1962.

21. Ibid., Jan. 16, 1962; Jackson *Clarion-Ledger,* Jan. 25, 28, 30, Feb. 1, 1962.

22. Ibid., Jan. 31, Feb. 4, 8, 10, 15, 1962; Greenville *Delta Democrat-Times,* Feb. 6, 1962.

23. *House Journal,* 1962, p. 47; *Senate Journal,* 1962, p. 38; Jackson *Clarion-Ledger,* April 4, 5, 1962.

24. *Senate Journal,* 1962, p. 660. A typescript of the official findings of the Lucas committee is at MDAH, RG 49, vol. 21.

25. Jackson *Clarion-Ledger,* April 20, 21, 1962; Greenville *Delta Democrat-Times,* April 20, 1962. For retrospective analysis, see Jackson *Clarion-Ledger,* Dec. 21, 22, 1967.

26. Greenville *Delta Democrat-Times,* April 25, 1962; Jackson *Clarion-Ledger,* April 24, 26, 1962.

27. Ibid., April 26, 28, 1962; Interviews 11, 19, and 20.

28. Interview 7; Jackson *Clarion-Ledger,* April 29, May 2, 3, 10, 1962.

29. Ibid., April 29, May 2, 3, 8, 10, 1962; *Inside World,* April 1962.

30. Jackson *Clarion-Ledger,* May 2, 3, 1962; *Senate Journal,* 1962, pp. 136–37, 670, 903, 1031–32.

31. Jackson *Clarion-Ledger,* May 27, 1962.

32. Ibid., June 2, 3, 1962; Greenville *Delta Democrat-Times,* June 3, 1962.

33. Jackson *Clarion-Ledger,* June 16, July 7, 31, 1962.

34. Ibid., July 31, 1962; *PR,* 1961–63, pp. 3–5.

35. Ibid., pp. 29–30, 39, 41, 44.

36. Jackson *Clarion-Ledger,* Oct. 14, 1962.

37. *PR:* 1933–35, pp. 46, 49–50; 1961–63, pp. 9, 11, 13.

38. *PR,* 1963–65, p. 5; Jackson *Clarion-Ledger,* July 10, Dec. 19, 1963; Greenville *Delta Democrat-Times,* Jan. 27, 1964.

Chapter 10: Caught Betwixt and Between

1. Greenville *Delta Democrat-Times,* Feb. 9, 13, 27, 1964; Jackson *Clarion-Ledger,* April 16, 1964.

2. Ibid., Feb. 14, 16, 27, Mar. 25, April 16, 17, May 27, 1964.

3. *Miss. Laws,* 1964, pp. 519–37. See also Saucier, "A History of the Mississippi Penal Farm System, 1935–1970," pp. 47–48.

4. Jackson *Clarion-Ledger,* Feb. 16, 1964.

5. Ibid., Feb. 14, 16, 20, 27, 1964.

6. Ibid., July 28, 1965.

7. Ibid., Jan. 26, April 17, Aug. 17, 30, 1966. For a later report of progress by Commissioner West, see ibid., Jan. 15, 1967. For an editorial praising the progress of the program, see Greenville *Delta Democrat-Times,* Jan. 27, 1967. See also C. A. Jones, "A Survey of Perceived Needs of Adult Education Faculty at the Mississippi State Penitentiary at Parchman" (Ph.D. diss., University of Southern Mississippi, 1978), pp. 65–68.

8. Jackson *Clarion-Ledger,* Oct. 29, 1967.

9. Ibid., Nov. 19, 1967, May 6, July 20, Aug. 24, 1969. For financial accounts, see *House Journal,* 1970, p. 503.

10. For accounts of the library, see *PR,* 1965–67, p. 47; *Declaration of Library Service* (Parchman, n.d.); *Dedication of Library Program, May 25, 1965* (Parchman, n.d.); and Jackson *Clarion-Ledger,* April 25, Oct. 22, 1965; April 20, 1969. See also an undated typescript entitled "Library" in the library of the Mississippi State Penitentiary at Parchman. For a description of the old striped uniforms, see Jackson *Clarion-Ledger,* Oct. 28, 1965. For accounts of the change of uniforms, see ibid., Jan. 15, 1967, and *Progress Report of the Mississippi State Penitentiary, 1964–1968* (Jackson, Miss., n.d.), pp. 28, 34 [hereafter cited as *PR,* 1964–68]. For accounts of the reception center, the diagnostic clinic, and the pre-release center, see Jackson *Clarion-Ledger,* Aug. 21, Nov. 23, 1969; and *House Journal,* 1968, pp. 157–58, 164–65; 1970, p. 505–6. For general comment, see Quarles, "A Study of the Mississippi State Correctional System," p. 21.

11. Jackson *Clarion-Ledger,* Feb. 16, July 29, 30, 1964; *PR,* 1963–65, p. 5; CMB 1960–64, entry of Dec. 14, 1964.

12. *PR,* 1964–68; *House Journal,* 1966, pp. 396–403; 1968, pp. 165–68.

13. Ibid., 1968, p. 170.

14. Interviews 17, 18, and 19; interview by author with a businessman who hunted dove at Parchman during the years of the younger Johnson's administration, Jackson, Miss., May 1982; Jackson *Clarion-Ledger,* Oct. 28, 1965; Mar. 10, 11, 14, 26, 27, 1966; *House Journal,* 1966, pp. 396–97, 1099; *Senate Journal,* 1966, p. 502.

15. Interview 21.

16. Jackson *Clarion-Ledger,* July 28, 1965.

17. Ibid., Aug. 1, Oct. 30, 1965; Interview 21.

18. *House Journal,* 1968, pp. 156, 170; 1970, p. 508.

19. Ibid., 1968, p. 167; 1970, p. 503–5.

20. Jackson *Clarion-Ledger,* Mar. 11, 1943; Oct. 28, 1965.

21. *House Journal,* 1968, pp. 157, 179; 1970, p. 503.

22. Ibid., 1968, p. 165.

23. Ibid., 1970, pp. 506, 508.

24. Jackson *Clarion-Ledger,* Aug. 1, 1965.

25. Ibid., Oct. 28, 1965.

26. Ibid., Mar. 14, 1966; Interview 21.

27. *House Journal,* 1968, pp. 161–62.

28. Ibid., pp. 155–56; Jackson *Clarion-Ledger,* Jan. 31, Feb. 1, 2, 1968.

29. Ibid., Feb. 10, 1968.

30. *House Journal,* 1968, pp. 155–71.

31. Ibid., pp. 185–87; Jackson *Clarion-Ledger,* Feb. 18, 23, 1968; Interview 18.

32. Jackson *Clarion-Ledger,* Feb. 15, 18, 1968.

33. Ibid., Feb. 23, Mar. 14, 20, April 5, 16, 1968.

34. Ibid., Feb. 23, 28, June 26, July 2, Nov. 19, 20, 24, Dec. 13, 1968, Jan. 25, 1969; Interview 18.

35. Jackson *Clarion-Ledger,* Jan. 16, 1970.

36. Ibid., Feb. 18, 1970.

37. *House Journal,* 1970, pp. 502–8.

38. Jackson *Clarion-Ledger,* Oct. 15, 1970; *Anderson v. Nosser,* 438 F. 2d 183 (5th Cir. 1971).

39. *Holt v. Sarver,* 309 F. Supp. 362 (E.D. Ark. 1970).

40. This account of the attitudes of state legislators is based on a careful perusal of the public record, on the general tenor of the press reports of the time, and on the assessments of all parties interviewed.

41. *Miss. Laws,* 1971, pp. 847–48.

42. Cabana, *Death at Midnight,* p. 58.

43. Ibid., pp. 43–44.

44. Ibid., pp. 52–54.

45. Ibid., pp. 70–71.

46. Jackson *Clarion-Ledger,* Feb. 22, 29, 1972.

Index

237